Anne Brewster lived in Perth fc. .v ui icii years and taught at Curtin University before moving to Syndey in 1999 where she now teaches at the University of New South Wales. In 1995 she was a Writer-in-Residence at the then Kalgoorlie College. Her two recent books are *Literary Formations* (1995) and *Reading Aboriginal Women's Autobiographical Narratives* (1996).

Angeline O'Neill was born in Sydney in 1968 and grew up in a series of small country towns in New South Wales. After graduating with an Arts Degree from Sydney University she pursued her PhD at the University of Western Australia, and now teaches Comparative Indigenous Literature, Australian Literature and Aboriginal Studies at the University of Notre Dame, Australia. She has found the experience of working on this anthology enormously enriching; in particular, her friendship with Irene Calgaret, Septu Brahim and Josie Boyle has been a source of support and inspiration.

Rosemary van den Berg is a Noongar woman who comes from Pinjarra, in the south-west of Western Australia and now lives in Armadale. She is married with five adult children and twenty-two grandchildren and she is considered an Elder among her people. She is an author and historian and has recently completed her PhD in Philosophy at Curtin University. She has written *No Options! No Choice!* (1994), her father's biography, and is currently adapting it for stage for Yirra Yaakin Noongar Theatre and Stages.

Cover image: Sandra Hill, *Water Dreaming* 1995, transfer, collograph, featherbark and watercolour on paper, 102 x 82 cm, the Edith Cowan University Collection.

Those who Remain
will Always Remember

An Anthology of Aboriginal writing

EDITED BY

ANNE BREWSTER   ANGELINE O'NEILL
ROSEMARY VAN DEN BERG

FREMANTLE ARTS CENTRE PRESS

Dedicated to
Irene Calgaret, Septu Brahim and Kathy Trimmer,
all of whom recently passed away. Their contributions
were an inspiration to us as we compiled
Those Who Remain Will Always Remember.

First published 2000 by
FREMANTLE ARTS CENTRE PRESS
25 Quarry Street, Fremantle
(PO Box 158, North Fremantle, 6159)
Western Australia.

Production Editor B R Coffey.
Production Coordinator Cate Sutherland.
Cover Designer Marion Duke.

Typeset by Fremantle Arts Centre Press
and printed by Sands Print Group, Bassendean.

National Library of Australia
Cataloguing-in-publication data

Those who remain will always remember

ISBN 1 86368 291 0.

1. Aborigines, Australian — Western Australia — Literary
collections. I. Brewster, Anne. II. van den Berg, Rosemary, 1939– .
III. O'Neill, Angeline.

A820.8089915

  The State of Western Australia has made an
investment in this project through ArtsWA in
association with the Lotteries Commission.

Contents

Introduction

Those Who Remain Will Always Remember grew out of a desire to
see Western Australian Aboriginal people better represented on
the national map. When we first started soliciting and advertising
for work, we were astonished at the amount of material
submitted. Clearly there are many Aboriginal people with
something to say who are choosing literary genres to do it. As
Mary Champion says of a favourite pastime at Kalgoorlie's Long
Park, 'everyone's telling stories'. We aimed for a broad representation of Western Australians from different regions,
backgrounds, age groups (Ethel Clinch, our oldest contributor is
over ninety), as well as a range of different genres. Although pan-
Aboriginality has a useful political role in certain circumstances,
as Denise Groves points out in her essay, we are also aware that
regional and cultural specificities and differences are important.
We have, for example, maintained the different spellings of
Nyoongah throughout the anthology as Nyoongah people come
from distinct regions and groups, a fact which is also reflected in
the different pronunciations of this word. (Rosemary van den
Berg's research has revealed that the word Nyoongah is itself a
misnomer; it was used by the groups in the south-west region to
designate 'man', while yorga is the word for 'woman'. The
various Nyoongah groups were then distinguished according to
region; Dr van den Berg herself is from the Bibbulmun people.

As editors we were interested in what genres the contributors
were using and how they were using them. One of the dominant
interests of authors is the (auto)biographical project. While a
number of different genres are mobilised as vehicles for
(auto)biographical writings including poetry, prose narrative is
the most popular mode for this type of narrative which is, in
some cases, fictionalised (Lorna Little, Dudgeon, van den Berg)
or dramatised (Pilkington); others are produced as life stories,
focussing either on the narrator or on family members (for
example, Clinch, Ellis, Colin and Betty Indich, Knapp, Tom Little,

9

Taylor, Torres, Murray, Penny, Quartermaine and Ward), sometimes from voice recordings (Chalarimeri, Brahim and Ward), or conversation (as with Colin and Betty Indich, where Colin narrated and Betty acted as scribe). These life stories are not always linear and shaped in the manner of western (auto)biographical writing; in this collection life narratives are sometimes fragmentary, episodic and syntactically fractured (Haynes, Ellis and Lockyer).

The (auto)biographical writings and life-story accounts in this anthology contain a wealth of historical detail: blackbirding in Broome, nuclear testing in central Australia, traditional bush practices, the 'dog' license, and the administration of Aboriginal people in a variety of missions including Wandering Mission and New Norcia. They defamiliarise the Anglo-Celtic version of Australian modernity by reading history in non Anglo-Celtic frameworks: the massive contribution of Aboriginal labour to the modernisation of Australia in the pastoral and other rural industries is documented; we see the birth of Australian multiculturalism *avant la lettre* in family histories such as that of Septu Brahim; the diasporas which resulted from the separation of children from their families and regional cultures are recorded; and the eugenics programs of the early assimilationist Protection Acts are compared to those of the same period in Nazi Germany (see Alf Tayor's extract from *God, the Devil and Me*).

While the generic boundaries of life story and fiction are sometimes blurred in these writings (Dudgeon, van den Berg, Lorna Little, Tom Little), fiction itself is relatively rare in this collection (a notable exception being Scott); we might speculate as to the reasons for this as regards the older generation, including a lack of familiarity with or assimilation to this particular genre and the generational specificity of the imperatives driving the production of life stories (such as their value as archival and pedagogical documents).

We were aware of a number of themes and interests dominating the fictional and life writing stories and other prose fragments, such as stories about ghosts and heroes (Slater, Deeble, Tom Little and Torres); those involving sporting careers (Knapp and Tom Little); and those relating experiences of gaol (Lockyer, Williams, Ellis and Deeble); indeed a number of the pieces in this collection were written while the author was in gaol. Incarceration and institutionalisation have historically been the experience of many Aboriginal people, whether in missions, goal and other corrective institutions, hospitals and the like.

Not surprisingly many of the writings — prose and otherwise — address themes of violence and police relations with Aboriginal people, and issues such as car chases, alcohol and drug abuse, gambling and domestic violence, which continue to afflict Aboriginal communities (Tom Little, Chalarimeri, Murray, Papertalk-Green, Penny, Taylor, van den Berg, Quartermaine, Trimmer and Taylor). Many of the young authors in particular (Chanelle Hansen, Jones and Tracie Pushman), are concerned with alcohol and substance abuse. There are also a number of mythic and legend narratives, such as Josie Boyle's legend of the Yaa Yaa-rrs, the young writer Chantelle Corbett's rendering of the Nyoongah Wagyl myth and Patricia Mamajun Torres' re-enactment of the 'devilman who has a tail'. Victor Deeble's and Tom Little's stories also have mythic dimensions.

In addition to life stories, fictional and mythic narratives, we have collected a number of statements, commentaries and essays. These include political, intellectual and ceremonial writings focussing on intellectual and property rights and cultural ownership issues (Eggington, Wilkes and Little and Little), Aboriginal identity (Groves and Scott), memorial performances (Bropho), racism (Pilkington, Yoka and van den Berg) and the intersection of Aboriginal and Christian spiritualities (Sahanna). We also include interviews with two prominent Nyoongah writers, Glenyse Ward and Richard Wilkes, and are particularly pleased to introduce new writing by a number of adolescents: Matthew Haltiner, Chanelle Hansen, Chantelle Corbett, Stephen Narkle and Chantelle Webb.

Just as we have aimed for a wide representation of prose writings, so the poetry of the anthology represents many different modes and themes: lyrical, ballad, anthemic; protest poetry, love poetry and political comment. It ranges from the haiku-like condensation of poems by Bropho and Jones, to the ghostly evocations of Stammner, the probing, interrogative address of Yoka, and the complex, ambiguous syntax of Fabien Hansen. Many of the poems bear evidence of oral and song traditions, for example those by Trimmer, Penny, and Chi.

Given the range of material we had a number of choices as to how we might order it and decided upon several broad themes, such as myths, legends, heroes and ceremony; history and myth; political commentary; yarns; here and now; and incarceration. We are aware, nevertheless, that these categories leak into each other; we consider the majority of the writing here political, for example, as all Aboriginal people (and indeed all Australians) live amidst the consequences of colonisation and the continuing effects of racism. Similarly, memory and history (collective, institutional and personal) are mobilised, for example, in the projects of fiction (as we see in the work of Scott) as well as in more overtly documentary or memorial writing.

In fact, an awareness of memory and the past saturates this anthology as remembering is an imperative for many of the authors. As Clinch suggests: 'those who remain will always remember'; for her, a lyrical evocation of 'home' equates with 'memory' and vice versa. For Clinch memory functions for the family to 'bring us all together again'. This consolidating role of memory has implications for the wider Aboriginal community (and indeed for Australia as a whole in the performance of Reconciliation). The act of remembering is a political act for authors such as Fred Penny; the reiterative lines marked with the change of tense — 'We were as one / We still are one' — indicate that the past functions as a point of identification and, further, that an affirmation of a continuity with the past is a vehicle by which a continuity and solidarity between Aboriginal people in the present is established. We see this double movement — a simultaneously retroactive or synchronic and diachronic identification — in many Aboriginal figurations of the past, such as Papertalk-Green's invocation of a pre-invasion utopian scene where 'time stops still'. Significantly we see this moment affirmed in younger writers, as in Kristy Jones' poem titled 'The Past Still Lives'.

Remembering is all too often a painful experience, however, as we see in many life stories. Chalarimeri describes a shift in his thinking which heralded the development of his political consciousness. He describes how in the 1950s and earlier 'we never ask questions'. The coloniser was synonymous with the police and with power: 'the first white person I ever saw was a police and they had a lot of power. That was the start of it, they had power, we didn't'. In this colonial political economy, Australia was literally a police state, and its modus operandi, terror. The hegemony of the police state was so complete at that time that as far as the Aboriginal people were concerned, 'nobody ever think that this was our country and why did they do this'; it was indeed 'very hard to fight against white people'. Chalarimeri describes how in the 1970s things changed for him, and he 'realised that the story we were told in the 1950s was wrong ... that's when I first realised that this was our land'.

This realisation represents a complex nexus; it is at this point that the false consciousness of the colonised disperses and the recognition that (post/neo)colonial power can be challenged is born; it also constitutes a moment of mourning; the point at which an awareness of loss is intensified. This moment of recognition and grief is profoundly ambivalent for both Aboriginal and non-Aboriginal Australians. While pain threatens to immobilise, it is necessary to animate the memory of the past in order to understand the social and psychic complexities of contemporary Australia. Chalarimeri articulates this moment of psychic crisis: 'When I think about [the past] now I don't like it, that's why I hardly ever think of it or want to hear about it anymore. It hurts people's feelings, and when you look back you go backwards. But in too many places trouble is still there today.' When the current Prime Minister refuses the 'sorry' word, we see before us the spectre of a haunted and troubled middle (white) Australia, an Australia which resolutely disavows the 'trouble [that] is still there today.'

The act of remembering the past is a point of the simultaneous convergence and divergence of Aboriginal and non-Aboriginal Australia. When Tom Quartermaine writes that 'we have to live with the past', the ambiguity of the word 'have' points to this simultaneous convergence and divergence. Where there is remembering there is also forgetting and when Aboriginal people remember it is often what the dominant culture chooses to forget. The historian Peter Burke has suggested that in official versions of white history it is the 'victors' who can afford to forget, while those who have experienced injustice are compelled to relive the memory of that injustice. The 'have' in Quartermaine's statement could refer to an imposition or unwelcome command: the dictate of a painful memory of injustice. On the other hand, the word 'have' might function as an exortation, a call for reform and social justice. And it is this exhortation which is equally relevant to non-Aboriginal people.

We have commented upon the significance of mourning in this anthology especially for those of the stolen generations. Much of the writing is indeed a performance of mourning. Calgaret and Stammner mourn their mothers, Sabbioni her child, van den Berg and Bropho their brothers. Eatts uses the occasion of a funeral to mourn the collective 'Nyoongar folk', and Riley mourns the banishment of the 'souls' of Nyoongars; they have passed through a 'twilight zone', as evoked also in Isaac's haunting poem 'Yellow Flowers'. Bropho's Success Hill ceremony, conducted for the young people for each of whom a tree is planted, opens with an invocation of the old people who have passed away; the stated purpose of 'bring[ing] back together all the people' once again works both diachronically and synchronically, with the Aboriginal youth as the target group in this exercise. (In Walter Eatts' poetry we also see this link between an affirmation of ancestors and the safety and wellbeing of children.)

While this ceremony enacts a ritualistic performance of memory, fictional and mythopoeic writings similarly perform memory. In Victor Deeble's 'Emancipation', Yinda's heroic escape from Rottnest Island similarly reminds the reader that 'escape this place he may, but as long as he lived he would never escape the memories'. Yinda does not live, but his heroic tale and many others like it live on in the literary imaginary of contemporary Aboriginal culture.

We referred above to Chalarimeri's coming to political conscious-ness. Another example of the recognition and discarding of false consciousness comes with Alf Taylor's reading of official white history, in the extract from *God, the Devil and Me*. He describes how, as a child in New Norcia mission, he and the other boys were 'told of Captain Cook fighting the natives to take control of their land. I used to look at the pictures of Captain Cook gallantly shooting the natives. I thought the natives were very bad people for not letting Captain Cook take over their land. Little did I know at the time, those 'natives' were my own people. Those religious people really fucked our heads up.' The painful irony of this piece is extended into a hilarious 'black' comedy where the young Alf mis-identifies not only with the Australian post-colonials but with the English colonisers. The scene is the visit to Australia of the English cricket team to play for the Ashes, which is worth quoting here at length:

I thought that Australia and England were first cousins, and England was far superior to their cousins. Also they, the white Australians that is, all come from Captain Cook. And we Nyoongah kids were told so much of the great Captain Cook by the nuns, we were a bit confused by the Captain Cook's team of England and the Captain Cook's team of Australia. So half of us barracked for England and the other half for Australia; I'm sure we were doing the right thing for the gallant Mr Cook.

After I got out of New Norcia in the early '60s, I was working with a group of wadjellas [white people] and I had not long run away from the place; I was about fifteen or sixteen. These wadjellas asked me where I came from. Without thinking, I said, 'England.' I thought Mr Cook would be proud of me, but these wadjellas walked away from me very unsure. I heard words of, 'I'm sure he's a nigger,' or, 'He's a nigger orright.' I mean I was a very fair-skinned blackfella; the only thing that was obvious was my blackfella nose and forehead. My skin was white as theirs, if not whiter; I had them fucked. And I also had a country I can call my own, Mother England. And of course the Beatles were just emerging, and I was proud to be associated with Mother England, my home country. Some of those white Captain Cook Australians were so stupid you could stick a firecracker up their arse and light it; they would turn around to you and ask, 'Hey mate, what's that burning up my arse?'

This extract, while apparently illustrating the mis-selfidentification of the young Aboriginal boy, also deftly turns the mirror back on Anglo-Celts. Their confusion over the young Alf's claim to 'Mother England' points to their own postcolonial crisis of identification. Taylor follows this story about cricket with a remark on the republic debate. Taylor's deconstructive reading of Australian post-colonial anxiety finds its culmination in his comment on the republic debate:

This republic debate that is going on today: to be quite honest, I would be neutral. I wouldn't vote on it at all. Don't ask me why. I guess reading what you've already read, just maybe the answer is in the story … Yeah, I'd like to leave it up to the reader.

According to Taylor's reading, the republic debate re-enacts the binary opposition staged in the cricket match between Australia and England which is, from his perspective, a showdown between 'the Captain Cook team of Australia' and 'the Captain Cook team of England'.

Just as Chalarimeri and Taylor brilliantly describe the process of a coming to political consciousness, the authors in this anthology indicate that the notion of Aboriginality is complex, processual and polysemous. Self-identification means different things to different people, and many of these issues are explored in the section with pieces foregrounding political commentary such as where Little and Little, Eggington and Wilkes talk about intellectual property, Scott about searching for 'ancestors in the archives', van den Berg, Pilkington and Yoka about racism, and Chi about resistance to assimilation and the pressure to become 'an acceptable coon'. Similarly Dudgeon's ambivalent and searching investigation of the 'Aboriginal industry', of black politics and Aboriginal leadership in her fictional piece 'Four Kilometres', turns a searing spotlight onto the tall poppy syndrome, on the 'pain and rage' which dog the difficult path to self-determination, on the guilt and ambivalence of the upwardly mobile and the complicities and false consciousness of the white social justice industry.

This anthology has taken four years to come to fruition and through it we have aimed to give Western Australian Aboriginal people special representation. We have worked together productively as a team, and this introduction is a reflection of our thoughts and discussions and the collaborative process we engaged in at each step of the way. The list of contributors reads like something of a who's who of Western Australian Aboriginal leadership. Several of the authors represented are acclaimed published writers with national and international reputations (such as Jimmy Chi, Glenyse Ward, Rosemary van den Berg, Doris Pilkington (Nugi Garimara), Patricia Mamajun Torres, Kim Scott, Richard Wilkes, Robert Bropho and Alf Taylor). Several others are well known in Western Australia as seasoned performers (for example, Josie Boyle and Kathy Trimmer). Many of the contributors have high-profile careers as community leaders, elders and spokespeople in areas of health, education, the church, the correctional services and arts administration. A number have been the recipients of literary awards. Sadly, during the course of producing the anthology several of the contributors have passed away, and we would like to pay tribute to Septu Brahim, Kathy Trimmer and Irene Calgaret for their great talent, and their commitment and contribution to the broader community.

Approximately half of the contributors have never been published; some are young and adolescent writers. We are very excited to be able to publish these people for the first time and wish them the best in their future writings; we know that we will be seeing more of their work in years to come. We thank the established writers for their support of this project and all the contributors for their patience. Our heartfelt thanks go ArtsWA and our editor and publisher, Ray Coffey, without the support of whom this anthology would not have been completed. There are others to whom we owe thanks: Diane Narkle, Julia Ravell, Adrian and Andrea Wood, Alison Georgeson, Julie Goyder, David Whish-Wilson, Tom Little, John Fielder and Jean-Francois Neron. And of course Jack van den Berg, Peter Lavskis and Paul Fournier who rallied in response to numerous small emergencies in the course of the book's production.

The Urba-rigine

You are black, you are brown and sometimes white
Eyes of brown, black, green and even blue
You are short, fat, thin but not just right
Big damper nose, pencil thin and hooky too

You look Asian, Pakistani, European and Indian
They call you Joe, John, Jim and even Mario
You're into Rock, Rap, Reggae and any other scene
You watch it on the television and hear it on the radio

They say to you, 'Speak to us some language'
You say, 'What you talkin' 'bout man?
I am speakin' my language
I talk same like you, white man'

You're stuck on a fence, you're in between
'Be like a black man' they tell you
And when you do and can be seen
They say, 'Go away, blacky, your way's not true'

Let me tell you people the road is hard
But be yourself, be proud, be free
They will not break you even though they've tried
Take pride in who you are
You are the Urba-rigine!

Bilyurr-Bilyurr Jarndu, The Red-Dress Woman — A Yawuru Story

In some of the areas around Broome, near Gabarragun and Malabaragun, the coastal sand hills near the Post Office and Prison, there sometimes can be seen the spirit of a woman dressed in red clothes. She has been called the Red-Dress Woman. There are also many stories told by the local people about seeing this spirit appear to them late at night or in the late afternoon, when they walked near Jirrinawula, the site of the Mangrove Hotel and across to the oval near the Shire Library and around near the old State School in Weld Street.

Some of my old people of Broome, who are now gone, had said that this was the spirit of a woman who had been killed in the time of early contact with white people. It was also said that her children were taken away from her and now she can sometimes be seen floating around very old trees and inside buildings, searching for her lost children and checking out any of the local children who are in the area, to see if they are her children. Others have said that she is connected to very strong 'Law business'.

When I was a child at Weld Street State School in the 1960s and 1970s, there were many stories told between the children about the sightings of this woman's spirit in the toilets, especially after school when most of the school was deserted. They would tell their stories about how they would be playing marbles near the old boab tree in the playground and then suddenly from out of the corner, behind the tree would appear this Red-Dress Woman and she would begin to chase all the kids, calling out after them. The kids, of course, would all be running away, yelling and screaming their little heads off in fright. After this experience, they would not stay late after school but go straight home.

I remember that when I told my grandmother and great-grandmother about this spirit, they would tell me not to be scared and say to the spirit, Go back to your own country in one piece, don't hang around here bothering us. But this is very hard to think about when you are shaking all over. It wasn't until I was much older that I was able to deal with the presence of spirits. I believe that the sighting of the Red-Dress Woman in Broome still happens today. She is also known to appear to adults to warn them of impending danger or to bring news of death in the community. Sightings of the Red-Dress Woman have been made, especially around places where there still remain very old indigenous trees in the traditional camping or ceremonial places in the town area of Broome. It is also believed that this spiritual being is linked to women's business and must be treated with respect if encountered.

Magarra-gudany, The Devilman who has a Tail — A Yawuru Story

In traditional times in the area now known as Broome, the Yawuru people had a devil dance that was performed around Jiljirigun, Manalagun, and Jirigun, near where the Foreshore Beach is located today. The Yawuru people from the Jugun clan group would paint their bodies and sing the songs of the devils. My grandmother's brother, Cass Drummond, said that he was just a young boy when he watched this dance being performed and sung. He can still remember some of the words from this song and he can chant the rhythm with the words. I also had an experience with a 'devilman', the Magarra-gudany, which means in the Yawuru language, 'having-a-tail'. This story happened when I was about twelve to fourteen years old.

I remember that it was during the high tide season in Broome. The water was really full and the waves crashed upon the small sandy beach. I was there with some of my girlfriends. We had come to swim and enjoy the water while it was full tide. We threw small stones into the water and dived after them, seeing who could find the stone first. At other times, we would run along the wooden planks of the bathing fence and do 'dive-bombs' into the water, splashing everyone who was near. We played like this until it was very late in the afternoon and the sun began to sink behind the hills and drop into the horizon beyond the ocean, leaving just a dull light on our side of the beach. I remember having so much fun swimming in the warm sea that even though I knew the sun had gone down, I just didn't want to move to start going home.

As I looked towards the right hand side of the beach where the mangrove trees grew around the small black outcrop of rocks, I saw a man start swimming towards us. As he got closer and closer to us girls, we began to notice that he was such a good-looking man and we started to stare at him while we were still swimming around in the water. He kept swimming even closer to us and waved his hands towards us saying, Hi! girls!

When he spoke to us, the hair on the back of our necks began to stand on end and a cold shiver went through the rest of our bodies. It was our spirits telling us that something was wrong, to be careful of whatever was out there. This made us very scared and we began to panic, we started to swim quickly back to the shore and scrambled up the beach. As we climbed up the sandy beach towards the bathing sheds, we looked back over our shoulders and we could see that the handsome-looking man was climbing out of the water and changing into an ugly-looking beast. We saw the horns come out of his head, his tail start to grow and his hands and feet turn to hooves with hair all over his body. When this happened, we all let out a terrible, frightened scream and ran as fast as our legs could carry us all the way home. We didn't stop running until we got home. From that time onwards, since that experience with Magarra-gudany, the Devilman, we never, ever stayed swimming until dark at the beach. We had forgotten that our old people had told us to come home before dark, as the spirits of the country would start to come out just as the sun sank down into the sky and the darkness began to spread across the land.

Legend of the Yaa Yaa-rrs, the Little People

Long time ago in Dreamtime Days there were small little Aboriginal people called the Yaa Yaa-rrs, that lived in the hills and caves around Murrin Murrin in Western Australia. Legend has it that the Yaa Yaa-rrs were good people and nobody saw them, but knew of their existence. Sometimes on a deep, misty, rainy day, you might have seen one when there was no sun, because, you see, these little Yaa Yaa-rrs lived under their Yaa Yaa-rr law, that they could not be exposed to the sunlight or they would die. The Wongi tribe that lived down on the plains often told their children stories of the Yaa Yaa-rrs, the little people, and how they could come and lay their hands on your forehead if you became sick, and you would get better. Sometimes at night the Wongi people went to sleep listening to the beautiful singing and dancing, for the Yaa Yaa-rrs loved to dance and sing, but only under the stars at night, and not let the Sun catch them dancing.

The Wongi people down on the plains went about their business each day, and the Yaa Yaa-rrs kept unseen up in the caves by day and went about their business at night, doing good things. One night all the little Yaa Yaa-rrs had a celebration and they danced and they danced under the Moonlight and the Stars. They were so happy with their dancing that they didn't see the Sun coming up. When the Sun rose, it caught the Yaa Yaa-rr people by surprise, and the sun froze them forever; captured them acting out their Dances in the Landscape, freezing them into Spider Orchids.

Success Hill Sacred Spring Ceremony 12/3/95

We're smoking this spring with paperbark and gum leaves to ward off unwelcome spirits.

In the name of Old Dick Nicholls and Angie Dyson and Granny Herbert Dyson, Tim Harris, Tommy Bropho (Old Nyinda), Isobel Bropho, Sissie Headland, Gracie Gentle, Gracie Narrier, Charles Nettles and Mary Nettles, Frank Narrier, Numbuck Dinah, Tunny and Mary Morton, Jimmy Sandy, Dennis Anderson, Freddie Anderson, Yabbie Parfitt, Joyce Parfitt, Joe Parfitt, Tommy Nannup, Dave Nannup.

These trees been planted here today — Sheoak, Redgum, Jarrah — in the hope the roots will combine together and form a protection roof over the top of the Sacred Spring.

These children standing here today, we hope that they will remember this event today.

In the name of my Grandmother, Clara Layland.

In the name of my Grandfather.

We the last of the River People make claim on this Spring that it should be protected on behalf of all Aboriginal People.

This spring was talked about in the early '40s by an Aboriginal man Dick Nicholls, Sammy Broomhal, Topsy Noolyi Brickhouse and we say that this is a Sacred Spring and should be protected.

Each tree will have a shell placed at the bottom of it.

Under this Redgum will officially be buried a Boomerang and a Grinding Stone and we Hope that they will be left there and the Redgum on top of it will protect the Spring which is the Milk coming out of our Mother's Breast.

We the Last of the River People hope that for many generations to come this will be remembered.

This tree planted today, we hope when Barry becomes a man, who planted this tree here, that he will come back here.

This Jarrah tree, we hope that when Louis becomes a man he'll come back here.

This tree is going to be planted by Freddie Frog and we hope that Freddie when he becomes a man one day he comes back.

This tree is going to be planted by Sam and we hope when he grows up and becomes a man that he will come back.

This Sheoak tree planted here by Noel, we hope that one day Noel will come back as a man.

What I will do, cover this where I smoked the bush, and that will become a Foundation stone.

****

Now you all bore witness to what happened here. This morning was a ceremony that took place by the Swan Coastal Plains People, the Last of the River People of Lockridge Camps and other Nyungahs.

A Ceremony to try to bring back together all the people. This is one Law of the Land. I suppose a lot of whitefellas will look at it and say that it's wrong, but they have Church of England, Catholic, Salvation Army and they talk about something in the sky.

Where this pad is, where you are sitting, the old Gillespies and Andersons and Kicketts, Ollie Kickett's mob, were living.

Top of the hill up there is a huge Jarrah tree. Under that tree are the Spirits of a lot of people: Teresa Jackamarra, Johnny Nannup, Dave Nicholls, Old Ollie Nettle (not Ollie Warrell). These are her Grandchildren here.

The Old Man who talked about this in the early days — well, spring, it's all water to us — he's saying, 'You know there's a well or a spring.' That's where we are having the Ceremony today.

We and the Land are one.

The Land becomes helpless when too many people want to strip it naked of its original beauty.

The Land has many things — Valley, Hills, Streams, Swamps, it has many things to offer.

The Race of People here today just ignore that and are eating away and will destroy it.

You can see the Jarrah, Stinkweed, Banksia, Bluebush, Pricklybush, Creepers, a lot of them refuse to die.

Anyway, that's the Ceremony of the Morning.

Munm-ury
the Teller

We were camped somewhere between Kulin and Bullaring, sucker bashing and root picking for a farmer. Twenty bob an acre was the going rate for this type of work. We were getting fifteen, along with our food and water. We'd worked two weeks straight and the old boy who'd gotten the contract reckoned we were due to let off a bit of steam.

The 'we' I'm referring to was made up of Pop-i Roy, a short, grey-headed man with a very abrupt manner; his daughter-in-law, Marge, who I think was about forty; a son, a couple of kids, seven and ten, and me and my missus. The work wasn't that hard but it must have played havoc with the women's backs; both pregnant but wouldn't stay at the camp. I think most bush women or women in general would rather be doing something than just sitting around.

I don't know what day it was or what month. The weather was warm and we were sitting around the camp waiting for Pop-i to come back from the farm; he'd gone to barter with the cocky for some stores. It wasn't the food the old boy would have to barter for, it was more like the grog. Not too many farmers would even think of adding booze to our grocery list, which was strange to me. I'd been brought up in the city and being banned from drinking in any hotel or pub was something unknown to me.

'Six bottles of beer — one for each worker,' Pop-i growled as he stamped back into camp. 'If the job wasn't almost finished and we didn't have a big pay coming I'd show him where he could shove his six bottles of beer!'

My missus picked up the store sheet and looked at it. Some things she'd asked for, for the kids, were on the list and she put it down again.

'Well did you read it for yourself? ... SIX bottles of beer!'

27

'Yes Pop-i .., Six bottles of beer ... but you can have mine ... and his ... if it makes you happy. That's right isn't it love?' She smiled at me and waited for an answer.

Being suddenly robbed of my one bottle of beer for a fortnight caused my brain to swing into action and I picked up the store docket and read it. The farmer's writing was crude and the list of stores was printed in a way that was easy to forge. It had no rhythm about it, so a few things out of place wouldn't be noticed.

'You want me to doctor this for you Pop-i? I just need a pencil with a black lead in it.'

'What do you mean doctor it?'

'Add stuff to it or just change some of the things around.'

'Ain't that stealing?'

'In a way I suppose, but you reckon the farmer owes us money and I reckon he's got no right to tell us how to spend it.'

'Show me how you reckon to doctor this thing.'

'Well, to start off, you could change that six into an eight and put a one on front of it; that would give you a dozen and a half beer.'

'Do you think they'd kick up at the store?'

'Not if you picked your time, get there late in the afternoon, when you know the boss is out in the paddock. The mob are wanting to close the store and if they do ring the farm there'll be no answer. They're more than likely to give it to you just to get rid of you.'

Pop-i looked over his shoulder to where my missus, who was his grand daughter, was standing. 'What was this bloke doing before you two met? Don't tell me,' he said with a wave of his hand.

We got served at Bullaring with less trouble than I expected. Pop-i was in his glory and even marched up to the petrol attendant and told him to put five gallons in the old car we were travelling in. Then marched off declaring that the boss would fix that up next time.

The five extra gallons of juice meant he could go and visit with his sister in one of the towns in the area. After a day of travelling on the open road with a mob of kids, grown-ups and a kangaroo dog, we were back at our camp. We'd left two of our workers behind in one of the other camps we visited and picked up another three. As long as the work got done it didn't matter who did it.

That night Munm-ury turned up. He was Pop-i Roy's sister's husband, who, although he was drunk, insisted on coming along. After a few arguments around the campfire I learned the hard way not to turn my back on Munm-ury, after getting clouted in the back of the head with a mallee root for talking out of turn, or giving lip to one of the elders of the group. Maybe the old boy was just seeing what I was made of. Anyway, after a bit of a run-in with him we got to talking.

'Where you come from boy, who's your mob?' Munm-ury was talking about my lineage.

'That's that Ida Deeble's boy ... married John Deeble long before the war ... you know her old boy. She used to be a Colbung ... Big Ida from Tambellup way,' his missus called out from where she was sitting by the campfire.

Munm-ury carried on, ignoring her. 'You're a Colbung then, boy.'

'No I'm not, my name's Deeble!' I shot back at him.

'Then Deeble's a Nyoongah name ... if you're a Nyoongah.'

'I guess it is, 'cause I'm a Nyoongah all right.'

'Names, names, they're all just names. Munm-ury meant something in my dialect once but it's just a name to me. Billbarn,' he said and his eyes sparkled. 'Billbarn,' he repeated and brought his hand in a clawed position towards my throat. I knocked his hand away and he got up from where we were sitting and called me to one side. I followed. 'Know what a feather-foot is, boy? Do they talk to you about the old days, down in the city where you come from?'

The name was not unknown to me. I had heard it around campfires around Wandering and Moora reserve and whenever Mum took me to Herne Hill sand dunes where our people used to camp, when I was a kid. Every time I had heard the name before it was from a young bloke like myself, told like a ghost story to scare each other. Tonight I had a feeling I was to hear something quite different.

The old boy and I were still within earshot of the others, who'd gathered around the fire chattering away among themselves. Pop-i Roy and Munm-ury's missus were rowing about their father. Apparently they had different mothers which made one higher in the clan than the other. Every time they'd start yarning it would end up in a row.

'Alex Billbarn could capture any woman he wanted,' the old

boy said, looking at the fire through the spread of his hands. 'Any woman that was not pure of thought or action, any woman could be caught by Alex.'

Munm-ury squatted, leaving me staring open mouthed into the space he'd just vacated. By the time I'd knelt down alongside and made myself comfortable the old bloke looked like he was asleep.

'Munm-ury, you okay?' I asked.

'I seen women after Billbarn was finished with them. He was an evil man, no two ways about that. You see, the magic of a spirit-man is passed down and now and then it falls into the hands of an evil one! Three stones, two black, one white, was what held his power. If they were placed in a tree, high up above the path where the women had to go to do their washing and bring water back to the camp, then a woman walking past would be suddenly confronted by the naked form of Billbarn, who was a handsome man, tall with a slender build and a crop of pure white hair. If the woman turned and fled she was okay but if her eyes lingered long enough on the naked form of Billbarn to coax one of the three stones from its resting place in the tree top to fall between her breasts, then a spell would fall upon her and she'd become Billbarn's. She'd be as normal as the others during the daylight hours, but at night she'd slip away to Billbarn's camp to do his bidding.

For a week she would do this until the magic wore off. Then she'd be returned to the camp at night after Billbarn had silenced her by twisting a length of thonging made from the tail of an old boomer around her neck until her tongue was so swollen that she could only make blubbering coughing and spluttering noises until she choked. No one ever got to know where he camped.

There's one yarn where the old girl reckons she was at the camp when something like this was going on. Seems one old lady spotted Billbarn hanging around the fringes of the camp one night and raised the alarm. The men and dogs took chase but ten yards into the bush, everything went haywire, men bumping into each other, dog biting dog, men knocking friends over with waddies; a real mess. By daylight they all thought Billbarn was miles away. Billbarn was far from miles away; the old lady who raised the alarm had seen his face and could identify him — not in this world but when we all cross over to be judged, where Billbarn was just another man. Then she could point out Billbarn

30

as a man who misused the powers entrusted to him, and he would be condemned to be an ant-hill and have ants crawl over him day and night or something like that.

This old lady had to be silenced. Her camp was at the bottom of a slope that ran down to the river. The old girl's legs weren't too good and walking to the stream for water was an effort. Billbarn swam up the stream until he reached her camp, then taking on the appearance of a long-tailed lizard, ran to the camp and under the tent flap. In the midst of changing back, two great red kangaroo dogs set upon him. The old lady saw two dogs fighting a giant lizard, then a man with a lizard head, then Billbarn. She screamed as the dogs drove Billbarn out into the clearing. The men came running with hatchets, rifles and spears. As Billbarn ran towards the bush all the men fired their guns and threw hatchets and spears. As they struck Billbarn's back they froze as his form changed from man to tree that grew before the men's eyes. Reaching a height of ten men, it gave forth a bloom of white parrots that instantly flew off. The men walked to the tree to get their weapons but they were buried so deep, the strongest couldn't pull them out. So there they stayed, a tribute to good over bad, I suppose.'

Munm-ury finished his yarn and bid me goodnight. I heard him talking to his wife as they were getting ready for bed. 'You didn't tell that boy the old girl's name?'

'No! I'm not that silly. Her mob wouldn't get no rest if they knew her name,' he said with a grunt.

I'd heard these types of stories, yarns, whatever you wish to call them, told a dozen ways … Men who turned into mopokes, men with hooved feet who knocked down walls to escape from holy water. None so graphic as that night! It could have been the darkness of the night or the invading stillness of the bush, but I think it was because Munm-ury was the Teller.

A few years after I'd heard the yarn, one of my sisters came home from the hospital with a new baby boy sporting a shock of pure white hair and bearing the name Alex. It was no surprise to me to see my mother tossing the newborn into the air, catching him and christening him Billbarn.

Emancipation

Yinda slid slowly into the water. He sat there half submerged thinking about the swim he would have to make to reach the mainland. There were many unknown factors in this dark expanse of water facing him. The men on the island had told him of fish, as long as two men and as big around as two of his biggest aunties. Fish that could take a man's body, shake it until it was dismembered, then devour it. The embers of the fire in the compound behind him burned with a dull light, but the fire of fear burned brightly in his mind. Escape this place he may, but as long as he lived he would never escape the memories.

Yinda had only been on the island for two weeks but the floggings and tortures he'd witnessed were indelibly printed on his mind. The Island of the Dead, his people had named it. Many from his family group had been sent there for breaking the white man's law, of which they had little knowledge or understanding. This reaction to law-breakers, black or white, was perplexing to him, but the idea of prisons and penal colonies was firmly entrenched in this new Australian breed, who were still deeply attached to the ways of England and Empire.

The sea had been calm when the boat that brought him here had made the crossing, but soon after landing a great storm had blown up. The size of the seas had frightened him, but not as much as the floggings. For the first time he'd seen a man's back stripped of its flesh; he vowed it would never happen to him. To make the swim would be dangerous but to return to the compound now was unthinkable. He had told the others of his plan. Yinda had been initiated into his tribe two seasons before and now his word was his honour. So he must make the swim or die trying. Now was the time.

Wading from rock to rock, he kept the low shrubs that lay at the water's edge between him and the lookouts posted on the shore. Slowly and carefully he moved towards the open sea. Though he was a strong swimmer, Yinda had never swum in the ocean. Where he came from, there were rivers, fast flowing rivers. One time he'd had to swim for his life after a croc capsized his canoe, another time when he fell from his horse while leading cattle to high ground. He'd swum the King River in flood, just for a dare. However, he knew very little about the sea with its currents and heavy swell.

On a hunting expedition gathering meat for the homestead station, two men from his tribal group had broken the arm of the station owner. He had fired the shotgun he was carrying at some valued tribal rock paintings. The Aboriginals in the party had tried to keep the owner away from the area of the paintings. Thinking they were hiding something of value from him, he persisted. When finally he saw what they'd been concealing, he laughed and discharged his gun, destroying a sacred site known to their people since their beginnings. The men struck the arm that held the gun seconds after he'd fired, leaving it dangling at his side like a useless rag. Drawing a hand gun he was carrying, he fired three shots in the air, then emptied it in their direction. The pain from the shattered arm caused him to stagger and the shots went haywire.

Yinda was in the group hunting less than a half mile from them. Hearing the three warning shots, he ran to help and was first to reach the conflict. After the owner returned to the station hospital he claimed he couldn't remember which of the men had broken his arm. He'd realised his actions were irresponsible and wanted the matter forgotten. 'One black is the same as another. Don't worry about it,' he told the police when they came to pursue the offenders. The Aboriginals, believing their actions were completely justified in the circumstances, wouldn't identify the culprits either. Frustrated by the wall of silence facing them, the police took them all into custody.

Yinda had escaped twice; once while they were still in the bush. Fearing the other men might be punished for his actions, he'd returned. Later, he'd jumped the fence of the make-shift gaol but only got as far as the local tribe's camp before getting caught. After that he had been chained to the fifteen prisoners already awaiting transportation, some of whom were strangers to him, and brought to this place.

While on the island he'd managed to steal two tobacco tins.

He'd made a leather thong from the hide of a dead rock-rat. The island was infested with these little kangaroo-like creatures. He had been told that the clinking sound and the shimmer of light reflecting from the tins tied to his ankles would keep the big fish away.

Other prisoners who had tried to make the swim in the daylight were run down by the guard, caught trying to wade out to sea. That's when Yinda decided to make the swim at night.

Throwing off the rough prison rags he'd been forced to wear, he slid further into the cold water. As he did a shiver came over him. The swim would be the easy part, he told himself. Staying awake while he swam would be his main danger. With a smooth, sleek motion he sprinted through the water until he reached the first outcrop, rested, then with another short sprint he reached the second. He clung there for a while, letting his body become used to the buoyancy as the swell rose and fell.

He looked back to the island. There was nothing but open sea from here on and although it looked dark and menacing, it could be no worse than what he had escaped from. Driven by the will that empowers men to flee from fear, he struck out for the mainland. His fear drove him out of the main channel where he could see nothing but the light that shone constantly from the mainland as a warning sign for ships coming to the harbour of Fremantle.

He'd been swimming for a long time, stopping now and then to take his bearings from the light. He didn't like putting his trust in something the whites had made but it was the only thing that he could see. All around the sea was dark. As he grew tired the tobacco tins strapped to his ankles came together making a scraping sound. In his weary condition it had the screech of a curlew, screaming for its mate in the silence of the night.

'This is telling me that I'm tired and need rest,' he thought.

He rolled onto his back, watching the stars, with the calm sea lapping lazily against his body as he relaxed. Even with his spirit in its darkened state, he could not help but marvel at the beauty and magnitude of the stars; it was as if they were placed there for him alone. He wished the whites could understand, but they had no time for trivial things, this new Australian breed. They had an Empire to help build and their Empire was built on blood, guts, sweat and hard work. Their tie with nature had long been suppressed. There was no doubting that some loved the country as much as he and his ancestors did, but their love was too often swayed by material things.

He could remember how happy the boss of the cattle station he worked on was, when an unusually large muster brought more cattle for sale than expected, and how his reaction changed when the next one fell short of its margin. Beef ... that was something that the whiteman had brought to this country that he could relate to. Yinda liked the idea of having meat that he didn't have to hunt for. Though its taste was bland compared with kangaroo, beef was one thing he liked about the whiteman and his food.

Lying there on his back, resting, watching the moon and the stars, he wondered what would be going on back on the island. Had his absence been noted? It didn't matter. They would not follow at night. That's why he had to reach the mainland before daylight. Once the sun rose they would come for him, for sure. Fear began to take hold; the vision of the naked back of a man who'd been beaten flashed into his mind. He cringed, then decided that thinking of his mother would be a better way to pass the time while he rested.

Yinda's mother was from the Midan tribe; his father was a Midan elder. Yinda wasn't sure which one of his father's wives was his birth mother; all three had nurtured him as a child but Marri was his favourite. She was the strongest and the one who fetched him the fresh-cooked yams and other bush tucker when he was a child.

Tears began to form in his eyes and made them sting. He tried to wipe them away but the salt water burnt them even more. It occurred to him that the sea was not unlike tears. He wondered if the sea was God's own tears. Knowing the way some of his people were treated, God would have reason to shed a lot of tears. Though the whites had done terrible things to his people, he had been told of the white men being put to death for stealing a few cattle too; rustling, they had called it. These men had taken just a couple of stragglers from a large herd and there were so many. The laws of the whites were indeed strange.

He was beginning to get cold. It was time to swim again. Swimming, though sapping his strength, kept him warm. If he got too cold he would cramp, so he swam. The time between each swim was getting shorter and after a while his strength began to wane. The need for sleep was beginning to consume him, but to sleep was surely to drown. He drifted off into a semi-trance. His body continued to swim as if by remote control. He woke with a start. Something was circling him.

The big fish he'd been warned of had come for him … better to die here than back on the island. He was ready. Though afraid, he did not panic. Something bumped against the tins strapped to his ankles. He jerked them away and gasped in fright. The action brought his head down and under the water. As he broke the surface coughing and spitting he saw a dorsal fin break the water in front of him then disappear. After what seemed like an eternity something slid past, brushing against the soft part of his stomach then nudged at his feet again. Yinda rubbed the tins around his ankles together frantically, waiting for the lunge that would surely come at any moment.

A school of flying fish leapt in the water to the left of him. Maybe this is what the monster was after. Something leapt out of the sea where the fish had landed. Silhouetted against the light from the moon he saw what he thought was a dolphin. A comforting chatter drifted across the shimmering water. He threw his head back and laughed. The dolphin answered him, chattering louder. The school of flying fish emerged again, this time off to the right, splashing noisily.

Diving this way and that, cruising as if it knew he didn't belong out there, the dolphin nudged Yinda's feet now and then. It played for a while, coming so close that Yinda could touch it, then disappeared.

'Go my friend,' he called into the darkness. Go fish and feed. You are proof that all creatures are not evil. Thank you for waking me.

Clouds began to cover the light of the moon. The stillness of the sea began to change. The waves and swell tossed him about. A loud thundering noise pounded in his ears. Though he'd been swimming all night he had no idea how close he was to shore. Was this a storm brewing? Could he reach land before it broke? As the wind blew harder, trimming the top of each wave that washed over him, he panicked. The darkness lifted and dawn approached. He swam faster, driven by the fear of pursuit and wasted effort. It seemed a lifetime ago that he had left the island.

Fear drove his body at a frightening pace. He could feel his heart beating in his chest and knew if he did not rest he would collapse. But his body would not listen to his brain and eventually he blacked out. The next thing he was conscious of was being rolled over and over in the surf. Big waves drove him, further and further up onto the beach. He clutched the sand with what strength he could muster. The water tossed him like a sponge torn from the bottom of the ocean and threw him onto land.

'Have I made it? … Is this a dream? No, I've made it! Beyond these sand dunes is the bush … and freedom.'

The realisation swept over him as another large wave dumped him onto the sand then threatened to drag his exhausted body back into the sea as it receded. Yinda struggled up the beach. Every muscle in his body had been pushed beyond the barrier of pain while swimming. Now he felt the strain of every movement. He knelt in the sand and, falling forward, he slept. A passing fisherman saw the black body stretched out on the sand and reported it.

Yinda was still there when the constables came. They took him to the watch house and from there he was sent back to the island. Two days later he was flogged unmercifully. As the last glimmer of life drained away from his body, the chattering of the dolphin came ringing to his ears. Others who watched him wondered at the smile on the face of the dying man.

Now he was truly free.

The Wagyl

A long, long time ago, before this beautiful country of ours was invaded, my ancestors, the Aborigines, roamed free and wide, living off the land. Having close ties with Mother Nature, they moved from one area to another as the seasons changed, knowing where there was abundant food and water and where their families would be safe.

Sitting around the campfire in the evenings, the old men told many stories about the Dreamtime and the spirits that looked after them. One of those stories I will always remember.

In the hills east of Pinjarra, a small town in the south-west of Western Australia, wildlife was plentiful and many species were thriving. Among them was a huge lizard which had a tail that was long and scaly. One day the lizard decided to travel to the flat plains below and he made his way down from the hills. His tail was so big and heavy that, as it swung from side to side as he was coming down from the hills to the flat plains, great deep furrows were formed. As the seasons changed and the winter rains set in, the water flowed strongly from the hills and got caught up in the big ruts made by the lizard's tail. It rained continuously for days and as the water ran rapidly, the trail left by the lizard got deeper and deeper.

When the lizard reached the quiet surroundings of the plains, he paused to rest in a shady pool. As he rested, the big volume of water caused by the rain came rushing down and flooded the flat country where the lizard was resting.

As he struggled to survive the flood, changes were made to his body. His form changed from that of a lizard to a long green snake. Because he had no legs and would have found it hard to move around on the land, he decided to make his home in the water. After the rain ended, the furrows made by the lizard's tail became a constant flow of water and turned into a river. The long green snake travelled up and down the river, which now was his home, and looked after everything around him, especially the Aborigines who treated the river as sacred and a source of food for their people.

After many years, the long green snake and the Aborigines began to respect and understand each other. Today, the green snake is called the Wagyl by the Aborigines, and treated by them as the protector of fresh water and the many different species of fish they depend on for food.

The Champion

On 15 October 1989, Rodney Champion died. His body was found under one of the trees on the northern side of the orchestral shell in Supreme Court Gardens. Police Constable Thomas, who found the body, said he'd seen him at 0715 hours that morning and it looked as if he was just sitting, leaning his back against the tree, looking out over the river towards the Swan Brewery.

'I called out to the old bastard, but I thought he was just being ignorant, like he usually is. You know what he's like first thing in the morning. I didn't push it because he's always snaky, especially if he's got a hangover or the DTs. When I went past at 0940, I could see he hadn't moved and he was too still so I shook him and he keeled over. That's when I called you guys in.'

****

Rod Champion was old even when I first met him as a ten-year-old boy in Pinjarra. He travelled a lot back in those days. Throughout the South-west and great southern he was known as a Mubbarn Man and visiting all the Nyoongar families and communities was a responsibility he took seriously. His duties included making sure the people were healthy, Nyoongar way, teaching the local custodians how to care for the sacred places and 'singing' the spirits of Nyoongar people who had not received the Nyoongar funerary rites when they died.

Born just after the turn of the century at Coolup, near Pinjarra, Rod had seen lots of changes to the country during his life. 'Hey, Koorlung, you know what Nyoongar means? It means Man, like Yorga means woman. When the first Ngidiung Warra bastards got here, they asked one blackfella, "Who are you?" The blackfella misunderstood: thought they said, "What are you?" so he answered, "Nguny Nyoongar — I'm a Man," so the Ngidiung thought our people were called Nyoongar. Our proper name is Bibbulmun and that means the people with plenty. We had plenty, too, before these Ngidiung Warra bastards got here. Maybe it's just as well we don't call ourselves Bibbulmun these days. Ngidiung made sure we got fuck-all now!'

I attended the post mortem at the State Morgue and the pathologist had a very difficult time determining the exact cause of death. While all of his major organs showed signs of ageing and some minor effects of alcohol consumption, none was so badly damaged as to be life-threatening or cause death. There was no sign of cardiac arrest, no cancer and no sign of internal or external trauma.

'I just don't understand it, Constable Kelly. It's as if he just decided to die, then sat down and did it! It's as if his body sat down and his soul kept walking. My father used to tell me this about the full-bloods up north. He reckoned they used to do it, but I never thought a Nyoongar could do it! The Coroner might order an inquest on this one.'

When I told my boss he couldn't understand why. 'What's the fuss over a dead Nyoongar drunk? Probably one bottle of VO Port too many, I reckon. Still, if the patho reckons there's no visible cause of death we'd better be prepared. Johnny, you take his personal effects and see if you can find any next-of-kin. You'd better do some background digging, too — find out a bit about him.'

I already knew plenty, like the fact that he had outlived all of his family, so there was no next-of-kin. I also knew that he had been the most respected man in all Nyoongar country for as long as I can remember. When I was a child, he had visited our house regularly and he and my father, grandfather and I would go bushwalking off in the hills above my home town. My grandfather used to call him Kongi and my father called him Mamon out of respect, which meant that he must have been considerably older than them. We would walk for miles and sometimes stay out for days, and the old man would tell us all the Nyoongar names of the animals — Yonga, Waitj, Wardung, Warlitj, Coorr, Coomarl, Coolbardi, Waggarl, Nyingarn, Kaarder, Yorna, Cooia, Gnuk, Jiljit, Chunyart, Gilgie, Djiti-Djiti, Ngulyaak, Kullery, Jerda, and plenty more I can't remember. The old man knew them all, and could tell stories about each one. In the evenings in the bush, the old man would teach us the dances of all the animals, and we would dance around the campfire until we were exhausted. Then he would tell us more stories until the fog filled my head and I fell asleep.

Later, I used to see him when I walked the beat in the city as a young police officer. He'd always come up and greet me and we'd yarn about the old days in the bush around Pinjarra and Waroona, where I'd grown up. He'd always ask what I remembered, almost as if he was putting me through some kind of examination, and I felt a deep, secret pride in being able to satisfy his questions when he asked them. 'Hey, Koorlung, how do Nyingarns make love?' he'd ask. 'Very carefully, Oldie,' I'd reply.

I went through Rodney Champion's personal effects. There wasn't a lot there, just an old backpack containing a change of clothes and shoes, a Commonwealth bankbook, a couple of combs, the ubiquitous harmonica — a Hohner Blues Harp, no less — some personal letters and five dollars, eighty cents in cash. I went through the letters one by one until I had read them all. Not one was less than five years old and all were from his daughter who had died about that long ago. He must have looked after them very carefully.

None of the letters was particularly sentimental. His daughter had written of her pride in being his daughter and her knowledge of the work he had been doing in the Nyoongar community, only briefly lamenting the fact that it kept them from seeing more of each other. The one letter that really struck a chord was the one in which she mentioned her sorrow in never having been able to give him a grandson to carry on his good work. 'Aunty' Coralie had visited our family many times when I was young and though we never talked about it, we all knew why she could not have children. As a child she had been raped by a drunken Ngidiung who had abused her, bashed her and left her for dead. That had happened in another town, where the man had been well respected, and he had never been brought to trial, even though all the townsfolk knew what he had done. If it had been a Ngidiung Yorga, they'd have lynched him.

Rodney had found his daughter. He took her into the bush and healed her injuries, Nyoongar way. Under his careful psychological counselling Aunty Coralie had recovered and during her life had relationships with several men, but the internal damage had rendered her infertile.

As I was looking through his bankbook, I found a small key tucked inside the flap of the plastic cover. I'd never have found it if I hadn't noticed that the cover felt a bit thicker than usual. When I removed the bankbook from its cover I found that Rodney had inserted an extra layer of thin cardboard inside the plastic sleeve and had slid the key in between that and the front cover of the bankbook. Obviously, PC Thomas hadn't noticed it either.

'Mate, all I saw was a bankbook with a few dollars in it. What's the hassle, anyway? If you'd walked the beat recently you'd know he used to go to the bank every pension day and take his money out so he could buy his flagon and get drunk. I'll give him this, though, he was always clean. Not like some of them.'

I took the key to a locksmith and he told me it was a type he wasn't familiar with. 'You might want to take it to a bank. They employ their own locksmiths to make all their keys, especially their safe deposit box keys. That way no one but the owners can identify them.' Now, what would old Rodney be doing with a safe deposit box key?

So the round of the banks began, and finally the Commonwealth bank in Murray Street identified it as being one of theirs. The bank manager was only too happy to assist after I told him that the contents of the safe deposit box would be part of a deceased estate. He went through his set of keys until he found the matching key and then we went to the safe deposit box section of the strongroom, where he unlocked his lock, then I unlocked mine.

'Do you want me to stay, Constable?' he asked

'Yes, I'll have to itemise all of the deceased's possessions and issue you with a receipt for them,' I replied. 'You'll have to witness what you're signing for.'

I took the safe deposit box to one of the tables, opened it and began removing the contents. The first item was a dark green stone, about the size, shape and colour of an emu egg. It was warm to the touch and gave me a strong sense of well being. I knew exactly what it was. Next there was a hair belt with feathers woven into it. I felt a funny, tingling sensation when I touched it, and a picture of the old man came into my mind. He was smiling. Then I found two sticks, about fifteen inches long and as thick as a pick handle. Both sticks had tribal markings on them which told people where the owner came from. The next object was a flat piece of wood, about six inches long and an inch and a half wide, with a hole in one end. Threaded through the hole was a leather thong long enough to loop around one's head so that the object could be worn as a pendant. The markings on the piece of wood signified a particular rank to which the wearer was entitled. I had seen all of these items before at one time or another, always in Rodney Champion's possession, and I had often wondered what had happened to them.

There were three items left in the bag after I had removed the cultural icons. One was a small calico bank bag containing twenty-three thousand dollars, give or take a couple of hundred, neatly bundled in stacks of hundred-dollar bills. It took us quite a while to record all of the serial numbers. The other two were both envelopes, one with my name on it.

I opened the unmarked envelope first and found the title deed to a forty-acre property five kilometres west of the townsite of Pinjarra, held freehold by Rodney Champion since 1960.

'The old boy obviously didn't trust banks,' said the bank manager, tongue in cheek, referring to the money. 'That money and the property'd be worth a fortune! I wonder who'll inherit it?'

Finally, I came to the envelope marked CONSTABLE JOHN KELLY 6139. I opened it and began to read:

Dear Koorlung,

As you know, I am the last of my family. I have no living relatives and my daughter was not able to bear a successor to take over my work. So I am leaving everything I own to you, because you were the best listener of all the young people I ever tried to teach about the old Nyoongar ways. The spirit is strong in you, Johnno, so I am confident you will know the significance of the contents of this box and what to do with them. You know the meaning of the egg, and the hair belt will be my connection to you. Every time you touch it, I will be there to help. The land and money you may dispose of as you wish.

Take the time to teach the little Koorlunga about your people and your country, Johnno, so that none of the history, Law and lore is lost. Wear the amulet with pride. You are ready to be a Mubbarn Man, and I will be here to help you. BE STRONG!

Rodney Champion
12 October, 1989

P.S. Anyone else reading this letter can take it as my last will and testament.

This last sentence had been countersigned by a Justice of the Peace.

'You're a wealthy man, Constable,' said the bank manager. 'If you need help or advice on how to use the money or develop the land, you call me, I'll be only too pleased to help!'

'In your opinion, is this likely to be a legal document?' I asked.

'I'm no lawyer, but it has been witnessed by a JP, so I should think so. From the sound of the letter, he was certainly of sound mind when he wrote it!' he said.

****

The Champion Centre, five kilometres west of Pinjarra, is a retreat for Nyoongar people to go and recover from alcohol and substance abuse, to receive counselling for various other mental and spiritual disorders and to take time out from the rigours of living alienated from their own heartlands by white occupation. The Centre runs on Nyoongar time and teaches Nyoongar culture, crafts and spirituality.

Recollections of the Early Days

I was born in Port Hedland, 1932. My father came from Java, of Arab origin. I'm not sure where he was born. On his entry form to Australia it said he was born in Malaya, but Malaya covered Indonesia, Singapore and the Malayan Peninsula at that time, so it could have been anywhere. As a matter of fact he never really spoke about where he was born, but where they lived. The family moved to Malacca (that's in Malaysia), but they were Moslems and Malacca was a Portuguese-Christian area. They weren't satisfied living there so they pushed on and went to Java, to a place called Surabaya and it was there that they took up land on the Surabaya River and settled down and worked the land.

They had oxen, chickens and ducks. They grew stuff in the gardens and used to take it to market every morning, seven days a week, sell their products and buy what they wanted. They were about twelve miles from town, from the markets, and they used to leave home about 3.00am and be there about 6.00am, I suppose, then be home by midday once they'd disposed of all their produce. That's the sort of life they lived from the 1880s to the turn of the century.

My father was twenty years old when he left his home in 1900 and went to Singapore and put his name down to work on ships. You'd go to the agents — there was a big English company there. You'd put your name down and they'd find you a job anywhere. They were calling for a lot of crew to go to Australia, so they put him on one of the ships heading for Australia and the first port of call was Derby.

It was just by luck. He only wanted to get on a ship and they wanted a shipping crew in Australia to man the pearling fleet, so about a dozen of them got on there that day and they ended up in Derby and then the company brought them by wagon back to Broome. The agents went around and disposed of them there to different owners who wanted crew. That's how they operated. They had their agents in Singapore — well, they had agents in Hong Kong, the Philippines, Ceylon. They would get cheap labour there. See, Australia had hardly anyone. The only labour they had here were Aboriginals and because they were inhabitants of the country, there were lots of things written about how to treat them and how much you could work them.

There was all this stigma then that they weren't much good, because the local (Aboriginal) people would fight back, 'cause they had their business to do too. You know, when it came Law time they wanted to go and do this and that and employers, who were mostly Europeans, said, 'No you can't do this.' So they'd rebel against them and run away in the middle of the night or spear them. They were touchy people to deal with. Anyhow, the companies imported these foreigners — indentured labour they called it, and I think they got about a shilling a day, yeah about a shilling a day was their wages. This was in 1900.

When my father first came to Australia he worked for Ted Norman, the biggest master-pearler in Broome. He was a deckhand for a couple of years and then became a tender in the third year, repairing sails and ropes and equipment and maintaining the vessel. In the first two days when they came to port they had to strip the ship of all the shell that had to be brought ashore and then repair all the things that needed repairing. By the third day everything had to be ship-shape ready to go to sea again, although you wouldn't go to sea, probably, for another week. Everybody had to show that they were committed to work.

My mother came from the Fitzroy Valley, up in the Kimberley Downs. She's from the Bunuba Tribe. I think she was born in 1906, but I'm not sure. Her mother was a full-blood Aboriginal. At the age of six months she was taken away from her and placed at Beagle Bay Mission till she was about eighteen years of age, I think. She was reared by people who lived in a 'colony' — Aboriginal people from around that area, who were taken away from Norman Creek and other surrounding places and ended in the mission. Their role was to foster incoming children who were very small and then they were put into the dormitories when they got old enough. These people belonged to the local region, the Ngulngul mob. The missionaries were German priests and brothers and Irish nuns.

When the girls were sixteen years of age they sent them out

from Beagle Bay into Broome and from there my mother was sent to Port Hedland to work for a local doctor named Dr Davis. She worked there for a few years and then was sent back to Broome. She applied to get married to my father and that took about three years to get permission from the local authorities. The police were in charge of it … well, that was the order of the day. They controlled Aboriginal people and at that time Aboriginal people were classified as stock — they weren't humans. You weren't a free person at all in your own country where you were born.

Well, I couldn't put a positive date on when my parents met, but my father settled into his house in Port Hedland and my mother was working for the doctor. He was already settled there in 1922 and she must've arrived there in 1924. The women working for the doctor were working seven days a week, twenty-four hours a day! Domestics in the house, you know. That was a common thing, all the white women had three or four servants doing the washing, doing the raking … cheap labour and they were contracted. My mother was contracted for twelve and six a week, but she only got five shillings.

The Department of Native Welfare had provisions that made it very hard for Aboriginal women to marry white men. It was very hard. It would take nearly three years to get permission and sometimes permission would not be granted. They may not have an office in your town, but they had a representative — maybe the local doctor or the manager of the native hospital. So if he didn't like you, you had no chance. The only thing you could do was, when he went on holidays, reapply straight away! That's how a lot of them overcame it and got away with it. You see, you were just like an animal, or something. It's been quoted that they were similar to animals, pests. Aboriginal people were pests.

Anyhow, my father came to Hedland early in 1922 and he bought a boat and three nets and took off fishing. He fished around the place, making a pretty honest sort of a living and then the publican offered him a job at The Esplanade — better than going out all night long, pulling these nets trying to get a feed. So anyhow, he took that on and that was in 1922 and he stayed there until 1942, when the local army swooped in.

Ooh, there was plenty of food at the hotel. All the leftovers at night! Their leftovers'd feed a hundred people and then, you know, with a bit of tea and sugar that the old publican used to give us, we were never starving and we fed ten other families too. You could get extra food from different places — someone might be out in the bush, might be fencing, and they might shoot a couple of kangaroos or an emu and they'd bring them in that night and everybody'd share them. That'd keep them going for two or three days. There was also an old cook at DeGrey, he used to bring in a quarter of a bullock when he came in for his holidays and say, 'Help yourself.' Well, in twenty minutes there was no meat left! Things like that, you know.

Things started to come good around 1939. There seemed to be a bit more money being generated in the community, but they were taking people out of the community, sending them down south to the war, all able-bodied men. But a lot of blokes got left behind, because they were manpowered like my father. The military had a base in Port Hedland. They came down and went to see the hotel manager and then came out to see Dad. They said, 'Tomorrow morning at 8.00am you've got to jump on the train and go to Shaw River' (which is halfway between Hedland and Marble Bar on the railway line). 'You've got to go and work out there.'

'Oh no,' he said. 'I can't go there. I've got all my chooks at home.'

'Don't worry about your chooks or the chicks. You gotta go.'

So then he said, 'Oh I've gotta wash the plates and who's gunna wash the saucepans?' Some excuse not to go! But Pickworth was the Captain then and he said, 'You're going.'

Once my father got established, we went to live out there for a while. He was a fettler, repairing the railway line. He stayed in Shaw River till he retired in 1945. There was a camp there — little huts and things for the families and plenty of water, millions and millions of gallons of fresh water. Oh, we had a garden about ten miles long! It used to take a week to cart the water from one end to the other. He grew everything. He went mad! We used to produce five forty-pound jarrah cases of ripe tomatoes a day; chuck them on the train and send them into town with cabbage and silverbeat and beans and turnips and you name it. Those blokes had their army camp right in the middle of town, where the old state school was. We used to send all that stuff in there and they used to send us bread, tinned fruit and tinned lemonade. (It was lemon juice in a tin and it was a favourite thing!) Every day they'd send four hundred loaves of bread up the track, 'cause they had a thousand crew working on the ground at Corunna Downs and they had two transport divisions camped just out of Marble Bar carting stuff from the rail there to the Corruna Downs airport. Some would cart fuel, some would cart bombs and some would cart food. There was over a thousand tonnes a day .going up to Marble Bar.

Well, we were supplying all this food and my mother and my godmother (she was next door) used to cook these bloody big pots of kangaroo stew or kangaroo rissoles and fresh vegies. There were a lot of soldiers and airforce people riding the train, going back after being on leave. They'd have a good feed and they'd leave two shillings. It was quite good there and they enjoyed it. My mother and godmother got recognition from the defence department over it! They never got any money or anything, but the authorities said, 'Oh what a good part you played.'

My father worked out at the railway for three years, I think, and then he was put off because he was sixty-five and the war'd just about finished. He went back and lay around the house driving my mother crazy! Then Mary Dakas, a local girl among the pearlers in Hedland, Australian-born Greek, became a master-pearler and pleaded and promised him everything to work for her. She said, 'Bring your son along too and we'll give him good money,' and my father's eyes lit up when she said good money, so we left Port Hedland and went to Broome on 22 February 1947.

I wasn't even fourteen when I went to Broome but I was a pretty big sort of a boy and got away with it. I signed on the dotted line and went to sea and then my father took crook and he went back home and I continued on up there. I continued up there in the pearling industry and used to send a lot of money back home, nearly all my money, I suppose. After the war we were on this percentage bonus for the number of shells you'd get. I was fourteen and I was getting more money than a bloke who was a foreman in the PWD (Public Works Department) or on the main roads. You had to be very hard and not be sentimental about it and waste your money. But a lot of those master-pearlers still did cheat a lot of people, like those full-bloods. They were only paying them half wages ... yeah, and these Aboriginal people, they accepted it.

There was what they call blackbirding. Yeah, give them cake and give them a good feed and what-not, or give them a drink of plonk and then chuck them on board and then head out to the ocean and make them jump overboard, dive in. That was blackbirding in those days. Once they got on open sea, just chuck them overboard. But some used to swim back to shore. Then they got a few regulations into the system in the twenties, where everybody who went to sea had to be signed on at the shipping office. So that eliminated this picking them up from the creeks and camps.

See, crew were a big problem to the master-pearlers: borrowing money, gambling, getting locked up … That was part of the culture in Broome, crazy! I read the papers now and see that people do this and do that, or you see people down the street singing out to people, abusing them and nothing done about it, but back then you only had to whistle at them or say something and they'd give you three months in gaol.

Other nationalities came into the system too, like Portuguese, Swiss people and Germans — adventurous types of people. Pearling was the name of the game in those days, so a lot of them drifted up into the north-west, especially those who had a little bit of navy background. Then they'd come here and they'd change their titles to an admiral or captain or some blooming thing. They might've been bloody deck-scrubbers when they were in the royal navy! They worked their way up into positions of managers and they got grants from some of these overseas financiers and set up their own business. There were hundreds of them, pearlers with only one or two boats, you see, and then they'd have a block of land and big gardens and half a dozen servants. People thrived on it, it was better than what they had back at home. They were all there: people from Timor, the Philippines and Malaysia, Singapore, Ceylon, India, Pakistan … you name it … Chinese, Japanese …

My mother was brought up with Irish and Germans and then she had the Aboriginal culture too. She had two cultures. But my father, he was a strict Moslem. He only had the one culture and he practised it very, very strongly and my mother had to fit in. Yes, we never ate pork or bacon and every Thursday night after he finished work at 9.00pm we'd be served up drinks — tea, coffee, cocoa and scones my mother'd have to make specially — and he'd read the Koran and we'd get into it. If any visitors came, he'd make them sit there and listen to him praying.

Well, my mother reckoned she was being slaved! She'd be grumbling about it. So about one or two in the afternoon she'd get her fishing line together and go down to the beach and she used to sit and fish till the sun went down. Some days she'd get forty or fifty fish, you know. She'd take them home and clean them and cook them and give a lot away to the nuns or townspeople, and then they might get something and give it to us.

There was a problem in the early stages, when I was born. I must've been over one year old when a visiting Catholic priest came around. This particular afternoon there was a church service on and I got christened with a few other kids from around town. Anyhow, one of the girls at that service was working as a waitress at the same pub as my father. She said, 'Oh, we saw your little son in church. He was christened.' He just dropped everything and blew his top and went out the back door, came racing home and went berserk. He raced into the tool shed out the back where he used to have a revolver and keep all his bullets, but when my mother and another lady there saw him going into this tool room, they just took off — grabbed me and away we went. We camped out at an old Greek lady's place, old Mrs Constantine's. Oh, it took him months and months to get over that. My mother was too scared to go back. Half a dozen people had to negotiate a deal, you know? He was a Moslem and I'd become a Catholic and that was it. That's why I say I'm a Catholic Moslem!

****

One of the major things I was involved in after I left the pearling industry, from about '57 to '59, was patrolling a section of the main roads from Onslow to a new town, Talgarno, which was about four miles away from Anna Plains Station. They were building a great big airport there at that particular time and there were over a thousand people working there. That was the town they were developing at the end of the launching pad for the Blue Streak rockets; the launching pad stretched from Maralinga to Talgarno. It was a British and Australian joint venture thing. You see, when India and Malaysia were granted independence and the British had to withdraw, they had to leave all their military establishments, so they were going to do it in Australia; right in the centre of Australia. They were going' to shoot these rockets off and they were aimed into Asia. It was a pretty big project and it lasted three years and then, when they got everything established, they superseded the Blue Streak rockets with something else! It was a shame — there was a nice town built out there in the desert with a great big airport. It wasn't opened up really. No, nothing's there now. You can see where the airport's been and where the foundations of the buildings were. They just sold all those buildings, just stripped them down. They took three or four to Broome and some to Port Hedland. Beautiful big buildings!

Well, they had a lot of trucks — something like twenty or thirty trucks a day coming up and going back, carting equipment and stuff. We had to patch all the roads up and then when we got back to Talgarno, I'd have to go out and down the track and do a sweep right 'round about a hundred miles out and pick up these old Aboriginals and cart them back in to Wallal feeding station or La Grange Station and drop them off there, because that was their language, their tribal area. I'd have to drive out there maybe once every ten days because when the time came and they were going to fire these rockets something might happen, might blow up.

It was such a big project, you know. I was pretty young then and it's a challenge for a young bloke. You lap it up, only one track right around and they knew there were Aboriginal people there, 'cause they used to sight them years ago. They'd see their smoke and sometimes they used to walk into the station. They had a fair idea how many people were there, but there were a few that got away from us. You know, probably the desert people. They'd just sit at the homestead there for three or four days and then they'd disappear overnight, back out in the bush. Then you had to run around and chase them. Once you got to know them you were satisfied once you had them on board. They didn't mind jumping on the back of the truck. They didn't know where they were going, but they always ended up in the same place and then they'd make an effort to run away again and I thought that was entertaining. Yeah, I'd say, 'Come on, you gotta come.' He'd jump up, chuck his wife on and dog, if he had it. I'd give them a drink of water or cup of tea and a bit of bread and they were happy. They thought they were first-class tourists coming home, the look on their faces!

****

We were lucky, you know. The greatest asset we ever had was the older people handing down the stories, Dreamtime stories.

People might laugh at it and say, 'Oh the Dreamtime, they're dreaming again.' That might be half of it, but the other half is telling us about different things that happened and how they happened. Traditional Aboriginal people have got to protect each waterway and the hills and the trees. This is what they've gotta do every year and it falls in with the weather. The initiation services start about the end of October or November. They go by their instructions from the moon and the weather and what the trees are producing and they go up into the hills and caves. There are some old drawings and carvings. They've got to watch these and look after them. In some places you're allowed to go and look, but some places women are not allowed to go and look and then there are women's areas where men can't go and look — even their own tribal men aren't allowed. They accept that, you see. The tribal men accept the women's Law. They say, 'That's women's business.' But when they have the initiation services, in the end the men and women come together, because these are their children who've gone through it all. The men've got one section of it and the women do the second section of it.

Everybody has to be educated about the Aboriginal race and their culture and Law. Yet, after saying that, I can learn for another fifty years about it myself and I've been living in it, practising it! I might even go two districts out, into my mother's area, and it's entirely different. It might take me fifty years to learn that, you see. So if you want to learn about Aboriginals, you've got a lot to learn! We've all got a lot to learn, even those people in the Bunuba tribe, and the Nyoongar down here, they've got a lot to learn about us. But I've seen some areas where people are not following the culture. They're following the white man's law and they just get up and rattle off about 'your culture' and 'your tribe'. See, they know a lot only because they speak to a few people around town and they read about different things.

Every time I lie in bed at night I think that one day if we all pull together, we'll achieve something. If you unite, you'll get somewhere. The nearest I've seen of that coming to fruit would be Noel Pearson. I thought, you know, people in every state would combine together and follow his promise and there'd be a united body to front up. That's the only thing that'll do us. For us to get on equal terms, I think the first thing we've got to do is get on equal terms with ourselves, with our own people. (We had a family reunion the other day. One hundred and fifty-four people were there and we probably had fifteen different policies on the same matter! That's only one family!) While we're fragmented we haven't got a leg to stand on. We're all over the place. Also, a lot of Aboriginal people are pensioned off. They get their fortnightly pension and they don't care what goes on outside the house. Aboriginal people like that are causing a problem for us.

There's a mass movement of people going from one area to another and there are a lot of inter-tribe marriages. This has broken all their culture down. There may be only ten percent of the people in the Pilbara following the Law and making their kids follow the Law and there's ninety percent of them who don't belong to any Law or any culture. They only pick up in little bits and pieces what they see their friends doing. That's destroying Aboriginal culture. Years ago, when people started to move in from their communities and they became entangled with the local community, they were forced to live under the rules and regulations and culture in each area and they were part of it. That went a lot better, but then it deteriorated too. Now any young bloke coming in and marrying into the community has no respect for his mother-in-law or father-in-law. You see, if it was under Aboriginal Law and culture, he'd have to respect to the highest degree and then if something happened, well they'd take their daughter back and then get ten men to go out and deliver the punishment — either belt him up with a green stick or put a spear through his leg. That's fallen away, although there are some young people still there who want to carry on with it. They give you your punishment and then you can go to the hospital and get treated. Then you know that you've got to respect these people under Law and culture. But that's mostly gone and now you've got the police coming in and delivering hefty blows to them, saying, 'You're not allowed to do this. We'll lock you all up.'

Lots of young kids aren't interested in their own culture. You might ask them one day something about it and they're lost, know only what they've read! By the time they're sixteen they should've already gone through the Law — that's the first stage. Now from there to the second stage, before they hand down any responsibilities to you, you could be twenty-five or thirty years of age. It takes a lot of time; when there's a Law meeting on you've got to go out there for maybe three weeks. No more television and no more town life! No more booze and no more drugs! You've gotta do your work for three weeks. While you're out there you're learning and it's coming back to you and you become accustomed to it.

It's a full time job, this initiation service! We're dependant on every fit young person to come back into the fold. The girls have got a lot to do, as much as the boys. The boys've got to go out and hunt kangaroos and turkeys and emus or go and pinch a sheep or bullock to keep that camp going with meat today and the girls've got to stay home and make the tea and the damper and look after the little kids and teach the little kids how to dance and sing. Normally, it's three to four weeks in each centre and they might have ten centres in one year. Normally it starts in November and then they go across to Woodstock, which is only about thirty miles away, and down to Roebourne and then up to Jigalong and across to La Grange, which is about four hundred miles away. You just try and shift two thousand people on the back of trucks! Some of them walk, cut across country, having fun as they go all the way. This is the true practice of Aboriginal initiation ceremonies. They come to a hill or a creek, you know, and they go and check those sites out. That's why everywhere you go where there's a hill or a waterhole you'll see artefacts and message sticks. A lot of white people can't understand that. Over forty thousand years they might go here and there and later they might come back and then they'll go the other way. They might take a long trip around. They're incredible, Aboriginal people!

There's still a lot of people who live in town and hold more Laws than the people living in the bush. They shed their bloody city clothes and don their paint and go out dancing and assist in initiations early in the morning, when the time is right. It's normally about three weeks and then they might have an overflow, maybe ten boys they couldn't do and they're pushed for time. They've got to go to Woodstock, so they'll go over there and try and do them over there. The custodians take them over there and then they might go to Roebourne, and because they started the system off everyone just keeps following. A lot of those old people get real happy when the Law season's on; a big feed all day long and then they're also helping train the younger ones, the little kids. They teach them how to serve the old people food and teach them the dancing and teach them the singing. They take them down to a shady tree and make a fire and they sit around there and it's great! The little kids enjoy it. I used to go and sit under a shady tree with my camera and take a few photos of them and see all these little kids there dancing and singing.

See, we're teaching young kids and we're handing something down every year to them and that's flowing through. It's nothing written. It's by word of mouth and actually showing what to do. I'm very proud of what I taught my own kids. They've taken it on and they can teach their kids now. Tradition will be handed down, and that's what all families should do.

My Brother, Des Parfitt

It was through the Dreaming
that we as Brothers came,
sharing everything we had
as we crossed the Plains of our Youth
to where we are now as Old Men,
and where you left us.

The Songs of Old that we sang
in the Nights around the Campfires
of the Swamps in the Eden Hill camp days,
will always be remembered
in the Coming Days and Nights.

It will be in each Raindrop that falls,
it will be in the North, East, South and West winds that blow,
it will never fade away, My Brother.

Thank you for sharing your life with us
as we passed through the Laneways of Yesterday.

You leave us now
but we will follow you when our time comes.

My Daughters, My Girls, My Life, My Everythings

My daughters, my entire life
You are so precious to me.
You will never feel the pain I have.

I don't know how,
But our lives will be shared,
Spent together, full of love, never to be separated
Like me and my Mum.

I will keep you with me.
They will never get any one of you
Away from me and your Dad,
We will never let that happen.

My history will never be repeated
My pain will be just that, my pain.
For you, my daughters, my girls, my life,
You will never be taken from me.

We will go together, to another place, another time.
I never suffered the way my mother must have.
She had no way to change
The things she could have.

For no one really cared how she or we felt
And the pain that kept us apart
Will not reunite us in our lifetime.
I love you, my mother — my three daughters
My girls, my life, my everythings.

No Time for Laughter

I never heard her laugh
But I did see her cry twice
That was all in my adult life I had
To share with her, my mother.

Her pain was as real as mine
We had no way to make up for
The lost years, lost chances
To love each other
With the special love
Of a mother for her daughter and
A daughter for her mother.

Together but apart we lost the chance
But never the love we should have shared
The bonds, the invisible bonds
Were there and still are so strong.

Even though she has gone
God rest her soul I loved her so
I never heard her laugh
If she did, did she sound like me
And did she think of me
As often as I would think and yearn for her?

And what would my life have been like with
A Mum, my Mum to
Love me
Just me
For me, Irene Calgaret,
Little Aboriginal girl, born in the forties
Taken in the fifties
To a mission made just for us.

We deserved better
Why didn't we get a little better
Or just a little of what were
Our rights as Aboriginal children
Black Australians?

My Country Oomarri

Ambrose told his stories while we lived at a piece of paradise called Walngga (McGowan Island Beach) twenty kilometres north of Kalumburu in the north Kimberley. We were there to record some of the oral history of the Kalumburu people, including Ambrose's.

We lived under a giant boab tree in a shack on a beach which had no front or back door, just a cement slab with a wooden structure holding up asbestos sheeting and a tin roof. Our room had no ceiling so the large green tree snake which visited one day in the middle of a working session could slither and coil up beautifully on one of the wooden rafters. None of the walls actually met the roof line, so we lived in fresh air twenty-four hours a day. The corners of the building were held together by tree trunks cut from the bush and there were plenty of generous gaps and no shortage of wildlife in our small room. We slept on thin swag mattresses on the floor and on three occasions I was woken in the dead of night by something cool moving next to my skin — a snake had come to share our bed. We only killed the first one in shock and fright, the others we persuaded to spend the rest of the night outside. Giant hairy spiders, foot long centipedes, and hermit crabs in the hundreds spread themselves everywhere — we were the intruders.

Ambrose's stories were recorded when there was enough money to buy diesel for the generator, when the heat was bearable and the flies not too insistent. The tiny old Apple Macintosh Classic computer and printer lived covered under plastic when they could not be used — which was from 8.00am to 4.00pm because of the heat — and when I typed the recorded stories into the computer, the flies in the day and other insects at night would crawl underneath my glasses. It wasn't easy. Compensation and inspiration were provided by the magic view across the bay to the Kul mountain shrouded in mist on the other side. The mornings there are incredibly serene and beautiful, the song of the butcherbird clear and so very sweet it could make your heart ache. In the afternoon a breeze would blow in from the open ocean and brilliant stars hung low in nights pulsating with sounds of life from the bush.

Traudl Tan

My name is Ambrose Mungala Chalarimeri and I belong to the Kwini tribe. I was born at Oomarri Waterhole, King George River in the Kimberley, and I live in the bush for a long time. Don't know which year I was born. First white people I saw is police and people used to run away in the bush, on the mountain. Police came on horseback on patrol, now and then, once every few months. When people used to go hunting, they found out from a long way police was coming, riding on a horse. They can see them coming and they knew it was the police. They were wearing a hat, an ordinary hat and proper straight but with a police medal on the front.

I had never seen a horse before. We knew it was an animal and we were scared. People ran away from the police and the police could not find them. The police would camp at the foot of the mountain and wait. Sometime people would go and talk to them. Men used to come and talk to the police tracker. They talked language too, might be Kwini language, because those fellas used to live in the bush before they were employed as police boys. Police could not go in the bush on their own, they never bin find their way. They mostly had police boys — one white police and two or four police trackers, Aborigines. They were people from Forrest River Mission like old Frank Martin, Victor's father from that Lyn River, he belong to Oombulgurri.

The police boys carried guns all the time, they would employ mission boys to be police trackers, well known to everybody. They never shot the Aboriginal people. They tell the people, 'We look after you fellas to come to the mission, to be civilised, not to be scared, we here to patrol not kill anybody, tellem.' People were scared of the policemen before, that's why they had police trackers to help them not to be scared of white people. They used to patrol from there to here, right around from Forrest River and come round here to Kalumburu.

We didn't know what a mission was. The police boys show us flour, tea, sugar and tobacco and explain what it is and where it came from. 'When you go to the mission that's where you get all this,' they said. Aborigines also had the bush wheat that make into a flour from millet called milalbo, nearly as small as birdseed. They usually have one flat stone on the ground like a basin and a round stone to grind the seeds and make into a fine flour. Instead of collecting seeds in the bush, which was difficult sometimes, the mission offer flour. It was more easy to get, just given. The same with the tobacco. The mission tobacco was better than the bush tobacco. Sometime that was hard to find and pretty strong, it could give you a headache. Slowly people find out what mission was. They first heard about it from the police trackers, later they went and had a look.

So we were staying in the bush all the time. When nothing wrong police didn't bother. People used to tellem what they doing, hunting, living here. Police tellem what they should do at that stage, make sure we don't kill one another, something like that, the white law. People wouldn't tell the police if they did have any real trouble. They scared of telling anybody, they keep it secret to themselves. Aborigines always like that. So police just came anyway.

My father took me down to see the police one time. I was afraid. Father told me that these policemen passing through, explain to us a lot of time what they were. 'Don't be frightened of the policemen, they are just here to see if something had happened.' Sometime someone carried story to the mission that somebody had died and the police went to investigate. The missionaries in either Forrest River Mission or here [Kalumburu] or Pago, used to ask the police to have a look around. My father was not scared of the police. He knew who they were, and the police and the tracker talked to him. Women stayed behind in the hiding place, they used to hide and not come out. Aboriginal people couldn't trust a white person, not really unless they knew who they were, the same person going up and down. They knew the police trackers, always the same men, but the people in the bush were on the alert mostly. They all knew about the Forrest River massacre in 1926, not long ago. We didn't understand the white person, what they said, it sounded strange. The police tracker talked English and lingo and my father speak lingo and the tracker could understand.

When rain time came we used to go to the cave, anywhere we think it was safe. They used to find the cave there, they would know where the cave is. We used to be close by and stay there for a while. Sometime when it was no cave we used to go and make camp out on the flat. We used paperbark because we can't find a cave, see. We cut it round and round again. They cut branches and made a humpie, made it round and round. Put the stick in the ground like a post, put others on top for the roof and put paperbark on the top. They used to put lot of big timber, some sort of a heavy wood, not stones, and secure it so it won't blow away in a wind. They never put stones. People used to dig the soil around the humpie so water won't go inside, see. They dug with a stick, that's how they also used to dig for yams. That's hard work. Men used to dig the trench. Sometime the humpies would be pretty big, like this room [four square metres]. My people, the Kwini people, are tall, that's why they built the humpies big. The dogs would sleep inside or outside. I used to have my own dog. Night time, sleep time, my dog used to sleep with me. We had about five or six dogs. When I was smaller I used to sleep with my mother. When I grew older, about four or five years, I used to sleep with my favourite dog.

We used to sleep on paperbark, paperbark is good, and we put grass on top of the paperbark, not spinifex, that's too sharp. People made some beds here and there in a humpie. We wouldn't worry about a ground cover. We only had one layer of paperbark and then grass. Mothers keep babies in a wanda, a basket made of bark. Humpies had a doorway and people could stand up in them. Humpies were out in the open, never under trees or near the river, never. People know something might fall on them, because lightning might strike too. Always put it in the open, not near the water because a flood might come. People had to walk to get water in paperbark or in some of the bark they used to make basket for baby. They made it round and carry the water in that, seal it with wax from the spinifex. Take the spinifex, green one, rich one, and put it in the fire and then you see wax fall down see, like a tar you know. No wonder mark remains when you drive over spinifex, it remains forever unless you burn it. Station manager always can tell if someone has driven over the spinifex because it leaves a track.

Sometime they camped near a waterhole for drinking. Sometime people would make fire inside or outside the humpie, or near the doorway, smoke go through the door. It's good for mosquitoes too, the smoke. Cave is pretty good — oh, sometimes they are small or sometime big. Sometime cave can be on top, little bit high so people could sleep there and watch out. That's where they used to watch out you know, sometime when people come from other country and make fire, they knew someone is there coming, lighting fires. People used to prefer caves because it's higher. They used to choose it whether kangaroo come in or not. The roo will go away. Cave used to smell when it's wet, rain time, smell different eh, smell nicely when water falls you know, smell like nature itself — of kangaroo camp there and spinifex smell or gum leaves. People cooked on the ground outside but if it rained they cooked inside. You find smoke there in places that I saw, there must have bin fire there. Sometime there was paperbark and we would know people were here. If people saw a cave where somebody has bin, leave that one look for nother one, or build humpies. They also used to build a stone fireplace. They watch the children if the cave was high up, so they won't fall off.

People lived in the cave long time as they liked, nobody don't tell them go this way, all depends where they like to go. The whole rainy season they stay there. When the rainy season came people would keep near the caves, they knew where to go then. Some did painting there on the rock. Nothing else to do. They would do the painting, and then go away. Painting is evidence of what was before, drawing is what they see. The painting was left there for the others to know that our tribal people has lived there. Many of our paintings are very beautiful.

When people have initiation or corroboree it's Law time. They don't have one place to do dancing, they go out to the flat. People travel place to place and ask one another what they do, what they do, and this man tell them, you better come and dance here. That's what they did when it wasn't raining. If food was left over it was hung in the tree or wrapped in paperbark for keeping. Paperbark is good because nothing touch it. They never carry raw meat, always cooked meat. When person was sick they tried to find medicine to save his life. They looked for the special plant, which grow a lot when it's wet. They break it and boil it in the hot water and put it on the skin or drink it. There is a lot of bush medicine, the old people know about it. Now people mostly don't.

I liked eating goanna then. We used to go hunt goanna with the dogs. Dogs find it and chase it. Sometime goanna go up the tree and then we stop and climb the tree to hit it so that it can fall down. Some people wait at the bottom to kill it. It was cooked in the hot ashes, cooked there for a long time because big one takes longer to cook. Then we eat it one part, someone eat nother part. It was there for everybody and each one chooses their favourite piece. Passionfruit I also like, the one that grows here, and that nother one berries. And that cunmanggu [bush potato], that is very good. I like to see some more, and bush honey, that was the most we used to eat, we call it wana. People also collected the green ant nests from the trees, get them quickly and squash them between their hands like they were clapping, or put it inside the water and squeeze it and bring it out and then eat it like that. Nother time they boil the green ants and drank the water hot like drinking tea. That was for colds and sore throats. We call green ants yilwei.

When it was really hot we used to go under the trees or put a humpie up, build it like a bow shed out in the open for shade. I loved life in the bush. It was pretty good because there was lots of food and as a child I had a lot of freedom and happiness.

DOG LICENCE AND STATION WORK

In the 1960s it was the old pound yet, and station job was very enjoyable. People used to love it, used to love riding in the bush and chasing cattle. They knew how to ride horses. Most people worked on the stations. There was other work too, main road jobs and shire work. In town they mostly worked on the wharf and people who live in town, they had to work there. Aborigines in those days lived only on the Reserve, nowhere else in town. They would be put in gaol for vagrancy if they had no job and were in town. They must have work and few shillings in their pocket.

The police asked them, 'You got a job or not?' Sometime they didn't. So the police tell them, 'Make sure you go away and get a job on a station.' In those days life was pretty hard and pretty strict too, I know because I was around. The police used to check up how many Aboriginal people are working in PWD [Public Works Department] and on the wharf. There was a list of the workers or they go to the employer and ask them. Aborigines were not allowed drinking rights in those days. People used to have a card with a photo so when they go to the bar they show them the photo and the card and then barman handed over the drinks. That was known as 'the dog licence'. [At that time dogs used to wear a special tag, a licence.] It was really a citizen rights paper, but it was called a dog licence to stir the people up, to make fun of it. On it was written, 'this man has full citizenship'.

People from Northern Territory came to Western Australia and they were barred from drinking at the pub because they had no citizen right paper. I think that they were always free there, that they could drink in Darwin without a dog licence. I never own one because I never drink in those days. It was like a passport, inside the wallet you keep it. Got name and date of birth on it. Only need that to go drinking at the pub in the bar, I don't think white people had one, only the Aborigines had that.

When I saw that I thought it must be good thing. People used to get into trouble when they supply alcohol to other people. If white people supply grog they could be in big trouble. If people had dog licence they would be in more trouble if they supply it to the other people than for getting drunk. People that supply used to go to gaol for six months or more. People that go and buy grog and take away, they get caught. People were not allowed to just give it to others or drink with them.

The police used to smell the alcohol and saw how people behave. When they talk to you in the street they can smell the alcohol. They ask you where you got it from. They then say you better come to the court. People used to be in gaol for a couple of days but this fella supplying used to go for six months, sometime twelve months. Because in those days they didn't have any help, see. It was only Welfare they had, not legal aid. Judge had the power when they sentenced the person to go in straight for twelve months. Welfare mostly helped pay people's fines, couldn't help in nother way.

Dog licence means to be like white people, just go in a hotel and have a few glasses. They said that to have this right you have to use them the right way. I knew it was only Aboriginal people who had a dog licence. It was for them to drink. I didn't think it was a discrimination. But it was really no good that only Aboriginal people were stopped in the street and ask if they had work or a dog licence. A lot of white people were working, there were lots of jobs for everyone then. We used to go for races to town. That's the only time we were allowed to go in unless we worked there. Nobody stopped people then, they knew it was races and didn't stop anyone. Then, nobody ever think that this was our country and why did they do this, nobody ever think that way. Maybe I thought they had more power than us, that's all. We never ask questions, we didn't know nothing about that. The first white person I ever saw was a police and they had a lot of power. That was the start of it, they had power, we didn't.

This is how the power was there. Once in Wyndham there was an accident in the street. One of the wharfies, that old fella, Barbara Gore's uncle, that big fella, Aboriginal fella, old fella Hilton — motorbike hit him. I was there and it happened in the 1960s and I saw the old fella walk down and the motorbike hit him. This white bloke came very fast, both of them got knocked out and an ambulance came. At that time I saw they came to save the white man first, that's what I saw and that old man Hilton was still laying down there. That white bloke died, he knocked his head against the road you know, and he was taken to white hospital. They helped the white bloke first. Instead they should have helped both, they helped one first only. Later on they took the old man to hospital. It was about an hour before they came for the old man.

The old man was talking but couldn't get up, couldn't move. Later on they came in a car, an ordinary car with an orderly, a white bloke. But he went back with the car and told them he needed an ambulance, he couldn't pick him up. He came from the native hospital, the Three Mile Hospital. He rang the doctor and said there is another old fella, he needs an ambulance. While people were waiting, they talked to the old man. 'You will be all right, they will be here soon.' Among themselves they said, 'Why couldn't they pick two persons at the same time. They only took the white man, they should have taken both.' People were angry. They were saying, 'What time are they coming?' and cursing the ambulance. A policeman was standing there too, waiting. He was stopping the traffic because the old fella was lying in the middle of the street. Later on I still had little idea about power. I didn't think about that, I didn't want to think about it. The Aboriginal man had a smashed knee, today he is still limping.

With the dog licence you were to be joined up and be treated like the white people. I didn't touch alcohol in those days so I didn't worry. The rules then was very strict, made by white politicians for Aboriginal people. It was too early for me to think about that much. I was too young then — we didn't know the rules of the white world, the government, the legislation. I had grown up on Kalumburu Mission, a very remote place, isolated.

In the town there were rules, the white law. In the bush we could make our own but not in the town. In the bush there was nothing to worry about until the police came along. The towns were white places except the reserves. In town were the shopkeepers, the wharfies, the bloke who look after the hotel — we just accept them. The older Aboriginal people, the pensioners who belong to the town, they moved away. They used to be kept separate out of town, where Welfare looked after them. It was the older people that like to live away from town because they had dogs with them and they like to live quiet, in peace all the time. Once a fortnight a bus pick them up to go shopping.

Reserves were built to protect Aboriginal people so white men wouldn't enter there. We were told that and I believed it then. Now I know that they didn't want us in town, or mix with them. I know that now, I know that. I know the real reasons, they didn't want us. It's too far behind to think about it now, you cannot go backwards. The rule is gone now. I used to live in a reserve but then it was too new to me. When I think about it now I don't like it, that's why I hardly think of it or want to hear about it any more. It was really bad. We don't want to look back at things that happen before. It hurts people's feelings, and when you look back you go backwards. But in too many places trouble is still there today.

Later I worked on Argyle Station owned by the Durack family. Then next door at Rosewood, then Mount Hart and Silent Grove. Aboriginal people like station life because they work in the bush all the time. Weekend they could go hunting goanna and fishing, that's what they usually did. They could ride horses and they were good at that. Living conditions were all right. We lived in tin houses, single and married quarters. White people house was much better. You see every station manager house is pretty good, you see lawn green and gardens. Some had brick houses and airconditioned. Aboriginal houses had nothing like that. Showers and toilets were built outside for us. One day Welfare come there and look at our houses and they write it down on paper what they see. Later on better showers were built, flash ones; before they were out in the open. Aboriginal houses were away from the homestead, about a mile or half a mile.

Pay was pretty good, about twelve pound monthly. Station get monthly wages, in town you get fortnightly. We had meals cooked but tobacco and other things you had to buy at the store.

Clothing, too. People eat their meals in the boughshed. I was working on the station in the garden then, and cutting wood. I never used to get much money but I saved it so I could go to Kalumburu on holiday. I saved a lot because I was coming to Wyndham for races. I worked in Number Two stock camp sometime. Truck the cattle to Wyndham, sometime I did mustering, dust all the time — I enjoyed doing that.

Ringers and everybody are more friendly because they work together all the time, more friendly than the white people in town. All station managers were white people. I was left there with the mechanic once when the others went away for Christmas, minding the station, and doing the windmills. Boss run me to Wyndham to the airstrip to go to Kalumburu. There were many mixed marriages of Aboriginal and white people, our women live with white blokes. Children used to go out to Beagle Bay mission for schooling. Later on they find it is too far so they built a school at Argyle Station. White kids went to Beagle Bay mission school too, they were all mixed then.

People were not allowed to drink on the stations, that was for Aboriginal people and the others. The most strict rule. No station allow drink in those days. If the white people want to drink they could always go to town. They go dry for six months then go to races and have a few drinks then in town. Nobody brought back a few cartons, nobody. You got to live with this rule, it was tougher in those days. Some would go into town at weekends and always drove into town, no planes then. Ord Air Charter was just starting. Only at Argyle they had one party with grog when one governor came there. Later on people from town came for a big party because the station was moved out. The bulldozer came and knocked all the houses down.

I was learning a lot about the real world outside the mission.

GETTING CHARGED UP, GAMBLING AND BEING LOST

Not marrying straight can cause problems. Straight means the tribal way, man from this way and the woman from nother way. That way they don't marry inside the same group. Jadangai means straight, melal is not straight. These days they don't mention it much, though some people still use it. Even before when people marry in the church the missionaries used to ask them not to marry crooked, they had to marry jadangai in those days.

When the old people are alive, they are the ones mostly carry rules. Some young people know too, but they see pretty girl, they fall in love with that one and forget about the rules. Some run away. I've seen lots of things bin happen that way. People get together and drink, they get charged up and go and buy more drinks and then they go to bed together. When they wake up in the morning they think about what they did, they think hard. When they don't like the person. They think I won't do that again, and go away. Falling in love and having sex are different.

Young people don't keep rules. They do what they like and keep going and going. When things break down life won't be any good for them any more, see, because the rules, Law is not there any more with them. Life is not what it used to be before, it has changed; yes it is worse now. Sometime when father run away you know, leave the kids alone, they grow up without control mostly, too much for the mother — kids go over her. They have their own way. They get into trouble with the police and get bad record. They learn how to drink, and get cheeky and too soon they find girlfriend. They get locked up for breaking and entering. Boys shouldn't have girlfriends before age nineteen or twenty. I see a lot of girls fall in love young, too.

Kids get into trouble for stealing cars, get drunk, walk around late night, mix up with different people, get mixed up in drugs, living off their parents instead of go out and work for themselves. They won't bother; they think is good life that way. They could go to a college or learn something. But they get into serious trouble, even murder and their family suffers, and they have to think about how to get out. Sometime they get worried and hang themselves; nobody is there to talk to them.

Other problems are gambling for money, playing cards. When they play all day, sometime they miss work because of it. Could be five or six people. Another house, another lot; many watch and when one is broke nother one takes their place. The one that wins walks away. The games can go on overnight to the next day. People play with up to one hundred dollars — lots of money for a start. One or two might be win two or three thousand. Me, I never like it from the start. Nothing wrong with playing cards, but they spend all the money and nothing left for kids; even the kids learn to play cards. The adults end up not having a cent. Parents are gambling too much. Gambling is one of the worst things in many communities, it is very widespread, like a disease. When they get paid the people go straight down the line to the house for gambling, that's what we see all the time. Then they sit there and what they got in their hand all the pay is spent. Sometime the kids wander around all day and night; the parents don't tellem, they're too busy playing cards. Dog barking there in the middle of the night and people see children walk around, parents still playing cards, so kids sometime sleep at friend's house.

That's why they have all the problems. Sometimes there's no money buying food. Instead of going to the store first they go straight to the cards. No money left for clothes, shoes, not enough to look decent. Mostly money always goes to the drain, just like you put them in the sink, you open the plug and the water runs out. When they win maybe one, two or three thousand they order a plane to go out to town, they spend everything straight out on drink. They go to Kununurra, Wyndham or Derby, those three places. Money can go in one full day among three or four people. They sleep any way in the bush. If that was me I'd sleep in a hotel and drink in a proper sociable way. I know of four thousand dollars leaving the community that way on the one time, no money left, the community is cleaned out.

Because you lose more in the cards, you have not a cent left in your hand, you lose right out, you don't get nothing. You get nothing out of gambling. With alcohol you can enjoy yourself, but not with gambling, someone else may win, and people can go higher and higher in debt. People don't want to work, they can get money without doing any work.

Mostly they go and buy a lot of drink for the others. I also bought drink for others a long time ago, I saved very little. Alcohol is a very bad thing in communities. When people get charged up they drink till they are drunk. They get silly in the brain and go argue with others and police come mostly then. Problem is they get into violence sometimes. If they drink and drink and go to sleep nobody wouldn't bother them. Drink leads to violence, people can drive around in the car and do stupid things, go mad and kill themselves or kill others, too. Family might get much worry if they see these things happen and do their best to stop them from getting into trouble. Is nothing wrong with drinking but they drink too much and they get silly.

People drink because they like the effect on the brain and because they have nothing much else to do. They have lost their old ways and culture. Long time ago in the 1950s when I was in the mission dormitory, people used to dance often at night. We used to go from dormitory to watch. Lots of people used to be around then, our people. Old people sometime they danced inside the compound when the Lord Abbot came from New Norcia. The dances then were longer, more of it and better in the way they were singing than they are today. The songs they had lots of meaning in it like about the islands and other places. In those days people had totems like turkey, other birds, kangaroo, dingo, lots of things. My totem is janggao, lizard. When people sing you got to have something to sing about, like little boy was in the waterhole, or dingo made a piss and it turned into a rock, or turkey was flying across the sky, all sort of a thing like that, or man in a canoe got lost by himself on an island, that kind of thing. People died off and now the next generation have nothing to sing about, and young ones are not interested or taught properly, so they don't know. The boys lived in the dormitory and nobody ever taught us much about our own culture. The old people also used to dance away from the mission in the bush sometime, different dances.

Only Sundays we used to go out. One of the old people took us hunting. When he killed a kangaroo he showed us how to take the guts out, then carry it over our shoulders and then cook it — dig a hole in the ground, make fire and put the roo on the hot coals later and cover it with hot stones, leaves and soil. It stays there like in an oven. None of the old people taught us much else, we only saw some dances. The mission didn't like old people teach us our culture. We lost that because of the mission. The mission had nearly all the children and there were not many around then anyway, they were at Forrest River Mission or at Kalumburu Mission.

Language, I never forget language, I can still talk lingo. But the young ones can't, they never bin taught before. When I was small and brought up in the bush I spoke my lingo. That was our language and that was our country and our parents taught us. My father spoke Kulari language, too. Later he learned English because he worked at Truscott Airbase near Kalumburu. Our language is called Gunin, our Kwini language. Nowadays somebody go to school and learn kids lingo in Kalumburu, but one hour a week is not enough. My grannies [grandchildren] wouldn't know how to speak lingo or their parents. My people lost everything; dances lost, music lost, medicine lost, songs and the language lost. Everything is going bit by bit, even the stories only remembered by the old people. When the young ones grow big they keep quiet. They live with alcohol, they're not interested. They don't think, 'I'm losing my culture.' Some don't notice that.

A lot of things bin break down. People not interested in the tribal way, they lost it all. Many were brought up in the mission see, some others stayed with their parents; they are all right because their parents teach them. Mission kids were only taught one way, mission side. They lose the other side, the tribal side. They didn't think of the other side. They know they couldn't keep up, they know they were losing. They couldn't keep going with that one.

Well, now people are independent of the mission but they're still dependent on government money. They are still lost. They are lost today because they lost their land, culture and everything. When you lose one thing you can't pick up something else so quickly. Maybe people don't realise that. I think the tribal and the modern way, some parts can go together, all depends where you live, doesn't matter who you are. If people have help they can pick up again, but many need someone to tellem and walk with them for a while.

MY COUNTRY OOMARRI

Little while ago we went to the river called Oomarri to have a look at the place where I was born. The Aboriginal name is Oomarri, not King George River; the name given by gardiya [white people] when they came. Certain waterholes got different names. The river only runs in the wet season. When the rain stops the water lasts for a long time. Later on, about July or August, the water settle down and stay in the waterholes. The river has two waterfalls, one we walked to when we were there, and the other further down. The river flows into the Timor Sea. I don't think we have Aboriginal names for parts of the sea. The sea hasn't got a name, only sections of the land have. I only know the river at certain places where the dreaming of that janggao [lizard] is, my totem, where I was born.

One day long ago when I was small, I went walkabout alone at the sea side. I wander away looking for oysters. Later on people came looking for me. I remember walking along the rocks. I went a long way, I didn't get hungry or hot, so the older women, they looked for me and found me and brought me back. I didn't think of any danger. I know I was at the salt water that side where the river come out. Many people used to live there at the sea, like old Manuela and her husband Joe Puruan.

Later we come back to that Oomarri waterhole. I remember playing in the waterhole in the bush. I never knew how to swim, only when I came here to the mission I learned how to swim properly. My brother Martin learned how to swim in the bush, I was the only one who didn't. Might be his father — my father's brother — learned him. In the mission Brother Ildephonsus taught us how to swim in the river.

I didn't remember exactly where to look for my country, my place at Oomarri. Last time I was there was in 1960s, me and Father Sanz, Francis Waina and two old people, who used to walk up and down to Forrest River Mission. Father Sanz wanted to find a road to Forrest River to transport cattle and he took me with him. We drove from the mission through bush without a road. There were no tracks of any kind. We came to the jump-up, that's the one we found a road through. That's where the police patrol used to come through. We went in a landrover. It was new from the Lotteries Commission. From there we went through Jiliwei and crossed over the Drysdale River. Later on we crossed that King George River.

We didn't camp at Oomarri then and I never thought this was my country or not. I never thought about it. Nobody told me it was. People didn't tell me this — they should have told me. That was in 1960s before I went to Home Station to work. I was around twenty then. I asked Father Sanz if I could come, I just wanted to go on the trip, no other reason. I was the only young bloke to go along. Francis Waina was the driver. I knew I was from the river somewhere, I knew this was Kwini land, but I didn't know exactly which place belong to me, and I didn't worry about the country then. Our old people used to live in the Kwini Camp when they stay in Kalumburu. That was humpies and tin shacks set up between the mission and Worraro Creek, and that was the only land I thought then belonged to my people because they camp on it. It is not used any more. Now I know that piece of land belong to the Bishop even in those days already, and it still does today. I don't think they need it — there is nothing in the paddock. The government give it to the mission. The government had no right to give that land to the mission. The land did not belong to the government, it belong to my people. They never ask if they can have it.

I found out later about my country when the old people were still alive in the Kwini Camp. They tell me now and then, 'You come from that place, that Oomarri.' I don't know about others then, if they knew where they come from. Later, a lot of people talk like that, where this one come from or that one. Only Father Basil — he is Australian — used to tell us where we come from; he showed us on the map where we come from. The Spanish missionaries used to talk a lot about Spain: 'We come from long way country, from the other side of the world, you come from this country, maybe you are Kulari, Walmbi, Kwini.'

They also talked about Europe. I remember about bullfight which is cruel anyway. They also told us about General Franco and that's how Spain is independent, how Franco and his men win the battle against somebody else, that's all I remember. They taught us about Columbus discover America, and how the English discover Australia. I think no one discovered this place, they only came here to take the place over. People were here before they arrived; no one really discovered this place. The Aboriginal people was here first, no one ever discovered this. We were here for a very long time. Just like Columbus, they said he discovered America. Other people were there already, the Indian people. It was not till the 1970s that I realised that the story we were told in 1950s was wrong.

I heard about land claim stories first when I was at Kununurra at the Kimberley Research Station, working on the cotton fields. Later, when Mr Whitlam came into power, at that time people was thinking in Kununurra that they should have blocks of land where they were born. They started talking about land, I know because I lived among them, the Mirriwung and Gajerrong people. They were not proper land claims yet, but that's when I first realised that this was our land, it didn't belong to the white people. Mr Whitlam was the only government then who wanted to give land back to the Aboriginal people. His word was pretty good and I thank him for that.

I became aware of talk about the land and getting it back from the white people, getting land for the Aboriginal people. I was wondering whether station people might be happy about this or not. It is very hard to fight against white people. They have all the land and we had it all taken away and bin left with nothing. All land was taken up by pastoralists, missions and the town shire, and later mining and exploration leases; no more free land available. I thought of buying a farm a long time ago to work and live on it. That's how I wanted to get some land, but I never had enough money. Farm is good because you can grow things on it, in the city you have no room to do that. Some of the people did get some land then, that was before Mabo. On the way from Kununurra to Lake Argyle there are little blocks along that road — those families that live there now got that land. I don't know how they got it, I know they couldn't pay for it. It was their land and maybe the shire gave it to them.

Back in the '70s when I heard the mining company was exploring for diamonds at Oomarri, and Berkeley River, the company was Tanganyika. From that time I never say anything, just carry on what I used to do. Later on I heard much more about the land claim right around. When I saw in the papers of that land claim going right around to Cambridge Gulf, I just thought, they can't do that. We own half of that way too. Later on I asked a few people at Mowanjum how they can do that and they said, 'No, we only go as far as Mitchell Plateau, Pantagin and all that way.' That is past Prince Regent River.

That was back in 1990 before Mabo, that came after properly. I wasn't interested much in Mabo, we thought it was just for the Murray Islands, should have nothing to do with our area here. Later on, two or three years ago, I found out more, but I still didn't like to hear about it. Others in Derby also said Mabo should have nothing to do with us, we all didn't know really. We couldn't understand what they were saying on television and in the papers about Mabo. While some people did say Mabo was all right, I was still not in favour. Later on people explained that we entitled to the land under the new High Court Mabo decision. I start to understand.

Now the mining companies are exploring for diamonds on my land. Used to be Stockdale before. Now the tenements are sold to Striker and Capricorn. Some of the diamonds they find on our country are coloured, green and pink. Striker has been there only lately. Exploration has been going for four years already. The mining company put some money already in the trust fund. The KLC [Kimberley Land Council] is holding that money in trust for the Aboriginal people. The money has to be spent on community development projects only. Our claim is called Balangarra Native Title Land Claim, one of the biggest in WA. The land reaches from Kalumburu to Sir Graeme Moore Island and near Wyndham, down to Oombulgurri and sunset side to Drysdale National Park and up to Carson River Station.

I am now recognised as a traditional owner and I bin going to meetings. At the meetings they talk about the land claims. The mining companies cannot just walk in to our land, they have to ask us and talk to us about what they do. Kimberley Land Council arranges meetings to negotiate with the mining companies and the government. Meetings are held in the bush, in Kalumburu, Oombulgurri or in town. There are lawyers from the KLC helping us. The meetings don't always go our way.

Some part of it is pretty hard to understand. The white people there talk a bit high, they talk a little bit higher word that some people don't understand, just like they work in the office or city people, how they talk. They talk lot of word that Aboriginal people don't understand, the older ones. Different words the white people use. After, the Aboriginal people don't know what the other people was talking, see, they can't follow that sometimes. Maybe they complain that the white people don't talk properly. We feel no good when you don't understand everything properly. Well, like that the KLC and the other gardiya think maybe it's all right because they keep talking like that all the time. The people usually don't bother to ask, they should but they don't ask, they say nothing. Well, I don't go much to meetings, if I go more I will ask.

Aborigines don't speak up much. They talk in different English sometime and that's why words pass them and they don't understand — they need help. They used to it, hear white people talk everywhere like missionaries. They bin brought up by missionaries, they used to do a lot of talking. But the missionaries side was pretty easy, they don't speak high high language. They live with us, they used to us, but these people now, they don't — they're separate all the time.

This time we went up to Oomarri, we drove along for about a hundred kilometres through Carson River, that's the road we

79

took then, right through to the King George River. We went with Dennis Howard and Margret, friends from Halls Creek. They recording Gunin language and we went with them. On the way we shot bush turkey. We cooked it in the evening by a creek, it was nearly dark. We plucked the turkey and cooked it in hot coals. We were tired and went off to sleep while the turkey was cooking. We couldn't find Oomarri straight away, so we camp just near a creek at the foot of a big mountain. There were very tall trees and in the morning the sunlight was beautiful through the leaves. At night it was full moon. In the morning we climbed up to see the view where we were. You could see the hills and nother hills and nother hills building up like that, and this side we could see the beautiful valley and the forest with the big timber on it. In the middle of nowhere the trees are untouched, nobody ever spoil it, it's all still there.

Finally we reached the Oomarri waterhole, my country. We camp there. I feel very good at that place. We saw a few rock paintings there, they were very old. That night we ate goanna. We live on bush tucker all the time in my country, we got it all from the bush, and only carried tea, flour, sugar and milk. One morning we walked to the waterfall. It was that hot! And later when we walk back, we run into a storm. We also found a bush apple, a white one and it was ripe and very nice to eat.

I thought maybe I was here when I was small, walking around there. I'm sure I bin there but it was too far gone to remember exactly. My brothers bin going there all the time. I did feel like I was coming home. I wish we could have stayed there longer. When the Wet is over we go back. I would like to build a house and live there. I wanted to know more about my country from long time you know, how my people lived there and where I was born. I was just feeling at home there. I can live there away from town, I can stay there, and it belongs to me that country, and I belong to that country.

The Home of Silent Memories

The home of silent memories nestles there between the caves and breakaways, which spread out forming a V where the water spills over into the pool. The swallows choose to build their nests with mud particles neatly glued to the ceilings of caves or buildings like little upside-down igloos. Their nestlings are safe from marauders but — sorry to say — not from boys with gings!

The finches come to drink, sing, and twitter in the trees, while the kingfishers make their nests in the mud banks. The perfume of the scenty-grass is wafted on the gentle evening breeze, stirring sweet fragrance of memories. The creek runs out past the homestead and into the dam. The water not held by the embankment flows away and spills into Lake Moore. One can still hear the pounding of the water as it cascades over the rocks and flows into the dam taking with it bits of debris, which bob up and down like little boats sailing on a rough sea. Before the rain has ceased, rain-coated and behooded, climbing over rocks, everyone comes out to see the welcome sight after a long dry season. At night Freddy-frog's band strikes up; a musical night can be expected.

So many memories like a large bouquet of flowers mingling and twining together, the willy-wagtails nesting in the peppercorn tree just outside the kitchen window, dad and mum taking turns at feeding the nestlings. Memories reaching the heart's deep recesses as they bring us all together again. Our children are there playing, laughing, and squabbling. But happy. Then comes time for school; the correspondence classes, then later, driving them to school. The memories are living because one dear man loved his family, who all were free to come and go at will.

Then it is shearing time again. We hear again the whirring of the handpiece, the throbbing of the diesel motor, the bleating of sheep and barking of dogs, as they fill the catching pens. The thrilling sound of 'Wool Away', bales pressed, branded, and ready to be loaded, then carted to the Wubin railhead. What once was carted by old camel wagon, is now carried by truck. The homestead still stands, the date palms and quandong tree growing by the front gate. The old peppercorn tree still reaches out welcoming arms. Everlastings — pink, yellow and white — making a patterned carpet in springtime. The flat stretches out like a white counterpane, Lake Moore gleaming in the distance, clouds tinted by reflections from the red clay lake bed.

In the homestead garden is the scent of stocks at evening, red and mauve poppies, sweet peas, morning glory, dolichos, seven-year beans climbing, twisting, winding together, just as these memories climb into our hearts.

The memory of the station stock brand, C.I.V, is seared upon our hearts as it was upon the flesh of the station stock. The smell of singeing hair still lingers about the old post and rail stockyards. Stockmen wheeling in young horses to be branded and broken in to the saddle. To watch the lasso whirl through the air and settle over the head of one as they gallop around the yard. Then, all hands to the rope. Well thrown!

The old slaughter yards and gallows. Galahs perched on the tank rim, nodding up and down, drinking their fill while keeping a wary eye. Others riding the mill tail as it turns slowly in the breeze. Sheep coming to drink from the trough, pushing and squeezing to get clear cool water flowing from the ball tap. They drink their fill and walk away contentedly. Yes, the date palm is still growing by the front gate, keeping guard over the memories that are locked within. Now time has passed on and many are no longer here, but those who remain will always remember.

Our Nyoongah Folk

By the side of the grave on that sunny day, in a sea of faces, I saw the grief etched on every one as I watched the tears flow down.

And my heart went out to my people, they seemed so lost and sad as they carried their pain, each their own; this sorrow that we share.

Yes, the hurt of our people was plain to see; so many of our people are passing away and our sorrow was showing the way.

It seems every day we lose someone and sadly soon we'll find that this generation of mine will all be gone: no more oldies to teach right from wrong.

Sadly to say, the young ones too are falling by the way; we are losing them now as never before. Yes, sorrow is with us this day.

The hurt for our people is cutting deep; our generation is nearly gone. It seems sorrow now is a way of life; who knows how long we'll be around.

Now as I stand by the grave on this sunny day, with each one feeling lost, I can feel the pain of our people.

And to share in sorrow with those who are grieving is the way of Nyoongah folk and I felt so proud as we stood as one while the earth was soaked by our tears.

Ancestors in the Wind

When the strong wind blows of a
summer night, our ancestors speak to me;
they are deeply disturbed by the way they see
our children wild, running free.

With no proper direction from dad and mum,
with no one to teach right from wrong,
our ancestors' spirits will never be at rest
until we learn to carry our load.

Only too late the folks realise
that things are out of control,
when children are facing the courts by themselves
without the parents being told.

We are a proud race of people, that's true, but a lot of
this belongs to our past, when our people of old,
our ancestors, shed their blood,
for this land that we toast.

Faces of our old ones are disappearing fast,
and with them true wisdom goes too;
we must salvage the things they have told,
and save them, whatever we do.

With many a trap set before us,
our old and young fall by the way,
through drink, drugs and pot. It's enough
for the strong to go astray.

We must not forget our folks who have fallen,
we must try harder to find a cure.
In the wind our ancestors are calling
before many more fall by the way.

You can hear the echoes in the wind of the night,
it's our ancestors calling a plea,
to look out for our children,
look out before we lose them please.

Yes, the wind in the trees is our ancestors of old,
watching out over their people, their land.
They're calling to us to cherish what we have,
the land, the trees, the seas, the skies.

It's the Dreamtime that's calling in the wind,
in the trees; it's calling our people to listen.
For our ancestors' sake we must do what it takes,
to keep all our children together and free.

Then the wind in the trees can peacefully subside,
and become quiet and calm across the sky,
when the wind finally stops to a gentle
breeze, we know that our ancestors are at peace
with the land, and the safety of our children
is won.

The Ring

At the age of sixteen, becoming a professional boxer seemed inevitable to me. There was just no way out. I had to find a way to stay alive, to protect myself from all the hurt I had suffered since I was born. My family being Nyoongah, and very poor, for us there were no birthday presents. The only time we had a special occasion was when it came to Xmas. Mum used to make a pudding the day before, put it in a wet flour bag, and hang it from a tree to set overnight. The next day we had pudding and custard.

My mum and my three elder sisters used to carry the washing across the paddocks to the nearest dam and I tagged along to try and help in some way. Sometimes my mum used to get so sick that she could hardly walk and so my sisters had to do the chores. When I used to follow them they made me carry their loads and if I dropped them on the ground, I was flogged. My sisters, especially the one that bullied me around, used to take to me as if I meant nothing to them. As if I wasn't their little brother, who had only tried to help.

She used to punch me really hard, in the middle of the back, knocking the wind right out of me, then leaving me just laying in the dirt, gasping for breath, and crying for help that never came. Her only way to make sure that I wouldn't tell was to keep on bashing me up. And I couldn't understand that, because she was my sister. Why was she hurting me like this?

I didn't really hold it against her, mainly because I was too scared to show it. Until one day, when she went too far, knocking me out cold, stiff as a board.

When I woke up, I lost myself in the scrub and cried. I cried for a long, long time and was too scared to go home. When I did make it home, my daddy was waiting for me with the strap to flog the living daylights out of me for not helping with the chores.

My sister used to get in first and tell lies about me, and she enjoyed it, simply because her word was taken before mine. I couldn't even speak up for myself. I just tried to live and understand why I was getting hurt all the time by the very people I loved and trusted so much.

'Not to worry,' as they say. 'Things can only get better.'

But then my daddy started drinking. And things got a whole lot worse. He used to come home late at night, full of booze, scowling at us like the devil himself. Then came my mummy screaming, crying out for me to go and help her. And so I used to try and get in the middle of them, and cry out to my daddy to stop hurting her. But he never did listen to me. Instead it just made him more aggro. And with just one swipe of his big backhand he would knock me sprawlin' across the concrete floor completely helpless and unable to help my mother. He wasn't a big man, but he was very, very strong, and even stronger when he was full of booze.

And then my other little brothers and sisters would start crying too, only to receive the same punishment dished out to me and my mother. But I never gave up. All I could do was ask Daddy why he kept hurting us all the time. Because we loved him and we wanted him and we needed him to love us as well.

I hardly ever went to school because Mum used to be sick all the time and so I had to go and cut the wood to make sure the place was warm for her. And when we had nothing to eat (which was most of the time), I would go to the rubbish tip and forage for food so as to make her some sort of soup to keep up her strength.

And then one day the welfare people came and they spoke to Mum and they looked at me. Immediately I started to shake, wondering what was going on. And when Mum came towards me I started to cry. I suddenly realised what was about to happen. These people had come to take me away and I grabbed for Mummy as hard as I could and cried out for her not to let me go. But all she could do was put her arms around me, kneel down and hug me, kissing me with all her love. Then she led me to the car, as the white man had ordered.

As we drove off, I looked back at her and saw the tears that were streaming down her face. Then she turned away and all of a sudden my whole world completely vanished. I could not see anymore, I could not understand anymore, and I was hurting from deep within.

Those people told me they were only doing good, but why the

hell was I crying so much? Why the hell was I hurting so much? And why was I scared like I never had been before? All that those white people were proving was that they were the superior race and that they had the right to come along and take us babies away from our mothers whenever they liked.

'A man in authority who oppresses poor people is like a driving rain that destroys the crops.' And so, yeah, I came to know who the oppressors were and I also came to believe that we, the Aboriginal people of this country were to be the ashes of their destruction.

When we finally arrived at my new home in Scarborough the family was all there to greet me. But I just didn't want to be there. I wanted to go home, and I kept thinking about my mother and my brothers and sisters who were still there, suffering, getting terrorised every night at the hands of my drunken father. I needed to be with them, to help them. And I wanted to explain it to these people, but I was much too frightened to even speak. As it turned out they were quite friendly, and the fact that I was black didn't seem to bother them. They just treated me like one of them, and they really did their best to make me feel at home. But this world of theirs was alien to me, and I reckon they must have seen it in my eyes.

And so Scarborough became my new home where I was never able to wag school, because two of my foster brothers attended the same one and my foster mum was pretty strict in so far as she only wanted to do her best for me. But little did she realise how my past upbringing had taken its toll. And no matter how hard I tried I just couldn't do, or be, what was expected of me.

But sports were a different matter and I excelled in mostly everything I did, like football, cricket, baseball and boxing. Our under fifteen football team actually won a premiership against Jolimont at Subiaco oval. Throughout the season that year, Jolimont had always beaten us by no less than twelve to thirteen goals. But that grand final day when we met on Subiaco oval, we just seemed to out-run and out-class them in every department. We went on to beat them by over eight goals.

Over the years at different times I've taken a look at our old premiership photo and it wasn't a bad side actually! My foster brother Trevor was extremely excited because he was our number one ruckman and that had been the first side he had played for that had ever made the four, let alone won the premiership. I myself was the number one rover and we combined very well, and it being a 'family affair' had made a big difference, no doubt in my mind, to our performance.

One of our other better players was Tom Hogan, who I reckon should have made footy his main bag. For some reason though he seemed to have a greater preference for cricket, and in my book proved more than good enough, going on to play for Australia as a left-arm spinner.

Tom used to come home where we played a bit of cricket in the back yard. We used to also have training sessions in the nets down at Abbett Park. I hated batting most of all because those bowlers were fast! Practically every ball used to be aimed at my head so I used to jump backwards out of the way. It was one of those times that a guy, Ken Mueleman, had come along and put a set of stumps directly behind me. Then he said, 'Righto young lad, I don't want to see even the cheeks of your arse touch those bloody stumps … Just keep your eyes on the ball, and when they come at you like that, just step inside 'em and put 'em away.'

I gave him something from under my breath but did exactly what he told me to do. And it worked — he was right! So every time I turned up for training, I opted to bat first, and I enjoyed it. I had the good fortune of being taught by someone that was certainly one of the best.

To keep myself fit I used to go on jogs from Scarborough beach to City beach, then back again and around a few of the closer suburbs. It was on one of those occasions that I spotted a few boys practising baseball. And so I kinda went over and asked them if I could have a bash with them. They pointed to the coach who was busy going through the motions with his pitcher and catcher. To be honest, I had been watching the pitcher the whole time I had been there. I just knew that I could throw the ball far better than he could. I had acquired my natural throwing skills growing up in the bush, throwing stones at rabbits and birds just to survive. Anyway, the coach seemed all right and gave me the okay to start training with them, Wembley baseball club. The first bloke I was introduced to was the pitcher, Ray Michelle.

No sooner had the coach spotted my throwing arm than he appointed me second pitcher to Ray. While Ray went on to become one of the best pitchers this country has ever produced, I just didn't agree with pitching to the catcher's instructions. You had to keep on looking out for how many fingers he was indicating with inside his glove. This was supposed to tell me what was going on around me, the opposition stealing bases and so on, and what sort of ball to throw, but as far as I was concerned, my natural instinct told me enough to know what was going on. All you had to do was look and listen to the crowd. They told me everything. It is exactly the same as watching tennis. All you have to do is watch the crowd's heads turning this way and that, like clowns in a side-show alley. It eventually led to the coach pulling me aside and saying, 'Look Al, it's either this … or that.' And so I took 'that'.

My whole life in general was becoming harder and harder to cope with. No matter how hard I tried to live up to expectations I just couldn't forget my family and the torment of their sufferings. This finally drove me to steal money from my foster parents, and head to the nearest pub where I got an older person to buy alcohol for me. I just couldn't handle it — it was too much for me. Their screamings were becoming louder and louder. So I'd get drunk and cry and cry.

By this time I had turned sixteen and my thieving and drinking were getting ever worse. I mean to say, it's pretty bad when a sixteen year old turns up in class with a bloody good hangover. Anyway, I frequented the beach many times during this period where there used to be a little side-show park. One day, I thought I'd go in and take a look around. I noticed a little green shed that was situated in the far corner of the park. I could hear these 'thumping' noises coming from over there. Being a little bit nosy, I guess, I decided to take a look.

As I stood in the doorway looking in I noticed this bloke with boxing gloves on thumping away at a punching bag that was hanging in the middle of the room. The flurry of his combinations and the force that he was hitting the bag with told me that he was pretty good at what he was doing.

After a while he stopped and came over and introduced himself as Ray Murray, saying that he was an ex pro-boxer from the eastern states and that when he wasn't running the go-karts he would loosen up on the old punching bag. Then he asked me if I wanted to get in and have a go. Straight away I said, yeah, brother, thank you. I was only too willing because I saw this as my big chance to get back at the sister who bashed me and my drunken father who had put my mum and brothers and sisters through so much hell.

And so I started and before long was to have my first fight in the ring. As it turned out Ray had also been a promoter but was about to retire simply because he couldn't find anyone interested in it. But I turned up every chance I got and he was always there to spur me on.

Anyway, Ray was pretty well known in the boxing circles and he contacted a few of his friends to put exhibition bouts on. He put me up against another Nyoongar, who had already made a name for himself. Ray was in my corner telling me that I'd be all right, to just go out there and do my best. But when the other bloke jumped into the ring, hey man, I just wanted to jump out. The nerves took over and I started to tremble and sweat like never before.

But Ray calmed me down and told me that he believed in me, and a few other things to get me back on track. Then the bell went with the referee giving his instructions — no hitting below the belt and all that — and then the fight began.

After the first few seconds my nerves were still raking me but then when he hit me with a heap of lightning quick combinations it straightened me up and I settled down enough to see out the first round.

Ray sat me back down and splashed water over my head. He told me to take in a few deep breaths, then offered a few words of encouragement. I took them all with me into the ring until the final bell went. Even before the referee had announced me as the winner I knew that I had won, and so too did Ray. I made him proud that night, and in his emotions he showed it.

And so, with the thoughts of my loved ones there still suffering, I made the decision to become a boxer. I wasn't going to stop until I was good enough to go back home and stand up for my mum and little brothers and sisters. Boxing took me from the little side-show park to football club bouts (Claremont, East Fremantle and Swan Districts) to standing in the tent at the Royal Show before finally taking me to the Embassy Ballroom in Perth. Along the way I won a few and lost a few but Ray was still there with me, and the strength that I got from this man was enormous.

It was a packed house in the Embassy Ballroom that night with Baby Cassius' fight the main event. Me and Ray had turned up and he had managed to get me on the card in one of the supporting bouts. I was supposed to fight a bloke by the name of

John Lawson. For some reason though he hadn't turned up and so Ray told me to hang around just in case someone else showed.

A couple of supporting bouts had already been fought and I had been pacing up and down in the change-rooms when Ray burst in, put his arm around my shoulder, sat me down, and said, 'Listen Al, we've got a chance, but it's a big one.'

I sort of looked startled and said, 'What do you mean ... big one?'

'Well,' he said, 'they've got this fighter over from Victoria, and he's supposed to be on the card as well, but the bloke who's supposed to fight him didn't turn up either ... So that leaves you both without anyone to fight ... Whaddya reckon? Give it a bash or what?'

Then I asked him, 'Well, is he a good fighter?' But Ray kept low-key on that one. All he said was that the guy was good, without telling me how good. If he had, there is no way in the world I would have gone out there. But he didn't, he just said, 'Listen Al, we've come this far — just go out and give it your best shot, I believe in you mate, you know that!'

When I held out my hands for him to start bandaging, he started smiling from ear to ear. 'Hey brother, you're not gunna get me killed are you?' I asked.

But he just shot straight back at me saying, 'All I'm doin' is gettin' him killed, okay?'

All of a sudden we heard the crowd erupt into a great explosion — the loudest applause I had ever heard — and Ray said to me, 'That's him, now it's your turn, son.' Straight off my nerves gave away and I followed him shaking into the arena.

The audience gave me a few little claps and cheers from here and there. Ray opened the ropes for me and I sat down on the chair in the blue corner. As Ray started to rub the vaseline over my eyebrows my eyes wandered over to my opponent's corner and there I made eye-contact with something that I can only describe as a satanic looking raging fucking bull. I swear he had fumes coming out of his fucking nostrils. I went cold all over, and through a twisted mouth, I whispered to Ray that this bloke was gunna kill me, man. Fucking hell! After this lot I'd be laying in hospital for about six months.

Well, at least I wouldn't have to go to school for a while!

Ray just pointed to the crowd and said, 'You see them, son? They all love him. He's got them. They are his strength and power and while it is they that have made him, it is they who will also break him. Inside this fuckin' ring here, son, he's by himself, an' you're gunna go out there an' make him fuckin' realise that, all right?'

I could sense a strange sort of emotion coming from Ray, the kind of emotion that could only come from someone of great knowledge and wisdom, spoken with the utmost sincerity. Then he put his arms around my shoulders and said, 'Listen son, you remember telling me about your grandfather? Well you are a big part of that great man, and you have his spirit, something that son-of-a-bitch will never break, okay?'

The announcement over the loudspeaker snapped me out of my dreamtime, as both of us fighters, in our respective corners were introduced. 'Ladies and gentlemen, in the red corner I give you a fighter already known far and wide, a legend both inside and out of the ring — the great Johnno Johnson! And his opponent tonight ladies and gentlemen, in the blue corner, hailing from the lower great southern — Alan Knapp. Please give them a round of applause!'

What fucking round of applause, I thought. It had finished already when they finished clapping Johnno. There was nothing left for me, brother, I was the underdog, the unknown. The referee was standing in the middle of the ring, motioning us both forward to lay down the ground rules. Just for that moment in time I felt a little comfort at having him stand between us. Hey man, this bloke was gunna kill me, for sure. I felt like a bullfighter, all dressed in red, without a cape.

Anyway, after all the formalities the ref told us to go back to our corners and wait for the bell. Ray quickly gave me a few instructions, then the bell went, and then I went — shoved straight through the fucking ropes! Right away the crowd was on their feet and roaring. The ref jumped in and kept Johnno at bay while I climbed back in the ring. He then barked a few more orders reminding us what his profession was all about and then the battle began again.

Still pissed off at being spilt out of the ring I wasn't about to let him get in first again. He was more of a slugger than a boxer and so I made up my mind to try and win the fight by outscoring him on points. Ray, to his credit, had me in 'tip-top' condition. I could run all day, so I figured if I could get in a few lightning combinations, and get out of it before he struck back, I might just make it. But his stance was like Fort Knox and I couldn't help but swear at Ray for setting me up like this.

Through his experience he read my confusion and charged at me again throwing haymakers from all angles. I tried to get away but the ring proved to be far too small. But I'd already been to hell and back and there was no way I was just going to lie down. The fight kept on at the same tempo, him chasing and me trying to score points, hit and run, until the end of the third round.

Ray told me to take a few deep breaths while he massaged my stomach and gave me a whiff of the smelling salts. 'Look, son,' he said, 'you're behind, but you're still in there! Take a look at him, son! Take a good fuckin' look at him. He's breathin' like a wounded fuckin' bull! He's goin' down, he's on his way down, son! Can't you see what you're doin' to him? He tried to take you out well and truly before this — but you're still here. I'm telling you, son, you're behind on points, but he's on his way out altogether … Just you go on out there and help him on his way!'

And so the fourth round began and with Ray's words still in my ears, I drove in a straight left, smashing him dead centre where his two eyes and the bridge of his nose met. Right away my face was given a spray job with the colour of his blood. And then I knew Ray was right. I was feeling more confident now of this bloke going down — but was he?

As it turned out, me and Ray were both fucking wrong! As he had looked in the first round, he was now looking stronger. And he came back harder and that put me in the hit and run situation again. The fourth and fifth rounds were fought just as hard as the first three and as I made it back to my corner Ray went to work telling me that tonight I had made him proud for even lasting that long. He told me to stay in there, as I was still behind on points and there was still one round to go.

As we met in the middle for the last round, the ref came between us and grabbed us by the gloves. He said, 'Listen boys, as you both know I'm supposed to be neutral, but whichever way it may go, go down fightin'!' Then he sent us back to our corner, to come out on the bell.

During those few seconds before the bell, Ray said to me, 'Hey son, listen — it's gone quiet all of a sudden, and everyone's lookin' at you. They're all starin' at you. That bloke in the other corner over there, he's a fuckin' legend, son. And if you pull this one off, what does that make you? So go out there an' do your best. Hold your head up high so everyone can see it! Let 'em all see it, and break their fuckin' hearts as well.'

I looked across at Johnno's corner where I could see his trainer, Brian Shipley, working on him, whispering something that didn't even seem to register. The look on their faces said it all. They had expected me to be long gone.

And then it came and I threw the first punches, straight left, then as he blinked, I hit him with a right cross that shook him head to toe. But he never even moved. Instead he came straight back with a right cross that landed square on my forehead, seeming to shake every bone in my body, from my head to my fuckingtoes. And for a second there, everything was darkness. Then there was light. Because I saw my sister and my father standing there in front of me, laughing at me, like they always did. My present was now my past and it all came back to me. And I could see myself, lying in the dirt, screaming for help, and I could see my drunken father, standing there with the strap in his hand, ready to flog me. I could hear Mummy screaming for the help I couldn't give her and all the silent tears streaking down the faces of my little brothers and sisters, too frightened to cry out in fear.

And then I lost the plot. There was no more Johnno — just my sister and father laughing at me, as all hell broke loose and I attacked them, and attacked them, and I just kept on attacking'em until they disappeared, right off the face of the fucking earth.

And now that they were gone, there would be no more hurting.

'Hey, son! Al! Listen to me, son! Are you all right? Come back to me here.' I recognised Ray's voice. 'What the hell happened there? You went off your fuckin' head! Here, take a whiff of this ... You're all right now ... Deep breath ... Deep breath — You're all right now.'

Then the feeling of cold wate, running over me. And the smell of salts, practically pushing up my nostrils. I started coming back to the present. The spinning was beginning to slow down and I could focus on what was happening around me.

'Ray ... Ray,' I slurred. 'What's happening?'

'Hey, son,' he said, 'You're all right ... You took a fuckin' batterin,' but look at him over there! After tonight, son, I'd go to war with you, and feel pity for the fuckin' enemy!'

But the reliving of my past had become my present. I was sick and tired, sick and tired of getting hurt. When you get hurt by your enemies, you recover but when it's by your own blood, well then, you just don't. It's there to haunt you for the rest of your life.

The whole place was in an uproar. The crowd were still on their feet, cheering and jeering, clapping and shouting things that were either for or against me. And it wasn't to cease until the ref took his stance in the middle of the ring and motioned for me and Johnno to join him.

Ray helped me to my feet and encouraged me to go forward. Johnno did the same, and as the announcement came, the ref took both of our hands. 'Ladies and gentlemen, I hereby declare the winner of this contest tonight, on a unanimous points decision — from the blue corner, hailing from the lower great southern — Alan Knapp!'

And then it erupted again, as the ref held my hand up, the crowd once again starting to roar. My whole body felt as though it was about to collapse, not only out of sheer exhaustion, but also because of the weight of all the sweat, mixing with the emotional streams of water welling up in my eyes, starting to drop, drip by drip. I could only describe what had happened to me as like being pushed by a bloody army tank, right from the top end of Australia's north, through the guts of the Simpson desert, right down to the very edge of the Great Australian Bight.

And I cursed the ref under my breath because I wanted him to hold up Johnno's hand as well. As far as I was concerned, neither of us had lost. Ray had come to my side and practically carried me from the ring, saying, 'Come on, son, I'll get you home.' Then he said, pointing at the crowd, 'Look up, son, they're all standing for you! Like I said, they made him, now they're breaking him.'

Back in the change-rooms, Ray expressed his pride by going back over the fight, round by round, especially the last one. Only then did he tell me who Johnno Johnson was. Apparently Johnno was a man who had already taken all before him. He had taken on the biggest and the best, in the ring, down at the docks, in pub laneways, and destroyed them all. Later on I was to see a photo of him standing there, surrounded by the likes of Lionel Rose, Baby Cassius, and of course his trainer, Brian Shipley. Thus the proudness of Ray — we had beaten the unbeaten.

And because of this I felt good, not just because I had beaten a living legend, but because I felt kind of proud for Ray. I didn't know too much about his personal or his past life, except that he had been a pug in Queensland, but I knew I was lucky to have someone like him to teach me enough to not only look after myself, but also to help me go in and win battles against the kind of people who, like Johnno, you can only respect for who they are, and what they are made of.

You Should Have Come Sooner

On Sunday at twelve o'clock I was debating whether to go to the trouble of having a shower and getting dressed for the day. After doing some very rudimentary housework and showing the nephew how to make a toasted cheese sandwich, I was looking for a quiet afternoon. Yeah, sure.

A woman walked through the open door. Her silhouette stood out against the bright clear blue sky. She clutched a rag wrapped around her head. Trailing behind her was the two year old she was looking after. She immediately started talking to my daughter in a strange mixture of Nyangumarta, English and Walt Disney.

Aunty walked unsteadily towards me and said, 'Murrkangunya. I got a bad headache. Take me to the hospital. It's really paining.' I couldn't see any fresh blood so I thought, 'Maybe it's a migraine or more than likely she's been hit with a stick.' I had a quick shower and we got on the road.

I watched her in the car. She was in agony. I couldn't help myself and I said, 'What happened?'

She named two young women and said that they had given her a hiding while she was really drunk. One woman had picked up a stick. This happened on Friday night, thirty-six hours ago. I then began to get very nervous about what was under her head gear. 'How big's the cut?' She showed me with her hands. My stomach lurched, but this was nothing on what was to come.

We arrived at the hospital, and I helped her out of the Toyota. When we got inside Aunty hesitated and peered through the window in the casualty waiting room. We could see five people. No marrugu (son-in-laws). Good job. We approached the desk and ended up having to ring the bell to get attention. We could see that the staff were busy.

I briefly told the story, simply and with some urgency. Name, birthdate, address and symptoms. I was hoping that she would be seen straight away. It worked. We were ushered into a cubicle.

The doctor was another new one to town. He asked some basic questions: 'When did it happen?'

'The other day.'

'You should have come sooner.'

I chipped in. 'What day did it happen? Today is Sunday.'

'Friday.'

The doctor looked at me quizzically. The rag came off and we could all see an ugly, crusty wound. Four' inches long and curved. He called the nurse over and said: 'Want to see a good wound?' Aunty covered her face with her hand.

The doctor left and the nurse had the job of cleaning up the mess. She spoke to Aunty, her senior by a good ten years. 'Can you have a shower, Sweety? Then you can clean up some of it yourself.'

I sat there and seethed. I couldn't help but wonder what was so sweet about having a gashed head. Why talk to an older person that way?

I was distracted by two-year-old Ms Donald Duck who had taken her dress off and was trying to slam dunk it into the next cubicle. I thought it was best to retreat and take her out for awhile.

I returned a short time later. The top layer of the wound had been sponged away. This revealed a seething mass of fat white maggots. The nurse was stoically practising chemical warfare and plucking them out with tweezers. Aunty was crouching lower, wincing and drawing in her breath. Finally a painkiller was given. Panadeine I think. I asked if she would be admitted and the nurse thought not. She said she'd be another half an hour. She added, 'At least there's no infection there.' Now that's what I call an optimist! I went away feeling sick and sorry for both the patient and the nurse.

Some time later (and I don't know how) Aunty walked to my brother's place. Ms Donald Duck ran down the driveway to her. I asked her where her tablets were. She had none. She knew she had to return to get the dressing changed. A crepe bandage was wrapped around her head. It slipped off within the hour. On the way home she said, 'It's my fault. I should have covered it up.'

Her head was numb and she thought it was much better. I explained that the drugs would wear off and the pain would return. Just lucky, I had Panadol; there are no after hours chemists in this town. During the night she was in severe pain. The next day I dropped her at the clinic and she said she would get to the hospital. I drove off to work in another town for the day.

On Monday night I woke to the phone ringing at 12.10am. It was my uncle. 'Murrkangunya. Your aunty is here. She wants you to take her to the hospital.'

'What about my kid? Do I leave her alone in the house?'

He was quiet.

'All right I will come.'

I drove over swearing all the way. Just feeling angry about leaving my daughter alone. Wondering why she wasn't hospitalised for a few days. Thinking about her pain. We tore into Port Hedland. I figured if I got pulled up I had a good excuse. She was feverish and clutching her head in pain. I knew one of the nurses. They worked swiftly. The doctor ordered an antibiotic shot, painkillers and antibiotic tablets. The pus in the wound was cleaned. The nurse was very gentle and explained what she was doing. I asked why she hadn't got painkillers and antibiotics before. No reply.

I did find out that the wound couldn't be stitched because it was left too long and that dead flesh was down in the crevice. It had to be removed. We went home.

On Tuesday we aimed to get the script filled, change the dressings and get some food. We went to the health centre. They are understaffed so treatment is only available from 11.00 to noon. We asked about the afternoon dressing and the Sister said she had no other ideas. But thought once a day would do. She was very surprised to see Aunty in this state and asked me why she wasn't returning to her own home in a little community on the edge of town. I sighed and suggested she must have her reasons.

Aunty told me she had tried Welfare a few days ago and they said they had no money for food. I thought we'd give them another try so that at least we could understand why they had said that. We had a bit of a wait and the duty officer explained that they had no money available but proceeded to contact St Vincents as this was an emergency. The child had to be fed. Aunty's cheque was not due for ten days. It was shame to have to grovel to get a lousy thirty dollar food voucher.

From Welfare I rang the local Aboriginal hostel near the hospital and explained Aunty's needs. They said they were full up as a group of people from Newman were coming in.

Did they have any other ideas?

No.

The Welfare officer suggested the Refuge; I hesitated. It's a bit more town-oriented and this was not exactly a domestic. But I would try there if necessary.

At Coles our junior helper Ms Donald Duck headed straight for the lollies. I put them back. We easily spent the thirty dollars and left quite happy. I felt a spray of water on my feet as we thanked the cashier. Our screeching Ms Duck wanted lollies and so left a puddle behind in protest. We pushed the trolley in haste.

At the chemist I handed over the healthcare number and two hundred and fifty dollars. This number had been procured earlier by going to Welfare, them ringing Social Security and being turned down. We went to Social Security personally and Aunty explained what she wanted. No worries. This was a good visit. Ms Duck slam dunked over those partitions with her dress. A lot of talent for a midget.

At 11.00am we went to the Centre for the dressing. Another Sister told us how to arrange for the domiciliary nurse. I left to get some air. I saw a friend who asked about Aunty. She saw her a bit charged up after she had been to the hospital. You don't get away with anything in a small town. I got a bit angry. Then I remembered what a good painkiller grog is.

Aunty thought her treatment was done a bit rough. Coming from someone who knows about pain, all I could do was feel sorry. I dropped them back at their friend's house not far from my house. I knew that they could come up if they needed me. I worried about the drugs and went to organise the domiciliary nurse.

At 1.30pm I got to work exhausted. Virtually all I could do was stare at the wall. I did not want to blame anyone. I was just so frustrated knowing we had got this far because of my talking and reading and writing skills. My mum's a nurse. I have taken lots of people to the hospital. I kept on thinking about all the other people on the bottom of the social dung hill.

That night I thought I would take her in to get a second dressing. But I could not find her. On Wednesday morning at 8.00am she walked in and said, 'When's the nurse coming?' Guilt hit me in the throat as I had not rung the hospital to make arrangements. I drove to the hospital and left a note for the supervisor hoping that Aunty would be where she'd said she'd be that day, that her tablets were safe and being taken. That she wouldn't drink or get hit.

That's a lot of hope.

Postscript: My darling Aunty, so kind and generous, lost her life through grog four years later.

Mixed Emotions

My name is Matthew Haltiner and I am a child of a mixed marriage. My father was born in Switzerland, in the city of Zurich. My mother was born in Pinjarra, Western Australia; Nyoongar Country. I would like to tell you some of the experiences I have had over the years as a child of a mixed marriage.

Having a white father opened doors to many wonderful places for my sister, my brother and myself. I have visited most of the capital cities in Australia and have been to many places in between. I have built sandcastles on Bondi Beach, swum in the Pacific Ocean in Cairns, visited Taronga Park Zoo in Sydney, driven through the Daintree Rainforest in Queensland, been to the snowfields of Mount Kosciusko, walked through the Snowy river, visited Adelaide, travelled to Ayers Rock and the Olgas, and even been to Darwin in the silly season. My mum always says no matter where she goes it's always good to come back to Nyoongar Country.

Unfortunately, not long after we moved back to Perth, my parent's marriage took a turn for the worse. Even though I was still small I could tell something was wrong. My sister, brother, myself and Mum all moved to a new house without our Dad. Mum said that even though we were without Dad she knew we would be all right because she always had her family and extended family who she could rely on.

Even though Mum has only one brother she has lots of cousins who are like brothers and sisters to her. I met my grandmother's brothers and sisters, their children and their children's children. That's just on my grandmother's side and I still don't know all of them. My granddad also comes from a big family and I have met countless uncles, aunties and cousins from his side of the family but I still don't know them all.

I have enjoyed the best of both worlds, being part Nyoongar and part Swiss. Although Dad has provided me with financial support, Mum has provided me with a caring, sharing, loving environment.

Even though my parents don't love each other any more I know that my parents love me. To me, as a child of a mixed marriage, the love of my parents is one of my most treasured possessions.

The Dance

Feet stomping.
Red dust flying.
Gum leaves swaying.
Boomerangs tapping.
Faces painted. Breasts painted.
Graceful bodies imitating
Kangaroos. Being Emus.
Arms moving in rhythm.
Side to side.
Low humming. High chants.
Mysterious. Wonderfully rich.
Time stops still. Goes back.
A refreshing feeling
flowing all around.

Bambaru Banaka

Around the turn of the century, small bands of Mardu people were leaving their homelands in the desert regions to settle at Jigalong. Why were they deserting their traditional lands? Was it fear of reprisals by the white labourers on the Canning stock route? That was one of many reasons, but the Superintendent at Jigalong, Mr A Hungerford, wrote in a letter to Mr A O Neville, Chief Protector of Aborigines, dated 12 September 1934:

> I got 5 more natives last week, two sick, two old and one man about 25 to 30 stone, blind poor chap. He is from Rudall river and cannot speak a word of English.

He added:

> The blacks seem to look on this place as a depot for all old or sick women with children. Now that the outside waters are drying up, a number of them are coming in from the desert country. (Department of Native Affairs — File No. 94/96)

****

Bambaru Banaka, her husband Tjirama Garimara, her two daughters, Bami Burunga and Tagoda Burungu, and her sons Balga Burungu and Toabi Burungu were out foraging for bush fruit and vegetables and hunting for goannas.

Bambaru simply means the blind one and Banaka is her kinship group name. She wasn't always blind, but like so many other desert dwellers she contracted trachoma, a contagious eye disease which feels like minute particles or grains of sand on the inner surface of the eyelids. The inflamed eyes were left untreated, thus causing blindness. The early explorers called this disease 'Sandy Blight'.

It felt good to feel the warm sun on her naked body once again. A few months ago, she, her husband and children were confined in their warm but cramped cave in the rocky hill several kilometres south of their present camp. Whilst living in the cave they were protected from the prevailing desert winds. Unlike the Aboriginal people in the south-west, the nomadic people of the desert region wore no articles of clothing made from animal skins, simply because kangaroos were hunted and killed for food and they were cooked in the ground whole.

On the west side of the same rocky hill was another cave which was used when it rained. Kangaroos sheltered in the cave on the east side, so before Bambaru Banaka and her family could move back in, a large fire was lit to kill and get rid of all the kangaroo ticks. For the next two weeks she and her family would continue to enjoy the freedom of their nomadic lifestyle.

As a young girl growing up around the Rudall River, she learned about the Gududjara country when her family moved from camp to camp in search of food in this desert landscape. She understood the importance of having a sound knowledge of the topography of the land. Her vivid memory and past experience were her most valuable assets. She imparted much knowledge to the younger women and girls because she knew that it enabled and ensured the survival of her family. They were the ones who were expected to carry on the tradition.

Her skills in finding and digging yams have been passed on and now, because of her affliction, Bambaru Banaka's participation in the gathering and searching of bush foods is limited to tasks such as grinding grain seed and threading fruit on sticks to be dried in the hot sun.

When bush foods become scarce (and that time is approaching fast) the family moves down and camps on the banks of the rivers where the kanyjamurra grow. Kanyjamurra or bush yam tastes like sweet potatoes. These yams are either cooked or eaten raw. Bambaru Banaka manages to use her wana or digging stick to find the thick tubes. Collecting yams is one of her favourite activities which she has not abandoned because of her blindness.

Collecting other fruits needs nimble fingers and good sight. Wamulu or bush tomato grow on grey–green shrubs a few centimetres high with pretty purple flowers and yellow stamens.

But the minute prickles along the stems are dangerous for the sightless and the children. This is a very common plant and found growing where Bambaru Banaka and her family have made their camp.

Since losing her sight Bami's mother, Bambaru Banaka, often sits in the shade of a large gum tree or windermarra tree, or remains at their latest camp in the company of her sisters, Mayu Banaka and Mayabingu Milungga, members of neighbouring clans north of Rudall River. The women, because of health problems and age, are assigned as child minders while mothers look for and collect food. This once proud and independent woman is quite happy to wait with her sisters and listen to and share stories or hear more recent family gossip.

****

The other women were doing exactly the same thing. The men would probably be cooking the game that they captured that morning. When the sun was high in the sky and the heat was starting to become slightly unbearable, the hunters and gatherers returned to their camp site. Their wirnis (coolamons or wooden oval shaped bowls) were filled with wamulu. A few minutes later Tyrama Garimara and his sons arrived with a cooked kangaroo. After a meal of meat and wild tomatoes washed down with water, everyone decided to rest awhile, but they were wakened by shouts coming from the north-east of the camp. It was old man Bayuka Garimara and his family calling in on their way to Jigalong. Offers of a meal were gratefully accepted.

The rest of the afternoon was spent threading the wamulu halves on strong sticks. At first the fruit is split in half then the seeds, which are black and bitter, are scraped out with a pirrkiri (a carved stick like a wooden knife). Later when the shrubs no longer have berries, the dehydrated fruit is placed on a flat grinding stone and when water is added the fruit is pounded until the flesh is soft enough to roll into balls and be eaten.

With the extra good rainfall of the past year, the desert had blossomed and bloomed for the first time in several years, resulting in a bountiful supply of bush foods. There were still plenty of wamulu nuts to collect. These would be buried at the base of a cool shady shrub. This way the fruit stays fresh for a few days.

The minyarra or native onions are found growing on river plains, river flats, clay pans and salt lakes. When the Gududjara and the Mandjildjara people go on their regular walks in the desert, they take notice of where certain plants and shrubs are growing in the area. This knowledge and information saves time and energy in fruitless searching and wandering about in such barren places.

Collecting onion seeds or small bulbs is a simple process, but one important rule must be observed. The minyarra plants must never be pulled up out of the earth. The Mardudjara people must always begin by digging a small trench in front along the edge of where the plants are, then they remove the packed soil underneath and roll the entire plant backwards to expose all the seeds or bulbs. These are shaken into a wirni to be yandied or separated later on. That is the correct way to gather the minyarra seeds or bulbs.

According to legend or creation stories and songs, if the minyarra are pulled by hand when it is raining, the ancestral beings will become very angry and will call lightning in the skies. The moral or message of that story is to do with conservation and preservation of food resources in a harsh desert environment.

The minyarra seeds are separated by a process called yandying; bulbs and seeds are placed together in a wirni, then shaken to and fro and tossed in the air, so that the light soil is blown away by the wind and the heavier seeds fall into the bowl. This is repeated until only the seeds remain. They are cooked in the ashes or can be eaten raw. Yandying is a highly skilled task and it is an activity in which all women of the nomadic society around Rudall River area become experts.

Spinifex and yuwinji or woolybutt seeds are collected by pulling the seedheads down over their wirnis then running them between their fingers. Once the bowls are filled, the women congregate in a clearing to winnow the grain seeds out. Winnowing grain seeds is a process that has been practised by women of all cultures for centuries, tossing seeds and allowing the wind to blow away the husks, leaving the seeds behind in the bowl. These are then taken back to the camp where they are ground into a coarse flour. By adding water, the flour is mixed into a paste that is either eaten like porridge or made into small mayi or dampers and cooked in the hot ashes. Either way it is enjoyable. It is interesting to note also that the grinding stone is an important tool that is taken with the family from camp to camp. It is carried on the head resting on a cushion made from emu feathers.

From the juicy, fleshy fruits of the bush or native tomatoes, the crunchy potatoes or yams, to the nutty-flavoured wild or native onions, and the emus, bush turkey and murrandus (goannas), this certainly has been a good season.

To all women of the hunting and gathering society, collecting and cleaning bush foods is a form of socialisation and recreation. It is a time for interaction, remembering the past by sharing happy memories of past harvests, the good and the bad times. Family gossip is passed on and there is laughter and bantering back and forth. But gathering fruit, vegetables and seeds is not regarded as solely a woman's role, and men and boys often participate and enjoy it.

The Gududjara and Mandjildjara people have lived in harmony with their land, as practising conservationists, taking only what was necessary. They learned from their ancestral spirit beings that if they took care of the land, the land would reciprocate by providing an abundance of food and game. The law of reciprocation is practised and obligations fulfilled by not only the Gududjara and Mandjildjarra people, but all Mardudjara people of Jigalong and the Western Desert regions. Preservation is the unbreakable golden thread woven into the fabric of life.

The nomadic lifestyle of Bambaru Banaka and her family and their movement is controlled by the seasonal changes. The seasonal cycle forces them to roam around their territory in search of food. When food is scarce they survive on small lizards, mice and birds. Now that summer is fast approaching, the fruit, roots, seeds and wama blossoms have shrivelled and fallen to the ground. The wama is a sweet drink made by soaking blossoms from the desert oak tree and cork tree and is greatly enjoyed. The traditional names for these trees are yumpalpa and palpinpa. Dust storms are becoming more frequent; pools, soaks and springs are drying up. Hard times are due. Bambaru Banaka has endured harsh conditions in the past and is prepared to continue to do so in the future.

****

It was a typically uncomfortable, hot day in the Rudall River area when Tjirama Garimara and Bambaru Banaka came to a very important decision. They decided to follow old man Bayuka Garimara and his family to Jigalong. What were the factors that brought about their decision to leave their homeland that particular day?

The couple agreed that they had endured the hardships of surviving in the desert in the past; that wasn't the problem. Other needs, both spiritual and physical, must be met. The most pressing need of the moment was finding suitable wives for their sons, Balga Burungu and Toabi Burungu. From information received from his brother, Bayuka Garimara, about a big meeting, Law business, that was to be held in a few weeks, the couple realised that there were not many desert groups left to hold ceremonial rites and rituals here in the Rudall River area. So they must move to the new Law centre. Ceremonial and sacred objects have already been buried at the Jigalong depot.

This is a special time for all the Mardudjara people including Tjirama Garimara and Bambaru Banaka and their family. This is the time when traditional and cultural rites, ritual and secret and sacred ceremonies are performed. At the completion of the special ceremonies, marriage between certain couples is announced. Choosing the right ngubas or spouses for their offspring is now a constant concern for parents.

Every child learns that Dreamtime beings handed down the belief system referred to as the Law, which includes rules for social behaviour, the codes and mores of Aboriginal society. The Mardudjara or Mardus (Martus) of the Western Desert have a unique kinship structure which provides a system of moral codes of behaviour, rules for socialisation and marriages. All individuals are categorised into one of five kinship or skin groups, Banaga, Banaka, Garimara, Burungu and Milungga. Each individual is born into one of these sections and cannot change or transfer into another group. Children are instructed at a very early age to conform to the kinship system, which is very rigid and complicated. The kinship terms are in constant use every day in preparation for more important roles when adulthood is reached. By that stage the pattern of behaviour towards other members of the clan and indeed the community, according to the kinship rules, is established. It is most important that obligations and commitments are fulfilled according to the kinship system.

A man must choose a wife from the right section; he cannot marry just any woman of his own choice. Marriage or union would be seen as incestuous and would never be accepted by the community. Many couples have eloped only to be apprehended and escorted back to Jigalong to face tribal punishment which means ostracism and public flogging. Finding suitable wives in the appropriate category means that sons must be present at the 'big Law business' meeting at Jigalong, where they will have the opportunity to meet their umari, or mother-in-law, and eventually their ngubas or spouses. Unlike non-Aboriginals, the nomads of the Western Desert did not have the time-consuming job of packing belongings then transporting them from place to place across the desert. Nor did they burden themselves with unnecessary tools or implements such as grinding stones. These would remain behind in the last camp along the Rudall River.

The journey began immediately after their meal of kangaroo meat, mayi (damper) and cool water. Bambaru Banaka and all the members of her family, including her kinship sisters, Mayabinga Milungga and Mayu Banaka, faced east and followed the river banks. Tjirama Garimara and his two sons had departed before the women, carrying their hunting weapons and a fire stick. They will all meet at a prearranged location at the soak on the banks of the almost-dry riverbed. The women walked silently, at first resisting the urge to look back at the homeland they were forsaking. Bambaru Banaka walked with her right hand resting on Mayabinga's shoulder, allowing clear space as they passed together through the grassy banks in the shade of the cadgebut (a thorny acacia) and river gums.

At noon, when the sun was high in the sky and the sweltering heat and burning sands made it impossible to walk any further, the women reached the designated soak. They waited there for the men to arrive. After a light meal of meat, damper and water they rested under the shady gum trees.

The siesta ended late afternoon. While it was still hot, it was more bearable, they continued westward toward 'civilisation'. They had already covered many miles and had further to go, so just before nightfall they made a camp and shared what could be their last meal. There wasn't much game around this arid, dusty and rocky land and everyone was disappointed that there was to be no fresh meat tonight, but there was always water to fill their stomachs.

These desert dwellers had no need for clothing of any description, neither did they possess rugs or blankets. Everyone was naked except for the adults who wore hair belts that covered their pubic area. They slept on the bare earth, relying on the fire to keep them warm at night. Even in the summer the desert winds can be very cold.

The next morning they filled up with water and hoped that the men would be successful today. The lizards that the women found were not worth the time and energy spent searching for them. The flesh on them was barely enough for a taste. Mice were in better condition, but the only problem was there was never enough to satisfy the group.

Bambaru Banaka and her family followed the Rudall River, walking slowly across the river flats until they came to wide spinifex plains with windermarra (mulga) and acacia trees scattered throughout a landscape surrounded by rocky outcrops which forced the group to walk in a wide circle around them. The barefooted nomads from the desert never allowed this huge obstruction, and the additional miles, to distress or upset them as they trekked over the dusty, red earth. Once again however, the heat forced them to pause and rest under the shade of the windermarra trees. Bambaru Banaka and her family group sat quietly listening to the cicadas and crows while the heatwaves were shimmering across the gibber and spinifex plains. It was difficult to sleep on an empty stomach.

As soon as it cooled down, spurred on by hunger, the group walked across the spinifex without resting. Their perseverance and determination was rewarded for, as the sun was sinking in the western sky, the tired, dusty, hungry and exhausted group reached the gates of Talawana Station.

Not having seen a station homestead before, the Mardudjara people from Rudall River became confused. They had no idea how to open and shut a gate so they climbed through the fence. Just as the last person cleared the fence a strange pale man wearing covering over his body came riding on a large beast. He was heading towards them. 'Look out,' warned Tjirama Garimara, 'it might be Marbu' (a flesh-eating being). The frightened group moved closer to the fence. 'Get ready to run,' ordered the old man.

They waited for a command that never came. When the stranger yelled, 'Stop,' everyone froze, not daring to move. Then he pointed to something a short distance away from the homestead and they saw smoke from camp fires. 'Go down there, that's the natives' camp,' he said. Although Tjirama Garimara had no idea what the person was saying, he understood the gesture when he motioned to them to follow him to the camps. They still carried their own firesticks.

That evening Bambaru Banaka and her family had their first big meal in two days. It was devoured with gusto. There was hot damper, tinned meat, salted beef and warm sweet milky tea. The new arrivals concentrated more on their meals than what Nalgo Banaka was telling them about what the life on a cattle station was all about. Perhaps tomorrow after a good night's rest they would show more interest in their surroundings.

Beside food and diet, there were other changes that Bambaru Banaka and her family were expected to make as others would be controlling their movements and their lifestyles. Tjirama Garimara, leader and highly respected elder, would become disempowered. His opinions as a Law man would not be sought and his customary Laws would often be disregarded by the foreigners. But despite the changes and adjustments, the Law business would take precedence over all other activities and the laws of a social system imposed upon them. The Mardudjara people of Jigalong and the western desert were determined to practise and preserve the Law and traditional culture.

These nomads from the desert would be ordered to cover their naked bodies so as to not embarrass or offend their white bosses. They would be given 'proper names'; in many instances their Mardu names would be anglicised or they would be simply given English names.

After two days of rest and nourishment, Tjirama Garimara led his small band of Rudall River desert people from the homestead and followed the rabbit-proof fence to their final destination, the Jigalong depot.

Apart from the food, horses and cattle, the greatest problem was becoming accustomed to the wearing of European clothes. The desert nomads were always glad when night time came and they were able to discard these unwanted garments for at least several hours.

****

At the conclusion of the traditional ceremonies, secret and sacred rituals, Bambaru Banaka and her husband, Tjirama Garimara, no longer had the uncertainty of whether their sons and daughter Bami would be married. Their eldest son, Balga Barungu's spouse was Mousie Milungga; Bami's husband was Willy Milungga; their son Toabi was given Molly Milungga.

Molly was present at the Law meeting and planned to return to Balfour Downs Station after the summer holidays were over. This allowed her in-laws to become acquainted, so Tjirama Garimara and his family established a camp on the banks of the Jigalong River. He also acquired a second wife and it pleased Bambaru Banaka to have a younger co-wife, because she was expecting her fifth child.

The 'native' camps were situated about fifty yards from the homestead on the other side of the boundary fence. That fence segregated the Mardudjara workers from their white employers and the white labourers. While Molly Milungga returned to work her husband and the rest of the family planned to spend some time with Nalgo Garimara at Murra Munda Station. Her mother Thumpy Garimara promised to warn the missus that her daughter had a new husband and that they had been married the right way this time. The high spirited independent young woman had a previous relationship with a Yamatji man named Andy Everett from Meekatharra who was also employed at Balfour Downs as a stockman, but after a miscarriage and a stillborn child, he broke off the relationship. He decided that he wanted to be free from complications and traditional family obligations.

One morning, Bambaru Banaka delivered a son. The station manager, a man named Joe Barker, called down to the camp to check up on both mother and son's condition.

'What's his name?' asked the manager.

'I don't know; no name yet,' replied Bambaru Banaka.

'Well,' said Joe Barker, 'call him Jacky Barker.'

So Ngidi, or the last child, was named Jacky Barker or Barga, and was cared for by his two mothers, Bambaru Banaka and Minnie Banaka. In no time at all it seemed the baby thrived and developed into a lively little boy who spent most of his time with Minnie Banaka.

Molly's husband, Toabi Burungu, and his family decided that they had developed the skills and learned enough about what is

115

required of labourers and station hands to enable them to make a significant contribution to the cattle industry. Each man was allocated jobs around the homestead. Tjirama Garimara, the station's gardener, was the first to undergo a name change; his 'proper' name now became Jimmy Garimara. Balga was given the name Peter and Toabi became Toby Burungu.

Bambaru Banaka's eldest daughter's 'proper' or English name was Pammy and Tagoda became known as Mona Burungu. Bambaru Banaka was the only one not to undergo a name change and was always known as the 'blind one'.

Under protest Molly moved in with her husband Toby and his mother Bambaru Banaka and father, Tjirama Garimara. She silently rebelled against her given spouse because she had already spent two years at the station and in that time had a half-caste boyfriend. Now she was forced against her will to be wife of a Mardu man from Rudall River, a Gududjara man. She was going through the motions of a dutiful wife to please her mother and the old people who gave her away to Toby Burungu.

Then, two years later in the summer of 1937, around Christmas time, a baby girl was born prematurely at the station. Molly Milungga named her Nugi, a name which didn't go down well with her employer, Mrs Dunnet. She scoffed at the child's name and ordered Molly to change it at once.

'It's a silly name,' she said. 'Change her name to Doris,' she ordered the child's mother.

Doris was almost a week old when Dr Albert Davis, the Medical Officer of the north-west, visited the station and when he examined her scrawny premature baby he announced that 'The child would not survive another week.' Weighing only three pounds at birth, Bambaru Banaka's granddaughter defied the doctor's respected opinion and prediction.

Dr Davis informed the Commission of Native Affairs of the child's survival on 19 September 1938: 'Thanks to Mrs Dunnet for her care of mother and child the latter still survives and probably will continue to do so for a while to come at least.' (Department of Aboriginal Affairs — File No. 345/37). Mr Bill Dunnet reinforced and supported the doctor's views when he wrote to the Commission of Aboriginal Affairs advising them that: 'The infant had grown wonderfully well and is now well and strong.' (Department of Aboriginal Affairs — File No. 345/37).

Three years later, Doris had a new sister called Anna, later

116

lengthened to Annabelle. Unlike her older sister, this baby was beautiful and plump and had been carried full term. Like all babies in the Mardudjara community, the child belonged to everyone. Three-year-old Doris became the eyes and companion for her grandmother, Bambaru Banaka. The child realised that she could control the activities and movement of the old lady and this attitude often got them into difficulties.

Bambaru Banaka allowed herself to be manipulated and persuaded to fulfil Doris's childish impulses and whims. Once Bambaru Banaka was led from the camp to search and dig for mata or wild sweet potatoes. The pair stayed longer than expected, so when the billy can of water was empty, Bambaru Banaka called out loudly for help. No one answered, so she continued yelling until her eldest son Balga Peter Burungu heard her and brought a bucket of water for her and his niece. He was so angry at this episode that his brother and sister-in-law were severely reprimanded. The toddler had no idea that her action could have put their lives in danger.

The child did, however, understand about aeroplanes. During the war, planes were often seen and heard flying to and fro from Perth to Darwin. One day Doris was playing a few feet from where her grandmother was resting when she heard the sound of an aeroplane. In fear and panic the child urged her grandmother to move and tried to hide her out of sight under the windermarra tree. When she was satisfied that the pilot or 'Japani man' could not see to shoot them, she sat protectively in front of her grandmother. When the planes were out of sight they returned to the camp. This action meant so much to Bambaru Banaka that a strong bond was formed between them.

Doris amused and entertained her grandmother with songs she had learned from Dallas, Mrs Dunnet's daughter. They enjoyed each other's company and communicated in Gududjara much to the disgust of Molly Milungga because she didn't understand them. 'You should speak Mardudjara' (a combination of Gududjara and Mandildjara). Bambaru Banaka found it amusing to listen to her granddaughter singing in English then translating it to the Gududjara language.

Concerns were expressed for Molly's health as she hadn't been well since the birth of her last daughter, Annabelle. She had been complaining of pains in the right side of her abdomen. She was examined and diagnosed as suffering from appendicitis. Dr

Davis recommended she be sent to Perth for an operation immediately. The problem was a lack of transport to get her there. The solution came in the form of a message over the pedal set (radio telephone) to Mr Bill Dunnet and it notified him that Molly and her children would be travelling with Mr Bill Campbell by overland mail. For the fare of five pounds, the woman and her little girls would be picked up from Balfour Downs Station on the 29 September 1940.

None of the family came to see them off, as they were all sitting in their camps with their heads bowed in grief, crying and weeping at the departure of Molly and her children for the long journey south. Having his wife and two daughters taken from him at the same time was too much for Toby Burungu to bear. Beside him, wailing louder than the rest, was Bambaru Banaka who had bright red blood pouring from a self-inflicted wound on her head, which was her way of expressing deep mourning for the departure of her loved ones. Doris watched them from the back of the mail truck, her little heart breaking, until her view was cut off when the truck went around a bend. Then a veil of thick mist fell in between, blocking out memories of her father, her beloved grandmother and all her other relatives at Balfour Downs Station.

Bambaru Banaka wept and sobbed well into the night, refusing to eat any food. At first light the loud wailing began again. Mr Dunnet was roused from his sleep, he glanced at the bedside clock, rolled over and went back to sleep. The next morning Bambaru Banaka and her son, Toby Burungu, left the homestead for Ten Mile Windmill, made a shelter and went on a hunger strike.

Twelve months later Bambaru Banaka passed away. She had mourned with her son for his loss of wife and daughters, but she especially grieved for her granddaughter, Nugi Garimara, the little one who became her eyes. She missed the little arms around her neck and the child's dusty kisses on her cheek. No one could replace the child who had shared her world, who had loved and cared for her and tried to protect an old blind woman in her own small way.

An Old Man's Story

In the shade of a twisted old Banksia,
By the side of a poisoned river,
An old man sat a moment, to linger
On thoughts from the past, of his people
Who walked tall with dignity and pride
Through a landscape rich with stories;
Of hope that should never have died.

He thinks of the old people, his family
And the love that they had for this land.
He remembers his wife, dark and slender;
Walking together, hand in hand
Over rocks, over hills and through valleys;
At one with all they surveyed.

By the fireside, at dusk he is standing.
In the darkness he hears once again the songs,
Sung from the soul with the spirit
Of the land, his Mother, for whom he longs.

Severed by the bolt of lightning
And crushed by the sound of a gun;
Ancestors became one with the spirits,
Now sleeping on hope of a rising sun.

The old man remembers the turmoil
That came with disease, death and gun.
Barbed wire, poison and rape
Took Mother Earth from her son.

Alone, tired and weary;
An old man can't understand
Why he's left alone with the memories
And a broken spear in a trembling hand.

Supreme Court Gardens, Perth

The benches were empty today,
Nobody sat on the lawns,
The rain has dampened everything,
People, grass, trees and birds.

The Nyoongahs are still the same,
Oblivious to everything around,
The spirits have dampened the souls
And their footprints left heavy marks in the sand.

I looked up to see where they'd gone,
It's as if they weren't even here,
Is it possible that mother earth has swallowed them,
Or have they become one with the trees, wind and sky?

What do dreams do? Is it a twilight zone?
Is there a doorway we all pass through,
Not knowing what's on the other side?
One Nyoongah came back then disappeared.

He's in the other world now, not dead!
Living here with urbanisation, yet
Living faraway, deep, deep down,
Down behind those mournful eyes,
And above that empty laugh.
Above the gentle blue skies
Below the concrete and the tar
Living beyond the touch of 'progress'
And away from the snarling jaws of
Civilisation.

Into the Light

(after Hans Heysen's painting of the same name)

He felt the stick in his hand, and might have drawn in the soil with it, the way she and the kids did. They used their fingers in the sand, or drew with charcoal on hessian, bark, scraps of paper. He had even found himself puzzling over meaningless arrangements of leaf, bone and ash.

Perhaps he should have drawn a map, himself, to show his children where they must aim and which way was forward. Or, more realistically, to indicate where the fences will be. But this stick was too big for drawing anything, save perhaps blood.

She had laughed at him, even as he struck.

He was an old fella, see. What sort of life had he made? Shepherd, prospector, teamster … farmer, almost. In everything he had been a pioneer. He worked best of all alone.

This country had failed him, despite its promise. There was no rain. You got a little bit of ground, and had to make do with that, had to make it produce. It couldn't, didn't; not enough to earn the money they now needed.

He'd partly fenced it. That was a first task for the bank, and to make something from the nothing that was there. He'd marked their domain off from the similar stunted stubble and bush that surrounded them. His gin-jockey self, his outcast wife, his insistently Aboriginal children. He had made them as an island, and they would be enough unto themselves.

But, change. More and different people. He and his own, it seemed they had somehow strayed and only he could lead them out of darkness and into the light. He was their shepherd, they should not want. He would uplift them.

But, ungratefully, she had refused to understand. And when the boys left, choosing their own way, she had laughed at him.

He went to his horse. The routine soothed him; bit, reins, saddle. Tightening the girth strap.

Then you go, she had said.

You first.

He took his first sip from a new bottle. The darkness was fading. Soon, the sun. He never looked back. There was nothing possible for him to say, he knew that.

The woman raised her head, spat soil from her lips, and watched him go. As, long ago a frightened girl huddled in a creek of piss tears blood had watched him approach.

Much later in the day the woman was still there to hear her boys, as they ran to her.

The dog hesitated, kept moving between the two of them. The man tried to call it, but his tongue clicked meaninglessly, and he could not whistle in any way the dog understood. It was the sheep dog, the silly one. The police had shot their good dogs.

Eventually the distance between the man and woman became too great, and so the dog stayed with the man, and the sheep it had collected.

He followed the road. He'd been among the first, the first white men. Fences ran either side, and as the rising sun showed the valley before him and the track scratching away to the south of a hill to his right, he realised that he rode between trees he'd ringbarked. Before him was one he'd missed. Not that it mattered now.

It was the sort of light that dissolved shadows. It was the sort which should have revealed angels. The sheep ahead of him were disappearing into it and the pale trunks of trees he'd killed — tried to kill — were smeared with red gore where the light struck them. The light filled his gaping mouth, and held his restless, stinging tongue.

He went into the light and there, soaring above him yet, were the remains of dead limbs which had fallen, clubbing the ground.

Once he had followed the arch of her wrist, the toss of her head, and there had been no path that he could see. Now a road led between these trees, and it showed him a view and a destination.

He swung away. The dog hesitated, then continued on with the sheep, sending them along the road. It looked to him, expecting commands. He gave none.

He realised he was on horseback. It must be that he was

checking the traps. Rabbit, rabbit, rabbit. Immigrants too, burrowing in more than miners. They were killing the country, taking over. But here he was, he and his little mob, living on them. His own kind.

They squealed in his traps, and he killed them with barely a tap, before peeling back the skin to show the blue-veined whiteness underneath.

Here, the bloody stick was still in his hands. He tossed it from him, and almost followed it, almost fell as a wave of giddiness rose within him.

The big slow horse leaned into a fence post, stepped through the wire, kept going. Large crescent prints pointed bluntly after it and the shrinking man on its back, swallowed and swaddled in clothes with a hat balanced on top.

It was an end. He'd passed the limit of any trap he may have set and, folding in on himself, had found this trace of an old trail. It was as slow as it ever was with a team, and he and Fanny walking, when she used to gather things and give him words for what she saw. Sometimes he'd pull her to the ground, and they'd thrash about beside the track.

They'd have to hurry, then, to catch the team. And she was livelier than ever, dancing ahead of his ponderous, plodding, grasping self.

The horse grazed, walking all the while from long years of knowing the weight on its back. The waterholes were larger than ever before, their surrounds chopped and boggy. The horse didn't know this, the man didn't see.

The sun passed them going the other way. Maybe he had it in his mind to get to where he had first met his Fanny. Where he had saved her — her, the only one — and put the red-flowing creek behind him. He took her in a wheelbarrow, past the edge of her world, and promised her another.

His tongue was thick, and sore at its flaking tip. It moved clumsily in his mouth as he mumbled, tongued his bits of prayer and broken promises.

He remembered following his shadow, and now was shocked to see it was his reflection staring back at him. He was kneeling beside a tiny creek, must have been there for hours. The light had faded, and tiny fish kissed and nibbled at the loose and puckered skin of his hands. Salt in his mouth, burning burning and oh, how his Adam's apple moved so painful. He turned his head, slow like a tortoise. A breeze touched his raw skin. Smoke? Was it fire?

There was her voice — and he could hear her boys — somewhere in the distance, in the smoke filling his skull. Justice, he thought. After all, it was he who had saved them.

The discoverers had tramped across burnt stubble and every step was a little explosion, releasing fine ash into the air. Now, as they stood together in a rough circle, facing inward, there remained at each man's back a series of small and ghostly clouds hovering above the last of his footprints. Gradually these faded, falling back to the black earth.

The men were held, as it were, by the landscape, which rose, surrounding them, from the small creek bed. And at the centre of their contemplation a charred body knelt as if in supplication, upon a small pad of fresh leaves. Its hands and face were immersed in a trickling fragment of smoky blue sky. Those who had found it placed tentative hands upon its shoulders and pulled. But the body did not, as they had expected, crackle stiffly onto its curved back and point its limbs upward. No. As attentive as had been the tiny fish the men watched the body tilt, and saw the way the carefully broken bones folded neatly onto one another until ... An arrangement of leaves, charred cloth, flesh, bone.

The discoverers fell back before a skull which, its grin finally grown full, sucked at the sun so bright bright bright.

Just Beach Land

Dedicated to my father Frank Corbett (Cobie)

This is my father's place, where the campfire burned,
The bright red flames showed me the way.
He has not left me
His spirit walks beside me.
Yes, I have fear only of the living.
I feel, smell the air.
Why do some fear the old fellows?
I don't, it's as if he's still here.
Night time has fallen,
The waves are calling.
I hear so many things
Far across the waves and ocean,
Peace has come until dawn.
Seagulls wait for breakfast,
Surfies wait for waves,
Fishermen look over the horizon. Another day.
It's dreaming place.
The waves tossing, getting louder,
The sound of thunder.
Don't worry, it's only the waves
Telling the fishermen again and again,
The break of the waves, and the big one that got away.
But with no doubt the fishermen will come back again.

He Couldn't Read or Write

You may have been born north
But the South Ellen's Brook was your childhood
With your brothers and Gran and uncle too.
My feet have travelled many places, so many schools.
You have always been my teacher
Though you couldn't write,
An X was all you could do.
Work you started, sun up until sun down,
A pitchfork in your hand,
Rows and rows of potato bags.
I look at those fields today, just dry grass.
I think a lot about those days and I feel a lot of pain.
Father, so much has changed.
This little old man with his old felt hat
Had tallied his bags for another day.
He was satisfied with a little grin on his face.
That's my father, Frank.

Shadow on the Wall

Last night you touched my pillow
I awoke from my dream
Sick and broken-hearted.
My dreams were of you.
Mother, come to me, tell me what to do.
You have entered into the garden,
Your spiritual world and place.
The phone rang near my pillow.
No more a shadow on the wall.
I knew she was gone.
Bye my darling,
I'll see you no more.
Next time stay a little longer,
Shadow on the wall.

Old King and Queen

One moonlit night old King and Queen
ran away from the Woorooloo Hospital
where they were meant to stay.
They came from the desert up Kalgoorlie way,
but were lonely and homesick most every day.

While the police cars and trackers on foot
searched through the night, old King and Queen
followed the pipeline in the moonlight.
Weary and sick they didn't mind.
They knew this pipeline would take them back home.

When they reached Kalgoorlie,
old King and Queen never came back,
the call of the bush was too strong for them.
Even though they are sick and old
they are happy and free,
roaming the bush up Kalgoorlie way.

Bud

Bud never got over
the death of his wife.
Drugs and alcohol
brought change to his life,
the emptiness and heart-ache
that time wouldn't heal,
the drugs and the alcohol
and the need for a meal.

Arrested and detained
in the lock-up one night
Bud never woke up
to see the sunlight.
A black death in custody
was what they said.
We all know the truth
But that's how it read.

His black mother prayed
at the end of that day
when it became known
how her son had passed away.
Her tired old face
showed the pain and the grief.
A victim of drug abuse
had now found relief.

atsic

all these gifts
the white man gives us
like atsic
     they're
         like
             time
                 bombs

Acceptable Coon

When I was young they sent me to school
to read and write and be nobody's fool.
They taught me the white ways and bugger the rest
'cos everything white was right and the best.

So I grew up in a white man's sense
and I found belief and I gained confidence.
No doubts were apparent in my little world
so I sailed on to big things with my wings unfurled.

My world was so rosy until I saw
that nothing that I did could open the door.
'Cos when you reach somewhere no matter how soon
you're nothing more than an acceptable coon.

Look down on the bucks look down on the gins
the old roads are evil and pathways to sin.
So learn all the white things they teach you in school
and you'll all become acceptable coons.

I know what I'm saying
I know that it's true,
that everyone here's turning out just like you.
You're doing the wrong things
believing it's right,
Australia's just churning out prototype whites.

Acceptable coons, acceptable coons
Australia's just full of acceptable coons.
Acceptable coons, acceptable coons
Australia's just full of acceptable coons.

Jangga Meenya Bomunggur
(The Smell of the White Man is Killing Us)

We the Custodial Owners of Nyoongah Culture, Respectfully representing our Traditional Elders, Spiritual Leaders, and Grass Roots Advocates of the Nyoongah people, declare a Stand of belligerent Confrontation on All People who for their own interests with no RESPECT, DIGNITY or INTEGRITY continually exploit Our Culture and Spirituality.

Whereas on multiple fronts varying interests have infiltrated the Sacredness of our Culture for the purpose of Desecration and Control, these interests reflect Anthropological Studies, Scientific Research, White Consultants, Eco Tourism, Student Studies, Medical Interests, Herbalists, Alternative Religious Practitioners, Humanitarians, Self Proclaimed Healers, Spiritual and Psychological Refuges, New Age Shamans, Cultists and Their Followers.

Whereas Our Significant Sacred Objects that bore the Storylines of our Origins have been Stolen and stored in Collections around the world.

Whereas various Animal Life with Totemic Significance is now known to be extinct, many forms of Flora which provided Medicine for Our People no longer flourish in abundance, and ochre pits rich in Ancient Paint used for Ceremonial Purpose have been destroyed.

Whereas the Skulls and Bones of our Proud and Strong People have been dispersed throughout the World as grotesque souvenirs or have been taken into World Laboratories and Museums for supposed experimental purposes.

Whereas Non-Aboriginal people, Wadjulla (white) Academics, Intellectuals and Theorists have enforced their Images based on Their Value Belief Systems distorting the reality of Our Traditional Values and Way of Life.

Whereas Non-Aboriginal People, Wadjulla, have assigned themselves make-believe Aboriginal Names to facilitate wholesale expropriation and commercialisation of our Nyoongah Traditions by all means of extortion.

Whereas Academic Institutions supported by Statutory Bodies mimic, duplicate and exploit Sacred Significant Traditional Art Symbols and meanings for recreational School Art Programs, encouraging Non-Aboriginal expressions creating alien story concepts.

Whereas Media, Film Industry and non-Aboriginal Art Expressionists continue to promote systematic Colonisation, Grossly Distorting Nyoongah Spirituality and Culture which reinforces the public's negative stereotyping of Nyoongah people and gravely impairs the self-esteem of our people.

Whereas individuals and groups involved in the New Age Movement, Women's Movement and Neo-Pagan Cults and Shamanism Workshops have all exploited the Spiritual and Cultural Traditions of Nyoongah People by imitation of Ceremonial Understanding and Meshing this with Non-Aboriginal Occult Practice in an oppressive manner.

THIS BREEDS THE IMPLICATIONS OF A FALSE IDENTITY FOR FUTURE GENERATIONS

This continued assault and misrepresentation of Nyoongah Spiritual and Cultural traditions requires immediate action to protect Our precious Spirituality from further desecration, contamination and abuse. Therefore we resolve as follows:

1. We will by the Blood of Our Ancestors nurture and protect Our People, Traditions and Spiritual Practice by whatever means.
2. We will by way of Traditional Protocol encourage All Aboriginal People to actively participate, to oppose Cultural and Systematic Genocide of Our Traditions and Way of Life.
3. We call for the strength of Unity of all Aboriginal People in urban and rural areas to identify and resist all abuses and exploitation of Our Culture utilising whatever tactics are

required in accordance with Aboriginal Protocol.

4. We condemn the Internalising of Our Own People who continue to profit from their own prostitution of Nyoongah Culture for their own gain and self-acclaim with no regard for the well being of All Nyoongah People.

5. We Oppose Stridently any Non-Aboriginal Authors with accumulated Cultural Information who impress their own Imaginative Theories and Fabricated Ideologies, claiming any Ownership or Rights to Speak or Act on Behalf of the Nyoongah Community and Our Culture.

6. We oppose Nyoongah Culture being exploited and used to create a false Illusion of Reconciliation as part of celebrating any activity regarding the Colonisation of Our People for political interests, i.e. Australia Day, Bicentennial and Ceremonial Celebrations.

MAY OUR CAMPFIRES BURN FOREVER

Description of the Declaration

The Declaration titled 'Jangga Meenya Bomunggur' was written by Robert Eggington, the Director of the Perth based Dumbartung Aboriginal Corporation, on the eve of a contingent of Aboriginal Elders who, representing Australia, travelled to the United States during January 1996 to participate in an International Press Conference regarding the controversial American author Marlo Morgan and the book titled *Mutant Message Downunder*.

The Declaration was initially presented at a Yokai meeting in Perth and endorsed by the Nyoongah meeting as the basis of the media campaign regarding intellectual property rights and cultural ownership issues.

The Declaration highlights the issues regarding various forms of infiltration and exploitation of Aboriginal cultural knowledge by entities such as the new-age movement, academic and government controlled institutions etc.

The Declaration has been included as part of Dumbartung's Wall of Shame initiative which shows further material examples of cultural exploitation regarding the:

Destructive impact of eco-tourism
Identity appropriation
Stolen cultural and ceremonial objects
Ecological knowledge
Tourist commodities and products

The philosophy of Dumbartung is to promote cultural development in respect of community and spiritual growth. There is no emphasis placed on evolving as a commercial arm of the so-called cultural industry as part of the funding criteria of the State Government's policy on art funding. This has resulted in the recent decision of the State Government to withdraw Dumbartung's funding and dissolve the State agency status.

As Aboriginal arts maintain an extensive and varying interest for many western countries, it is imperative to strengthen our commitment to the central need of working towards the empowerment of the rights of ownership of our people over the oldest living culture on the most ancient land mass on the face of the earth.

To What Extent is Contemporary Aboriginal Identity Political?

Since the late nineteenth century the colonisers have had a preoccupation with observing, analysing, studying, classifying and labelling Aborigines and Aboriginality (Dodson, 1994:3). In what Marcia Langton (quoted by Johnson, 1993:34) has interpreted as a 'legal and administration obsession', the search for an appropriate characterisation has led to a variety of definitions of Aboriginal peoples. Commencing with the colonisers' first impression of the indigenous peoples as being 'the most wretched people on earth' (Dodson, 1994:2), mainstream society continues to employ a number of essentialist measures to gauge 'racial difference'.

Government policies attest to crude scientific and biological determinants to categorise Aborigines. The 1905 Aborigines Act is a classic example of the ways in which Aboriginality became defined in accordance with the concept of 'white blood'. What followed was a number of 'hybrid' classifications such as 'half-caste', 'quadroon', and 'octoroon'. The Assimilation policy emerged when it became evident that the Darwinian notion that Aborigines would simply 'die out' was proved wrong.

Such essentialist practices can be understood in terms of Foucault's theory of knowledge (Groves, 1995:18). According to Foucault, discursive practices and, by extension, the essentialist, racist practices historically used to categorise and institutionalise Aborigines, are:

> characterised by a delimitation of a field of objects, the definition of legitimate perspectives for the agent of knowledge, and the fixing of norms for elaboration of concepts and theories. Their effect is to make it virtually impossible to think outside them. (Young, 1981:48)

What this means is that it becomes difficult to consider Aborigines in any form other than those prescribed by dominant discursive practices. Although definitions such as those mentioned above may be considered obsolete, similar discursive practices are still in place (Groves, 1995:18). Consider the 'traditional/urban' dichotomy in which 'traditional' Aborigines are considered authentic whilst urban Aborigines are seen as 'empty vessels, drained of their content by European culture' (Jennings, 1993:12).

More recently, the Australian government's response to the High Court decision on Mabo provides another example of the State continuing to pursue such essentialist practices. The success of Native Title depends on the ability of plaintiffs (indigenous peoples) to provide 'proof'. If they have:

> continued to acknowledge the laws and to observe the customs based on the traditions of that clan or group, whereby their traditional connection with the land has been substantially maintained, the traditional community title of that clan or group can be said to remain in existence. (Bartlett, 1992:1)

Thus the obsession with the categorisation of indigenous peoples continues — the 'authenticity' of Aboriginality is now legally determined on the basis of the ability of indigenous people's being able to 'prove' their spiritual connection to country. Yet no recognition or compensation exists for those indigenous peoples whose 'spiritual relationships' with ancestral lands were severed as a result of them being forcibly removed and relocated by the State. It is as if they have been forgotten.

Such forgetfulness is what Brown terms 'refracted knowledge' (1987:61). That is, rather than having to address 'black' political issues, the colonisers surround themselves with 'comfortable and familiar' images of the colonised. For the colonisers, Aboriginality has become essentialised in a series of 'familiar' metaphors — postcards, teatowels, Aboriginal gnomes and, more recently, in television commercials, as 'ochred, spiritual, and playing the didgeridoo behind the heroic travels of a black land cruiser' (Dodson, 1994:3). As Brown so eloquently states, 'it is as if a camera has been pushed through a gap in the Mission fence' (Brown, 1987:61).

Such essentialist practices provide excuses for the majority of white Australians to remain ignorant of Australia's 'black history'. The definitions put forward by the State say nothing about the ways indigenous peoples define themselves. They dismiss our histories, cultures, politics and efforts to decolonise.

Yet like many other colonised peoples we recognise the fundamental need to claim our identity. Aboriginal peoples, like other colonised peoples, see it as one of the most important processes of decolonisation. As Albert Memmi states, 'the colonised's liberation must be carried out through a recovery of self and autonomous dignity' (1965:128).

INDIVIDUAL AND COLLECTIVE IDENTITIES

Australian historian Bob Reece says that when the British invaded Australia there were no 'Aborigines', but rather six hundred identifiable groups of people possessing sophisticated technology, social systems, geographical knowledge and linguistic skills (1987:1). Upon colonisation, there followed a process Albert Memmi terms 'depersonalisation'; that is, the coloniser homogenises the colonised. The colonised are never characterised individually but rather as an anonymous collective. In effect the Aboriginal people or indigenes of Australia became the 'Australian Aborigines' (Reece, 1987:14). Eve Fesl says such practices denied the existence of specific indigenous 'nations' (Fesl, 1987:16).

In contemporary societies indigenous peoples consciously take active steps to decolonise both individually and collectively. Whilst we publicly acknowledge our specific identities as Nyoongars, Wongis, Yamatjis and Bardis etc., and make conscious decisions about the appropriateness of our speaking position such as acknowledging whose country we are in and whether we have the right to speak about particular issues, we consciously claim the coloniser's term 'Aborigines'. We claim the latter as a national process of solidarity. Where once the colonisers named the colonised 'Aborigines' as part of a process of oppression, Aboriginal peoples have reclaimed this term as a form of resistance. It is in this collective sense that we unite to

138

share our experiences as colonised peoples, our need for equality and justice.

Since the 1970s the United Nations' interest in the plight of indigenous peoples internationally has increased. More specifically, in 1972 the United Nations Sub-commission on Prevention of Discrimination and Protection of Minorities commissioned the Study of the Problem of Discrimination to examine the criteria governments use to define indigenous peoples (Dodson, 1994:4).

The study concluded that indigenous 'identities' were being constructed according to non-indigenous peoples' lifestyles and values. As a result indigenous peoples were generally identified not in terms of their positive attributes but rather in terms of what they lacked. Whilst non-indigenous peoples were seen as 'developed', indigenous people were regarded as 'underdeveloped'. Furthermore, indigenous peoples were considered 'primitive', uneducated and unable to speak the language of the non-indigenous population (Dodson, 1994:4).

Australia is one country which is recognised for enforcing such naive categorisation. For instance, consider the Western Australian Government's enforcement of the 1905 Aborigines Act which resulted in children being removed from their Aboriginal parents and extended family and placed into welfare institutions and the institutions of 'white' families (Groves, 1995:18). The basis of such horrific legislation was the primitive/civilised dichotomy, that is, Aborigines being considered 'primitive' peoples and whites 'civilised'. This ideology of 'we (the State) know what's best for you' is prevalent throughout the many policies and laws inflicted on Aboriginal peoples by the colonisers.

Even today indigenous peoples, on a daily basis, are subjected to non-indigenous scrutiny of their identity. Part of the problem is that many non-Aborigines continue to 'identify' Aborigines in terms of 'Wadjella-ness', that is, assessing Aboriginality by adopting non-Aboriginal criteria. This is a practice Edward Said has termed 'othering'. It is what he describes as:

the culturally-sanctioned habit of deploying large generalisations by which reality is divided into various collectives: languages, races, types, colours, mentalities, each category being not so much a neutral designation as an evaluative interpretation. (Said, 1978:227)

In this instance non-Aborigines are white, Aborigines are black. White represents clean, pure and innocent; black represents dirty, bad and evil. It is no wonder that non-Aboriginal people become confused when we contradict our labels, then say to us, 'Really, well you don't look like an Aboriginal.'

The UN study rejected any definition that relied exclusively on either descent or cultural characteristics. It is recognised that classifications according to biological and scientific theories have been widely discredited. The study recognised the inappropriateness of defining indigenous peoples according to a fixed 'imagined culture'. The identities and cultures of colonised peoples are not static but are continually adapting to societal change. Thus it would be foolish not to consider the ways colonisation has influenced the lives of colonised peoples. The study stated that while cultural considerations are important, they could not be considered absolute (Dodson, 1994:5). It concluded that:

the fundamental assertion must be that Indigenous populations must be recognised *according to their own perceptions and conceptions of themselves* in relation to other groups. There must be *no attempt* to define them, according to the perception of others through the values of foreign societies or of the dominant sectors in such societies ... [and] artificial, arbitrary or manipulatory definitions must, in any event, be rejected. (Dodson, 1994:5)

As Dodson says, the right to control self identity is part of the broader right to self determination, that is, the right of a people to determine its political status and to pursue its own economic, social and cultural development (1994:5). The current UN Draft Declaration on the Rights of Indigenous Peoples states that:

Indigenous peoples have the collective and individual right to maintain and develop their distinct identities and characteristics, including the right to identify themselves as Indigenous and be recognised as such. (Dodson, 1994:6)

In 1980 the Australian government responded to the United Nations' findings by adopting the following working definition on Aboriginality:

An Aboriginal or Torres Strait Islander is a person of Aboriginal or Torres Strait Islander descent, who identifies as an Aboriginal or Torres Strait Islander and is accepted by the community in which she or he lives. (Dodson, 1994:5)

Yet whilst such 'official' definitions exist, the identities of Australian indigenous peoples are continually challenged by non-indigenous societies. Responding to racist and ignorant allegations can be time-consuming and costly in terms of the energies and finances involved. This is particularly so if Aboriginal peoples choose to challenge within the existing structures of the State, such as courts. Yet in the past five years our spirits have strengthened. The spirit, tenacity, and achievement of Eddie Mabo have become inspirational for many of us.

REFERENCES

Bartlett, R. *Resource Development and Aboriginal Land Rights Conference. Papers*, 1992, University of Western Australia and Murdoch University, Perth.

Brown, K. 'Representing the Oblivious: An Analysis of the film *The Chant of Jimmy Blacksmith*' in *Aboriginal Issues Course Reader*, 1987. Murdoch University, Perth.

Dodson, M. 'The Wentworth Lecture' *Australian Studies Journal* No. 1. 1994. Institute of Australian Aboriginal Studies, Canberra.

Ely, D. *Photofile* No. 40, Nov 1993.

Fesl, E. 'How the English Language is Used to Put Koories Down, 1987. Deny Us Rights, or is Employed as a Political Tool' in *Introduction to Aboriginal Studies Course Reader*, 1987. Murdoch University, Perth.

Groves, D. 'A Critical Discussion of Race and Tracey Moffat's *Bedevil*', in *bur-ran-gur* (court out), 1995. School of Architecture and Fine Arts, Perth.

Jennings, K. *Sites of Difference: Cinematic Representation of 1993 Aboriginality and Gender*, 1993. Australian Film Institute, Victoria.

Memmi, A. *The Colonizer and the Colonized*, 1965. Souvenir Press, London.1965.

Reece, B. 'Inventing Aborigines'. *Aboriginal History*. Vol. 2. 1987.

Said, E. *Orientalism: Western Conceptions of the Orient*, 1978. Penguin Books, London.

Young, R. *White Mythologies*, 1981. Routledge Press, London.

Yellow Flowers

When I had returned home from America
I had a dream that I was standing
In a field of golden brown ripe wheat
On a clear day under a blue sky
In the brilliant light of a golden sun.

The wind started to blow like an arrow
And the heads of wheat started to lean over
In a straight line coming towards me direct
As it came from the east like a knife blade.

When the wind reached me it stopped
And started to move in a clockwise direction.
The heads of the wheat leaned over but
As the wind moved around me they stood up.
When the wind completed the circle
All the wheat started to vanish.

The red clay soil became dry and dusty
Then long cracks and furrows appeared.
They ran across the land as far as I could see.

Later on it started to rain very heavily.
The rain didn't splash on the land so dry
But fell into the cracks and furrows
And it splashed upon seeds in the furrows.

Beautiful green shoots started to rise up.
They grew before my eyes and leaves sprouted.
As well as the brilliant green leaves
Large yellow sunflowers started to unfold.

In front of me the plants and flowers grew
But they only grew in half a circle in front
From my right to my left hand side.

I suddenly realised that all the yellow flowers
Were all turned and standing perfectly still.
In the complete silence they were all looking
They were all looking directly at me.

It was only then that I looked more deeply
And from behind the brilliant green stalk and leaves
I saw black ants who were peering out
From their hiding places.
They were all looking at me and together said
'Don't bring the machinery. Don't bring the machinery.'

Then the black ants all started to cry.
Tears fell from their eyes and from the flowers.

The Past Still Lives

You tell us to forget,
to move on and look to the future.
But the past still hurts us, chokes us,
every time we see old pictures,
hear stories from our people
and read the journals of the invaders.
When I close my eyes, I can see the faces of the old people,
the expressions I see will haunt me forever.
Made to wear chains around their necks,
cutting into them, deep.
The horror still lives inside us,
their children's children,
permanent memories in our hearts.
We won't forget, can't forget.
They were proud people,
still deserve to be proud people.
We won't throw away what they fought for.
I will stand up and be counted
with my people any day,
teach my kids what little I know
and I will never be guilty
of what the invaders were guilty of.
I hope I never hurt anyone
as much as Australia's history
has hurt our people.

Brick Walls: A Comment on the Challenges Facing Indigenous Artists

There is currently a furore over the apparent misappropriation of indigenous art, literature and culture by non-indigenous people. Recently, we have seen such alleged examples as Mudrooroo, Elizabeth Durack and Leon Carmen. Mudrooroo, it has been claimed, has made a livelihood and established a high academic reputation based on the perception and projection of his Aboriginality, even to the extent of accepting prize monies for competitions involving indigenous writings. Elizabeth Durack has been known in the past as an artist of great renown, whose studies of indigenous people and their culture have great value. However, in the eyes of many people, she has sullied her fine reputation by entering artworks under the name of Eddie Burrup into a travelling exhibition of indigenous art and being paid for it. Leon Carmen has written a prize-winning novel about an alter-ego who is a middle-aged indigenous woman. This work has received critical acclaim, and it is significant that the author didn't reveal his true identity until after the prize had been awarded. In each instance, the perpetrators of these appropriations of indigenous culture have, it seems, tried to shrug off the fact of their exposure. Mudrooroo's only statement before disappearing from public view was to the effect of 'what will be will be'. Elizabeth Durack 'couldn't understand what all the fuss was about.' Leon Carmen implied that 'anyone could write a Black Story.'

The art and literary establishment may claim that the works of these artists are of sufficient merit to stand on their own, but this does not excuse the fact that these artists have misrepresented themselves as indigenous artists and have received acclaim for being indigenous. It also conveniently ignores the fact that indigenous writers are in the process of establishing a niche in the literary world from which they can rewrite themselves and their culture into the history of Australia. It is apparent that the establishment has, in each case, neglected to carefully and thoroughly investigate their backgrounds to establish their connections to the indigenous community. If the establishment accepts that these artists have the right to exploit indigenous art and indigenous people in this way, there can be little hope that genuine indigenous artists will ever receive fair and just treatment at the hands of the establishment. Unless the establishment makes a clear and unequivocal condemnation of these individuals, it leaves itself open to the claim that anybody who is non-Aboriginal, can produce 'indigenous art', and that impugns the efforts of all indigenous artists.

Indigenous artists have to provide a high level of proof of their indigenous status when they apply for Arts Council or any other funding to pursue their careers, so it is adding insult to injury for them to see their works rejected in favour of these non-indigenous artists who fraudulently misrepresent themselves. Indigenous artists who wish to receive project funding have to place their level of proof on a legal footing by signing a statutory declaration which cites the artist's connection to the indigenous community. This usually means going to an indigenous agency, being sighted by its board of management and having one's indigenous status confirmed by Elders who know of the family connections. The penalty for lying on a statutory declaration, which amounts to contempt of court, is very severe. Should not the same rigour be applied to competitions, particularly where awards and prize money for indigenous excellence are concerned?

ATSIC has a definition of indigenous status which is used for official purposes:

A person of Aboriginal or Torres Strait Islander descent who identifies as such and is accepted as such by the community.

This definition requires indigenous people to prove three separate elements of their identity. Firstly, they must prove that their descent, or lineage, includes indigenous antecedents. Secondly, they must prove that they identify as an indigenous person and are involved in the indigenous community. Thirdly,

147

they must also prove that the indigenous community accepts them as a full-status member.

In the Nyoongar community in the south-west of Western Australia, a person is identified in the following ways:

1. With full indigenous status.
(a) According to birth. A person born into a clan, group or community. For such a person, identification is complete and unconditional, even if they should reject or be removed from their clan, group or community and become part of the mainstream community, so long as their connections are known and can be established.

(b) According to kinship. An indigenous person who, by marriage, becomes associated with a different clan, group or community. If such a person adopts full responsibility for the culture and customs of the clan, group or community, they may have full clan status conferred on them, according to local custom. Any children from such a union would automatically be considered part of that indigenous group as well as the other parent's group (similar to dual citizenship provisions).

2. With conditional community status.
According to habituation. Where a non-indigenous person moves into an area occupied by an indigenous clan, group or community, and subsequently accepts the culture and customs of that clan, group or community, such a person may be granted conditional community status. However, this would be subject to their having learnt the cultural protocols and conventions governing that clan, group or community, and would depend on the extent and context agreed upon by the clan, group or community. Further, the conditional status conferred upon that person may have no significance outside that particular clan, group or community.

There are a number of factors which impinge on the ways indigenous people identify themselves. Dislocation and dispossession have made it exceedingly difficult for many people of indigenous descent to prove the identity of their ancestry. This can often be remedied by inquiring within the indigenous community, because often the Elders will know the family connections. Inquiries can also be made with the appropriate government departments because, being bureaucratic in nature, they usually keep records, which can sometimes help establish or disprove those links.

Within most indigenous communities of our experience, intellectual property in the culture and art traditionally resides in the whole community as an entity, and does not accrue to any individual or agency outside the community. Any individuals using any of the information for their own purposes (for example, artworks or literature) would need to have obtained express and detailed permission from the community prior to usage. This is not the case in the mainstream, where the person who writes, draws or records something is generally considered to be the owner of the copyright. Once someone owns the copyright on any piece of work, it cannot be copied or reproduced without permission for the author's lifetime plus fifty years. If a non-indigenous author records indigenous cultural material at twenty years of age, then lives to be ninety, that cultural material is not available for use by the indigenous community whence it came for over a hundred years. Given indigenous morbidity rates, that could mean four or five generations, time enough for those indigenous people to forget.

Non-indigenous researchers, writers and artists have been known to appropriate indigenous culture in the past by being the first to write, paint or record the material. No credence has been given to the strong oral tradition on which indigenous culture is based, nor the prodigious capacity of memory which enabled indigenous elders to retain their cultures and pass them on to successive generations. Until this issue is directly addressed, indigenous culture and arts will continue to be pirated by cynical, self-seeking non-indigenous people, who make their reputations on the backs of indigenous Australians.

That is why we consider this anthology to be so crucial to indigenous culture. By taking part in it, we take the opportunity to make a contribution to the growing movement of indigenous writers who are writing indigenous Australia back into the history of this country. Some great writers lead the way. Here in Western Australia the list includes: Jack Davis, Sally Morgan, Glenyse Ward, Doris Pilkington, Rosemary van den Berg,

Richard Walley, Jimmy Chi, Richard Wilkes, May O'Brien, just to name a few. If this sounds like an honour roll of Australian indigenous writers and artists it only indicates the depth and talent of Western Australian indigenous art. Because of the recency of our exposure to non-indigenous culture and influences (as recently as thirty years ago there were still indigenous people in Western Australia who had not seen a white person), our indigenous culture has remained strong and this shows in the calibre of the artists above. This anthology has brought together a new crop of emerging indigenous writers from Western Australia, whose ambition it should be to take indigenous writing and history into the mainstream.

The Howling

The dogs are howling in Rivervale tonight.
No, it's not a full moon — what moon there is
is hidden by clouds and rain.

No, the dogs are echoing the baying
of a mechanical hound as it runs,
screaming through the night.

You — Hound, I see the bloodlust glow in
your shining eyes! Will you be sated or
will you, thwarted, savage some other, less nimble prey?

Will you run, fatalistically overdosing on your own
adrenalin? Will this rush have an end,
or will it kill you?

And you — the Hare, my brother — will you
be taken tonight? Will the hound
tear you apart, or will you escape?

Hound, you are also my brother, each
rending bite you take at the hare
rends me also, my soul bleeds freely.

Hare! Hound! Brothers, I have seen you walk
together in peace. Must you now kill yourselves
and others in this mindless game?

Will the dogs of Rivervale sing dirges for you
or for some other innocent creature?
The dogs of Rivervale howl too often.

Yamitji Rich

Uncle often said — Yamatjis are rich people
Some probably laugh — but I knew what he meant

Rich did not mean dollars or gold
Rich is spiritual. Rich is knowledge.
Listening to wind bring weather reports
watching animals and birds with messages
from loved ones or of something to happen.

The land has strong rich stories
imprinted all over its face.
Stories handed down for thousands of years
(Sure is something to boast about)

Rich meant being able to sit
all day and read the land
learning from the land
listening to the land
respecting the land

And being rich in
all this knowledge.

Domestic Violence

They all say it with ease
'Leave the bastard.'
But what about the kids?
Where will they live?
How will they be fed?

Sometimes it's easier to stay
take the punches, hits, verbal abuse
Doesn't seem to hurt after a while
The kids have a bed
They all have a feed
There is no shame.
Escaping thoughts sometimes enter.
Flee. Run where?
No education. No money. No hope.
The next day always seems better
Thinking the hits will stop today.
Most times they never do.

Yeah. They all say it with ease
Leave the bastard.
Yet a lot of women
Are just not that strong.

One Sole Parent

Left school at thirteen.
Teased and taunted
Teachers blamed her,
Nobody else — just her.
Baby expected at fourteen
No man. No marriage
Nobody told her about this.
It was harder than
Playing house with dolls.
An alcoholic at twenty —
Without knowing it.
Everyone drinks
Everyone fights.
She is no different.
Doesn't know any difference
More kids at twenty-five.
Men have been and gone.
She is still alone.
She feels like a fifty year old —
And sometimes looks like one.
One sole mother.

Culture Way

Homeswest give ole man
ebiction notice yesterday
he bin sick long time
diabetes, kidneys
Homeswest reckon he
got too many 'lations
visiting, making big noise
and trouble late at night
he can't tell countrymen
'Shoo, shoo,
Go away'
That not his culture
that not his tradition
Where that Homeswest ALO now?
That the one should help him
where that Aboriginal housing mob
to explain cultural ways?
Ole man being shoved back

Anderson Street way
that not solve anything
Homeswest must be too lazy
to accept that culture way.

Government Paper Talk

Paper shuffling from tray to tray
lets the government man have his say
talk about how the money is spent
talk about where it all went.
In an ivory tower trying to solve
all the problems that have evolved
not giving time to think
need an answer before you blink
consultation process done
public servant goes home
thinking the government has won

We Still are One

Why does the white man think he knows
Everything about the black man
He say, 'Do this and do that
And one day you'll be just like I am'
We tell him we been livin' and dyin' our way
For thousands and thousands and thousands of years
But he say, 'You cannot live like that any more
Now you gotta live like the white man.'
I would love to have been with my ancestors
Running and playing through the virgin bush
Being as one with the land, the animals
And the sky
All brothers under the sun,
We were as one
We still are one.
So why don't they leave us alone
We still call this land our home
Come on all you black people
Why don't we unite
Come on all you black people
Let's stand up and fight
Come on all my brothers
Come on all my sisters
Let's get together now
We've got to show them how
We've got to show them now.

The Hurtful Legacy of Racism

Racism is a problem that arrived with the first fleet in 1788 and, like the rabbits, foxes and other feral animals that were transported here, it will never be totally eliminated from Australia. Those of us who have been victims in the past of either blatant or subtle forms of racism know just how cruel and disturbing that experience can be. We know how the colonists, with their contempt and superior attitudes, contributed to much of the bias, ethnocentricity and negative stereotyping in our history books. Today, school children, including Aboriginals and Torres Strait Islanders, are consistently exposed to this kind of offensive stereotyping in the pages of history books, and that, unfortunately, is a legacy of colonial history that will remain on the shelves of schools, municipal libraries and other resource centres.

Throughout European history in this country Aboriginal people have been victims of racial discrimination in one form or another. But it is the laws and legislation of the 1905 Act that had the most devastating effect in the past, and still have an impact today. The 1905 Act introduced the most inhumane and offensive caste system. Under that caste system Aboriginal people were graded and segregated according to the shade and colour of their skin, then placed in the corresponding institutions or incarcerated in settlements, where they were subjected to language and cultural genocide.

All 'part-Aboriginals' (or 'half-castes') were destined for the Moore River Native Settlement because Mr A O Neville, Chief Protector of Aborigines (1915–1940), saw this grading of Aboriginal children as a positive move towards assimilation. This scheme's main objective was to encourage the Aboriginal inmates to seek spouses from white or near white individuals. He envisaged that this policy, based on controlled racial inter-marriages, would lead to a gradual breeding out of Aboriginal genes.

It may have been seen as a good idea then but no one imagined or perceived at that time what repercussions and effects this would have on future generations, and what a fatal impact it would have on the Aboriginal people of Western Australia who were deprived of their history and their values.

The indoctrination, deception and misinformation which proliferated behind the locked gates of those government institutions gave birth to the most damaging effects in this so-called new Aboriginal society — discrimination against their own people. Many institutionalised light-skinned Aboriginal children grew up with the belief that they were superior to their black-skinned relations whom they despised and were ashamed to own.

The links to their families, their history and cultural past were severed and for many, like my sister Anna, the alienation caused permanent damage, from which they would never recover. Anna was only two years old when she was taken away from our mother and because of her skin was classified as a quadroon or a quarter-caste. She was placed in the Sister Kate's Children's Home in Queens Park, Perth, while I — the half-caste sister — was admitted into the Moore River Native Settlement.

A few months ago I was thrilled to receive a contact address and phone number for my sister Anna in South Australia. Immediately I rushed a parcel to her containing newspaper clippings of our mother's long trek from Moore River Mission in 1931, and copies of my two novels, *Caprice: A Stockman's Daughter* and *Follow the Rabbit Proof Fence*. I waited eagerly for her reply and the prospect of reuniting my mother with her baby daughter. But, alas, the reunion was not forthcoming. The parcel was returned unopened and stamped clearly on the envelope were the words 'Rejected by the addressee,' and 'Return to sender'. My sister Anna will never know the pain of those words. Reluctantly I relayed Anna's rejection to our elderly mother. In a very soft voice she replied, 'Oh well, she is dead. Let her be dead.' Racial discrimination hurts. Racist policies destroy families.

Meanwhile, the flames of racial bigotry and hatred are being kindled by Pauline Hanson, the Independent Member of Parliament for Oxley. Her misinformed racist views and comments, in the print and electronic media, cause great concern not only for the two target groups she attacks, the Asian and

Aboriginal communities, but for the wider Australian community. Yet in her simplistic manner she denies being a racist with comments such as, 'How can this be when all I want is equality for all Australians?' (Peter Rees, *Sunday Times*, 4 May 1997.) That may be true but, as George Orwell reminds us in *Animal Farm*, 'Some are more equal than others.' So what is her definition of equality? Does that include recognising and accepting injustices of the past?

What is even more frightening is that the media informs us that her One Nation Party has adopted an updated or modernised version of the White Australia Policy. Russel Ward tells us the White Australia Policy was not embodied in any single parliamentary act. In fact the White Australia Policy is merely a form of words widely used before and long after 1901 to describe a racist attitude towards the immigration of coloured people.

At a meeting in Perth in May 1997 details of Ms Hanson's policies included treating all Australians equally, free from the multicultural and Aboriginal policies, repealing the Native Title Act, abolishing ATSIC and reversing the Wik Decision. Her policies are clearly racist. They reek of contempt and superior attitudes and, worst of all, the divine right of the white supremacists. We, the indigenous people of this country, do not need Ms Hanson and her supporters destroying our efforts to improve race relations, opening up old painful wounds. Her speeches are filled with misinformation, unjustified accusations and criticisms; her aim is to create scapegoats for those who feel they need them. And, of course, we know who the scapegoats are in this case: the Aboriginals and Torres Strait Islanders and Asians.

The Asians and other immigrants are blamed for the unemployment and economic problems. But that is not true, according to Andre Malan (*West Australian*, 1 May 1997): 'Fortunately for us the numbers are growing. This is injecting a lot of money into our economy and creating quite a few jobs, particularly for our young people.'

As for the accusation that Aboriginal and Torres Strait Islander organisations and agencies are wasting taxpayers' money, this is an exaggeration and is untrue. Whilst there may have been a few who have exploited and manipulated the system, the number is minimal. This negative stereotyping is damaging to the positive image that we are trying to establish, not only in our local communities but in the wider Australian community. The Aboriginal and Torres Strait Islander people would like the public to know that we are justly proud of our individual achievements in the arts and sports, that we are equally proud of our success in business enterprises, of our skilled professionals in occupations of responsibility and trust. As taxpayers, and business men and women, we make a considerable contribution to our country's economy.

Ms Hanson has revealed her self-righteous agenda to the nation. Now it is up to us as fair-minded Australians to ensure that her One Nation racist policies be returned to the past and remain buried forever. So let us all work together and form partnerships to fulfil the Australians for Reconciliation vision of 'a united Australia which respects this land of ours; values the Australian and Torres Strait Islander heritage; and provides justice and equality for all.'

Disputed Territory

Looking for ancestors in the archives I came across this from very early this century:

> Freddie, who never demeaned himself by work of any kind, was something of a labour agitator and on one occasion I looked him up at the native camp ... (I) found him sprawled on his back reading the Bulletin, with spectacles on his bitten off nose. This attitude, together with his ape-like face and limbs, gave a general effect which was truly comic.

These words of the pioneering pastoralist repelled me, obviously, and made it abundantly clear that I didn't belong as part of his anticipated readership. And yet — to be horribly honest — in a perverse sort of way I was intrigued by the bristling, aggressive attitude of the writer. It seemed to be the same sort of mind that could claim 'the only good half-caste is a dead one', and speak of the dangers of the 'educated native'. There is this desperate desire to belittle. Why?

It is as if the writer himself feels threatened, and therefore makes this aggressive attack on 'Freddie's' character: labour agitator (what could be worse!), ape-like, comical, sprawled on his back, spectacles, bitten-off nose ... Why all this vitriol?

The archives elsewhere reveal that Fred McGill, as a young boy, was one of John and Alexander Forrest's guides on their trek across the southern coast of Western Australia. Just after the turn of the century a regional newspaper mentions his thank-you speech after a 'charity feast', and letters to the Aborigines Department refer to him organising work parties to cut long wooden clothes props and the like. In 1897 he was writing letters to the newspapers:

I write to know why we cannot obtain some of that 5000 pounds voted by the West Australian Government for our support and do crave through the columns of your newspaper for some assistance. Some white people as a rule are very good in giving us old clothes and necessary food. Many thanks to the so charitably disposed, but, on the other hand, should I send any native brethren to buy goods — bread in particular — some of the business men hold the article in one hand while the other is held out for money and, in nine cases out of ten, no change is given.

And elsewhere:

I worked as a sort of missionary amongst my countrymen and I went about preaching the doctrine of obedience.

And:

There were plenty of blacks out there as well as kangaroos, opossum, wallabies and rats. The blackfellows were somewhat wild (in some areas), but beyond that they were quiet. They were wild because of white men shooting into their camps.

Fred McGill, also named — so these sources tell us — Tickenbut, seems an educated, literate man; and a tribal man. I think of such a man reading the *Bulletin*, with its masthead proclaiming, 'Australia for the white man.' How difficult would it have been to read such a thing, to read any of the English language texts of the time? And I wonder how he was allowed, by those sorts of texts he read, to think of himself as an Aboriginal person. What did the word 'aborigine' mean to him? His Coolgardie letters indicate a wider sense of identity than with his own mob, even though he clearly regards himself as different from those he is arguing for. And how accurate a picture of him, and his thinking, do we get from these renditions; even from his own writing?

I reckon this image of Fred McGill, especially when set against the representation I have quoted, suggests something of the problems an Aboriginal person faces in engaging with 'literature' and formal education; you get the point-of-view of the colonisers and their representations of Aboriginal people; and you occasionally get the thoughts of Aboriginal people but these are usually from within the constraints of that colonising language. Oh, and of course, people such as myself are researching from a similarly constrained position. There are all these deceits and dangers of 'paper talk'.

But, for all that, I believe my own formal, mainstream education and the process of writing fiction has helped develop my own sense of Aboriginal identity.

I think this must be an uncommon experience. But then again, I've gotta be a very singular Aboriginal person; I am forty plus, and alive; I am employed on an average income; I am university educated. Oh, and also, of course, I have fair skin.

In this essay I hope to offer something of a thank-you and reply to those people who have said such things to me as, 'You feel it, here?' — and, tapping my chest — 'If you feel it, say it.'

I grew up, in the sixties and seventies, thinking of myself as 'of Aboriginal descent', a perception I received from my father, and one which partly reflects his own predicament. As I understood it then, being 'part-Aboriginal' had something to do with the difference in quality between my father's own mother (Nyungar) and father (Scottish). It also had a bit to do with not participating in the racism of the neighbourhood, and with not being defined only as 'working class'. When I was very young, it was also about being a fighter with my fists. That changed, perhaps mirroring changes in my own father's life of which I was not fully aware.

But there was also a sadness, provided by certain empirical realities; there was something of the smell of defeat. My own sense of Aboriginality was a strange mix of pride, shame and isolation. A private thing. A thing at the heart of me, albeit a thing I could not put into words.

This may not be orthodox, and so it is important to stress that I speak only for myself here.

In attempting to explain my own sense of Aboriginality and my writing I need to discuss, as briefly as possible, something of my own life experience. It is hard to know where to start, given that it is these concerns which fuel a lot of my fiction. However, since it is from my father that I take my sense of who I am, I will start with him.

My father was already isolated from his Nyungar heritage. He was the only surviving child of a Nyungar mother, who herself died when he was a boy. Subsequently he spent some time at New Norcia, which he only rarely mentioned and that was briefly and with hatred. His own father later 'reclaimed' him and there was a series of stepmothers, as my grandfather went through a series of failed marriages. In between times my father lived with an aunty, who had married a European man, and also with his Nyungar grandmother who had apparently evaded living on reserves or missions and the like, at least in the time my father spent with her. She, apparently, alternated between living in a house and in a tent in the sand dunes of the south coast. This woman, who had married a white man sometime before legislation made that difficult, had her remaining children fostered out to white families after her husband died.

I mention these things briefly to indicate degrees of isolation and even denial of Aboriginality within my family. Isolation and alienation are words which I think most accurately indicate my own life experience and that of my family closest to me. It was a blend of sullen resentment, and frustration, and some mix of pride and shame that I inherited from my father rather than an attitude of denial, although there seems to have been denial aplenty within my mob in the interests, I think, of avoiding the impact of legislation aimed at Aboriginal people earlier this century.

For a lot of my childhood and youth my father was away for two weeks at a time working on the roads. My mother is a timid, quiet, woman who had no family where we were living. When my father came home we'd go away camping, into areas adjoining or on the edge of his people's traditional country. But I can't remember him ever stating this fact, nor was there anything in the way of stories around the campfire, although as he got primed with grog, he'd try. There would be a repeated refrain about the importance of family, yet it seemed there was only us; the nuclear ones surviving. He'd get sentimental, and he'd sing a lot, especially when he was drunk.

My father used to swagger and the only time I remember noticing a change in his body language was when he was talking to older Nyungar men or women. But, for myself, there was not a lot of contact with a particular Nyungar community as such. There were few relations; and these were similarly stranded as ourselves. Sometimes, there'd be young kids staying with us while their fathers or mothers were in prison. One of the old fellows lived over the road and used to bring them to us, but that stopped too, after a baby died soon after returning to its mother, and my mother got very upset.

I think working on the roads must have provided an important part of my father's education. A few years back a Nyungar elder, who I'd gone to see in trying to trace my family, told me my father used to visit her all the time in those years he worked in her country, the same area we used to return to on the weekends when he came home. And, also only a couple of years ago, I heard that the gang he worked on was referred to disparagingly as 'The Boongs' Gang'. My father was promoted to 'leading hand', and I suppose — in the sixties, before most Aboriginal people received citizenship rights — may have done the grog runs. He would have been in the fights around the campfire, had to get men up for work in the morning.

I often wonder about what authority he had to wield. Fists? Sackings? And what reply did he give to the challenge; who's your mob anyway? Himself isolated from heritage, from kinship, because of historical processes and continuing ultimatums. And then returning to his wadjella wife, and his children to whom he would try and impart the feeling in his heart, for which he had not the right words.

But this is already more than I meant to write. And as for me, the boy, I was clever and quiet. There were scholarships and free education, and there I was heading for a new and — for the times — accommodating university in the city.

My father died before he was forty. I had this icy silence in me. At university — a quiet one, a loner, a reader. When I could I chose to look at other parts of the world — other colonies, other 'coloured' peoples. I know this seems ridiculously naive, but there were few ways of thinking about myself available at the time, in such a place. There were no such areas of study as 'Aboriginal Literature' or 'Aboriginal History'. I was wondering, how come I'm alone here.

Callow and ignorant? Yes. Education, though, affects not only what you think but the positions you're put into. I became a high school teacher, and went to teach in the wheatbelt. As a teacher, far more than I ever did in my ignorance and isolation as a student, I experienced how racist such places can be. I heard teachers talking about the Nyungars, and saying how much easier it was if the kids didn't turn up. I saw that a Nyungar could stand all day at the back of a queue unless he or she asserted themselves. At a district high school the police took some very young kids into the office, alone, without notifying their parents, because it was 'obvious' they'd done some shoplifting. Any dissenting voice belonged to someone leaping on the 'Aboriginal band-wagon'. And if you were Aboriginal yourself? Nah, you're not. And laughter.

I moved into a house, a relatively plush one, reserved for principals, because no other teachers wanted it. There was the problem with the neighbours, see? That was racism. When I left I wish there had been others around to laugh with us when my neighbour said it was a shame we were going, because we were the best neighbours they had ever had.

I applied for a position as an Aboriginal Liaison Officer, and I remember standing at the counter listening to some boss in the back room saying to the receptionist, 'how dark is he?' And the same fellow looking at me incredulously, 'You know it's a big drop in pay?' I didn't get the job. And, in truth, I realise now, I was applying more from my own deep need to be accepted back into a Nyungar community, than for what I was able to offer.

More recently a non-Aboriginal accountant working within Aboriginal Education said to me, 'I can't think of any reason why anyone would want to claim an Aboriginal identity other than for remunerative purposes.' And I am not sure how to reply to someone so far away from me. Could they hear anything I might say, share what I feel?

It was in that little wheatbelt town, working as a teacher of English, that I started writing seriously. It was because the work made me think about writing, and because of some sort of politicisation that was occurring within me, an increasingly intimate rather than intellectual awareness of division in 'our' society. And I wondered how come I usually seemed to be standing with, and listening to, people not my own?

My first novel, *True Country*, I have come to understand, began in that time.

I applied to teach in a particular Kimberley community because a family name seemed to lead there, and probably as part of a psychological quest of my own. In many ways that was naive, but ... well, I was naive.

I began writing *True Country* when I returned to the city after some years teaching in the Kimberley.

The title comes from the words of a Midnite Oil song:

We carry in our heart the true country
and that cannot be stolen
We follow in the steps of our ancestry
and that cannot be broken.

For some reason I kept those words beside me when I was writing, and also the title of the song; 'The Dead Heart'. I was not really conscious of it then, but I was writing and exploring the space between the intent of those lyrics, and the title of the song itself. And at the time I felt constrained by what an Aboriginal writer was supposed to do.

I was acquainted with various ideas of what Aboriginal writing was, or rather — as most often was the case — what Aboriginal writing should be. I read that it should be about overtly political action and agendas, and the raising of issues of exclusion and inclusion; and the empowerment of one's people. Whatever the validity of these notions the very discussion of them inhibited me. Was my writing revealing my Aboriginality, or revealing the absence of it? Who was I writing for? What purposes could my writing serve? This is a recurring problem — particularly now that I have been published — and partly arises from my own insecurity, but also — I believe — from restrictive and limiting definitions of what it is to be Aboriginal, and what is allowed of an Aboriginal writer.

It was for those reasons, and a desire for integrity rather than out of diffidence that I made the biographical statement that I did on the cover of *True Country*:

Kim Scott ... of ... Aboriginal and British ancestry ...

And quite frankly, all the time I was writing that book I was asking myself: Who am I, with this icy silence around my heart?

I know that in writing *True Country* I became aware of how my formal education's stories interfered with what I was trying to say. As that novel begins, so did the writing of it, but more so with a sensibility akin to that of frontier stories, of pioneer stories, of an individual consciousness seeing Aboriginal people as 'the other'. That sort of thing.

The realisation that this was what I was writing, and that what I was writing was not true to what I felt, was enormously depressing to me. At the same time I was playing around with ways of writing versions of 'Aboriginal English' in an attempt to capture on the page some of the poetry it has when spoken. And I was exploring aspects of my own experiences; remembering, and re-creating.

The 'Aboriginal English' helped make a different sort of story possible, and helped to free me from the way of writing in which I had been educated. It allowed me to get closer to an expression of a sensibility that seemed more accurate; that seemed more like what I felt. It was not just that one version of English was better than another, but that one broke down the dominance of the other, and that their juxtaposition — even the attempt to fuse them — allowed the expression of something else all together.

And perhaps it was the very act of moving between the surety of those two contradicting sets of words in the song lyric — the 'dead heart', and 'we carry in our hearts' — that seemed to be the most affirming thing. Giving words to the silence between the two seems like an affirmation of who I am. That song lyric, incidentally, concludes with, 'the dead heart lives here'.

My writing has often been a process of making public what is essentially a private thing. Fiction allows various disguises for this. But whatever surety I may feel inside — in my heart, at my core — about who I am, there is something about putting it into words, or testing it against outside realities that always induces doubt and insecurity.

Perhaps this is a measure of the extent to which I have internalised the values of the dominant society. What has become increasingly clear, however, is that this is a society that does not allow the possibility of being part-Aboriginal. Such is 'our' society's division, and its history, that one is either Aboriginal or not. There is no middle ground.

'Speaking from the heart', beyond saying 'yes', is no simple or straightforward thing. There are mazes to get lost in, minefields and booby traps to avoid, mirrors to learn to look away from if what I carry to someone else is to be true to its origin.

My current writing project is an historical one. An act of sheer stupidity, I have often had cause to think. My research has been predominantly archival, and using written rather than oral sources. And my starting point is the sort of social experiment, over a number of generations, articulated by A O Neville, Chief Protector of Aborigines in WA for a number of decades, in his self-published book *Australia's Coloured Minority; Their Place in Our Community*. Despite the title the book offers no place for that 'coloured minority' and it reveals the ultimatum delivered to Aboriginal people in that era: become white or die. It seems very similar to the ultimatum currently delivered by people such as Pauline Hanson as far as I can see.

More recently in my writing it seems that I achieve what 'feels right' to me by taking on the very language I encounter in my research — as offensive and painful as that often is to read — and through various 'literary' and imaginative means trying to 'defuse' it. Sometimes it even seems that such a process helps to thaw that icy silence around my heart. This may be the result of rewriting internalised values, or merely the result of attempting to give words to that silence.

Again, sometimes, in writing and rewriting the language of the archives, it seems possible not only to defuse, but also to hint at what that language can't say; as if something existed behind and between the lines. In a slightly different way, the quote with which I began this essay contains much more, I am sure, than what its author ever intended or was able to do.

And Fred McGill's own words add something else to that, again, whereas that written 'voice' of Tickenbut's, if presented on its own, gives such a shallow sense of what he must have been like, and of the ways, presumably, he was able to think.

It is as if there's a presence outside of and greater than the language, outside of the story. It's as if using the tools of the colonising society, but writing from a different motivating impulse, or spirit, means you end up with something else. And, surprisingly, it may provide a way to write about spirituality without being hijacked by other, predominantly new age, concerns. As a writer becoming increasing constrained by self-consciousness, and also as one of those struggling at the fag end of a process of attempted assimilation, this is an exciting possibility.

Earlier in this essay I said I wanted to speak of how formal education and the process of writing had helped develop my own sense of an Aboriginal identity. More and more, this is because of increasing access to published information, especially that from Aboriginal authors. Most recently, as someone versed in the formal education system, and working within that system with Aboriginal students, it has been through shared experiences. I recall, particularly, standing on the back of the Wargyll out in the 'wheatbelt'. We had tasted of the water running from the wound where the Wargyll had been speared, and were high up in the air, with the breeze on our faces and looking out over land where we could see a series of small and futile circles a tractor had described. We could hear the bleating of sheep far in the distance, see their pale bodies. We were together, then, and even with cleared paddocks before us and the sounds of sheep in the air; we were not in any place known as the 'wheatbelt'.

Identity is a fluid and shifting thing, which is not to deny the power of spiritual essences. As a writer, however, it seems to me that my identity is about articulating a position I inhabit at an intersection of histories and peoples, and it is an obligation to speak for those people in my family who history has silenced, and by attempting this to step forward with a heritage largely denied me.

It heartens me to know that the country I am descended from is boundary territory; between peoples, between desert and sea. In some of the maps — to the extent that you can ever trust them — it is even that labelled 'disputed territory'.

The place I write from is also a particular and specific historical place, which might also be thought of as 'disputed territory'.

And so, when someone taps me on the chest and says, 'You feel it?' my answer is 'Yes'. But, to 'speak it from the heart' is a harder thing. The private, becoming public, can be ambushed or even hijacked. You can find your words used against your heart. Yet, for a heart iced-up and barely pulsing, the tapping can help thaw it; and the listening bring it alive.

The March

The Black Red and Gold
marched past
'What do we want?
Land Rights!
When do we want it?
NOW!'

My search has ended here
This was the answer
to all the questions
I had ever asked myself
Pride swelling
thoughts dwelling
on all the injustices of the past
and present
of being born black
of the lack of direction
we need this Unity
we must convince the
opposing majority.

The march filed on still orderly
then I heard her
white middle class blue rinse set matron
'They should all be taken out in the
desert and blown up!' she said
my anger broiled in the sun and
it was very difficult to halt the
impulse to swipe that
doyen of 'respectability' who also
seethed with the anger of prejudice
and then I pitied her.

Experiences of Racism

For most of my life I've lived with racism. I became used to it as a child and when I grew older, I learned to cope with it in my own way. It is not a nice feeling always being the butt of some white person's cruel jokes, bad-tempered moods or just plain nastiness. To be called names just for the kicks it gave some of them and for the power they wielded over an Aboriginal person was degrading and belittling. They liked to see the black person squirm. It boosted their own morale and gave them a sense of what little power they possessed. They lorded it over us Aborigines. They were white and knew everything. We were black and knew nothing. One minute some whites were friends, the next they didn't want to know you.

I learned to ignore them until I reached the breaking point, then I lashed out at the perpetrators with words or actions which didn't cast me in a very good light, but it made me feel that I was in control of the situation and I could hold my head up high and say, 'That'll teach them to call me derogatory names.' I had my self-respect back and I knew I handled the situation the best way I could. Those people would think twice before making me the target of their racist comments. That happened when I was a kid and when I was an adult. After all, there is only so much a person can take before retaliating. But, in my older years, I've found that there are more ways than one of getting my point across, ways which do not involve fisticuffs or violence. As one grows older, one seems to gain more wisdom, so that fighting becomes a waste of time and effort. There are more ways than one to skin a cat, as the saying goes, and now I resort to the written word to express my disgust at the racism I encounter. My experience with racism over the years is written on these pages.

Back when I was a baby at the Moore River Native Settlement, I did not know the first thing about being Aboriginal, or a native, or black, or a boong, or a dirty nigger or a coloured person. My education in racism was to come later.

When I was five, we moved to Pinjarra where my education really began. Strange people frightened me. When my parents went into town to get our stores for the week, I would cry if a white person came too close to me. I would hide behind my mother's skirt and peep at the stranger with a white face. Likewise, if a black or brown person came near and spoke to my parents, I would cry and hide. I had no truck with or trust in strangers. I was a little bushie and only trusted my own family or the extended family I knew. Life was free and uncomplicated. There was no racism in my life, just brown, black and the few white people who spoke to my father.

My problems began when I started school. By this time my mother had given birth to two more brothers, which left her with little time to mollycoddle her older children. My three older sisters were my protectors and I revelled in their spoiling me. I began my schooling in 1945. My three sisters and I walked miles to go to school. This is where my education in racism began.

My oldest sister, Junie, took me to the infants' grade (as it was known) and left me in the hands of the teacher. My mother and older sisters had coached me in the ways of the school. They all told me I must be good, whatever that meant, and to do as the teacher told me. I was not to fight the other kids, as I did my immediate older sister, Bibby, but was to sit quietly and learn my abc. June, Lorna and Vivienne were my mentors, guardians and bosses. When my parents weren't around, I had to listen to what they told me and do as they said. Life was starting to get complicated for me what with all these orders, but nothing my parents and sisters said had prepared me for going to school.

When I walked into that classroom and saw a sea of white faces sprinkled with dollops of black or brown, I freaked out. I shrieked, I screamed, I yelled and grabbed Junie by her skirts and would not let her go, never mind the teacher telling Junie to let me go, to leave me. Junie had no say in the matter; I was not going to let her leave me at the mercy of this strange white person and all those staring faces. She was my last link to my safe world and I did not want her to go. If she did go, she was to take me with her. My poor sister, what I must have put her through that morning! But finally, after much persuasion, threats and cajoling from Junie and the teacher, I succumbed to the inevitable. I was now a school kid and it was my first taste of life outside the home. It was also my first taste of the blatant racism which was to dog me for the rest of my life.

When Junie finally got out of my clutches and left me, the teacher showed me to a seat at the back of the classroom where the other black and brown faces sat. I wanted to sit near the door where just maybe, I could escape and run home to my mother, but it wasn't to be. I was placed down the back and told to stay there. I really thought it was so I couldn't run out of the room and flee home to Mum. Gullible me! I learned later that all black and brown kids, the Aborigines, that is, sat at the back of the classroom. Not knowing the politics of racism, I went to the back of the classroom where the teacher made me sit next to a brown-faced girl who was to become a good friend one minute and a fighting foe the next. In time, I was glad I sat at the back of the classroom. I did not have to have all those white faces staring at me. It was bad enough when I did something wrong and was made to stand in the corner with my back to the class, knowing that the other kids were chanting dunce, dunce, double dee, go and learn your abc. The first time it happened, and I turned around to face the teacher, every eye was on me, as all the white kids in front of me turned around and stared at me. Some laughed, some sniggered, but all the black and brown faces had their heads down, hiding from me in my shame. I felt so alone.

One memory I have of this fateful year was of coming out of school early believing that I was late and that my sisters had left me behind. I knew I had to go home and I also knew how to get there. My parents had come into town from the farm where my father was working to do some shopping, and to visit friends and extended famil. I did know the way home and, because of this mix-up, I was to put my knowledge to the test. I decided I had to go home alone without my sisters' company.

Once my decision was made, I had fun walking through the main street of town and passing over the bridge which spanned the Murray River. I spent time on the bridge trying to see if any schools of fish like mullet or yellowtail swam in the dark green water below. Then I was on my way, passing the butcher shop and the hotel. I knew I had to turn a sharp left when I passed the butcher shop and head along that road for home. I went by the four or five houses where white people lived, keeping a wary eye out for any dogs which might feel like biting a six-year-old girl. I walked and ran along the road until I came to the Ngarrdie Bridge. I had heard stories about this bridge and the wurrdatji (little hairy man) who lived under it. This wurrdatji liked to eat little children, especially those who travelled by themselves. I was full of fear as I galloped over that bridge expecting at any time that the wurrdatji would get me.

Fortunately, I saw neither hide nor hair of him and breathed a big sigh of relief when I made it safely to the other side.

After a spell to catch my breath, I continued on my way home until I passed a farm house where some ducks and their babies were walking outside the fence which enclosed the place. They were so cute that I began to chase the babies to try and pick one up to cuddle it. Suddenly, I heard a strident voice yell at me, 'You leave that duckling alone, you little black thief. Isn't anything safe from you niggers? Must you steal everything that you see? Nothing is safe from you people. Go on, scat, before I sool my dogs onto you, you dirty thieving little Abo.'

I looked up in fright to see a white woman walking down her garden path towards me, dropped the duckling and turned and ran. When I heard the dogs barking, I ran for my life, crying with fright by this time. I ran all the way to the safety of my mother and home.

I was terrified. I did not know what I had done to deserve that white woman's shouting and her cruel words. She looked like a ghost as she seemed to float up the garden path in her long dress. She was definitely the stuff that nightmares are made of and for weeks after, I gave that place a wide berth when going to or coming from school or town. That was my first confrontation with racism in all its raw negativity.

Over the years, I learned to live with racial prejudice at school. I remember slapping a white girl at the old Perth Girls High School, where I was sent to study for the high school certificate, because she had called me 'black'. She never called me names again and later we became fairly good friends. The woman at the Aboriginal girls' hostel where I lived, never let us forget that we were natives and that we owed white people (her) for the very air we breathed. She wasn't too bad, in retrospect, but I think having control over people in New Guinea made her treat us with disdain. I think she felt that it was her lot in life to show us the errors of our ways, when we forgot we were trying to live like white people and went back to being Aboriginal and wanting to go home. I suppose it was hard for her looking after a mob of teenage Aboriginal girls with all their petty bickering and adolescent mood-swings. However, she controlled us with two iron fists and never let us forget that she was boss. Still, I like to believe that we turned out pretty decent citizens when we reached maturity and, I suppose, in a way, we have her to thank for it.

After I left school, I went into nursing-aide training at the Royal Perth Hospital. I was seventeen and fresh from high school. Talk about being a gormless teenager! I knew nothing about life and hardly knew what made boys tick. Although by this time, I had my father, four brothers and uncles and boy cousins, to me they were neutered beings; sexually they were taboo. And while I had my crushes on boys during my early teenage years, at this time I still did not know about 'the birds and the bees'. I had my theories, as my friends did, but getting down to the nitty gritty was a bit scary. My generation, while growing up, did not receive any sex education at school and the mere mention of 'sex' was enough to send our mothers into a tizzy. So when I saw my first nude male in the course of my training, I nearly died. My friend Bessie was working on the same ward as me and we'd also been friends at high school together and at that hostel. Well, this day, we both had to bed-bathe a young white male who was going for an operation that same day. To make it worse he was a policeman and both Bess and I knew how policemen felt about Aborigines. You should have seen us — blushing like tomatoes and that young police constable was no better off. I washed him while Bess dried him, but we made sure he both washed and dried his private parts, as sick as he was. He didn't know where to look and we didn't know where to look. I knew if I had looked at Bessie, I would have got the giggles, and vice versa. We strove hard not to look at each other and we were too scared to look at our patient, who was just as embarrassed. That was the first time in my life that no direct eye contact was made between me and the people I was talking to. After we'd bathed and dressed him, made his bed and saw that he was resting comfortably, we cleared away the wash bowl and dirty clothes and headed for the pan room. Bessie and I took one look at each other and burst out laughing until we were nearly crying. That poor policeman! I bet that was the first and last time that he was totally at the mercy of two young Aboriginal girls.

The hospitals I worked in until I married were pretty good in the ways of not promoting racism in the wards. The sisters in charge ensured the patients did not refuse our treatment of them because of the colour of our skin, although sometimes real crotchety ones, especially old white women, were hard to please and some refused by saying they did not want to be contaminated by blacks touching them. I remember a ward sister telling off one old girl who refused my Florence Nightingale ministrations. I didn't feel put out by her refusals; some others in the ward welcomed my tending to them. They knew I'd do things for them and spoil them when other staff members wouldn't or couldn't be bothered. Old men and children were my favourite patients though. They were only too glad to have someone to talk to and to give them attention throughout their illness. They felt better and I felt better which is what nursing is all about, to my way of thinking.

So far, racism hadn't played too big a part in my life. I knew it was there, but I was young enough not to care what people thought of me. I was Aboriginal — so what? I had a tongue in my head and I could stick up for myself if necessary. If people didn't like me because of my skin colour, that was too bad; that was their problem, not mine. Facing racist taunts was old hat for me. I grew up in Pinjarra, remember? On the whole though, my nursing days were not too bad. They had their ups and downs, but I only had myself to look after and at that time I could handle anything. If I couldn't, as with the break-up with my boyfriend (not lover), I went home to 'The Old Place' to lick my wounds. My mum and dad would sympathise with me and my younger siblings would soon take my mind off my loss of esteem in the love department. By this time, Mum and Dad had ten children, six girls and four boys altogether, and Dad had bought a five acre block of land on the outskirts of Pinjarra, which we called 'The Old Place'. Anytime any one of us children wanted to go home and have a break from the rat race of the city, they would welcome us home and always made room for us. Even when we married and had our own children, there would always be room for us to go home and get away from it all. Just to rest and gird our loins for the next onslaught of tackling the outside world was good for the spirit. I miss those days! I miss my parents! But times change and I became a person in my own right.

For me, things changed when I had my daughter, Leanne, and married my husband, Jack, and had our other children, Diane, Sharon, Peter and Valerie. I now had others to care for, people who were and still are, very precious to me. It depressed and saddened me to hear of Jack being called 'boong lover' and 'gin jockey' because he was a Dutch man married to me. Whites could not get it through their thick skulls that Jack and I loved each other and they would sling off at his choice of partner. He and I did not care. If they laughed at Jack to his face, they had to be prepared to back it up with their fists, for he was no slouch when it came to fighting for what he believed in, and he believed in me, our marriage and our children and by God, he was prepared to fight for us. Even I learned to fight for our principles and tackled both black and white who called us racist names. We taught our five children to stick up for themselves and to fight for what they believed in and not let anyone put them down. We had the right to live in this country and no one was going to belittle us because we had a mixed marriage and our children were half-Dutch and half-Aboriginal. Our way of tackling the cancer that was racism was to face it head on and be damned to those who didn't like it.

Yes, my husband had his fair share of abuse from both Aboriginal and white people, for neither understood that we could live together and be happy with our lot. We accepted our differences, including the colour of our skins and our cultural backgrounds. Jack was European, a merchant marine and a man of the world. I was Aboriginal and only knew my Australian world; I had lived and worked in the eastern states for a couple of years before I met Jack and married him. We were both adult, loved each other, so why couldn't we marry? The archaic Native Welfare laws and policies which forbade whites and Aborigines to marry never stopped us. We got around this by going to Melbourne where we married. Western Australia was so backwards in its treatment of Aborigines.

Our lives have changed again now and our children have all grown up and are married and, between them and their spouses, they have given Jack and me twenty-one grandchildren. The old days of our youth have gone when racism was a black and white business and we knew where we stood. Now racism has taken a more subtle twist. It is called a new racism, or a new racialism, and it belongs to the 1990s.

How do we handle it? We are middle-aged and we can't fight racist jibes like we used to, nor are we inclined to tackle this issue like we did when we were young. With the policies of multiculturalism now in place, we thought we could sit back and watch our grandchildren grow up in a country which had learned to accept Aboriginal people, as well as the ethnic groups who migrated here to settle permanently and to be treated with equality, just like other Australians. How wrong we were! Racism is alive and well and thriving in Australia, thank you very much! One Ms Hanson has set the dogs of dissension loose to snap at the heels of Aborigines and Asians alike and our status as citizens of this country counts for nothing as racism again rears its ugly head.

When the ex-Prime Minister, Paul Keating, was in power, everyone had to abide by politically correct rules and mind our ps and qs and not say anything derogatory to others for fear of getting rapped over the knuckles and taken to court. This meant having to pay out big sums of money if found guilty of breaching these rules. This was a great fear for the white people, some of whom found it impossible to curb their racist feelings and lashed out, especially at the Aborigines. Everyone had to be on their best behaviour, white, black and in-between. Big brother was watching us, so look out!

Our current Prime Minister places his values on freedom of speech, so much so that Australia stands in danger of speech 'libertarians' making derogatory comments about Aborigines and Asians without redress for those groups. These bigoted people use freedom of speech as a ploy to express their hatred of the other and they disregard the common courtesy which should be shown to another human being regardless of the colour of his or her skin and cultural heritage. Pauline Hanson is living in cuckoo land if she thinks Australia is a white country. It will never be so long as there is one blackfella, one Aboriginal person, left to walk this land. Our country does not belong to Asia, nor is it European. Our country and our people know it will always belong to the Aborigines.

Nevertheless, are Aborigines living on false promises of equality? For the racist elements in Australian society never let us forget that they believe they are superior to us. Their ancestors took the land, language and culture away from our Aboriginal ancestors, who were left with nothing, not even their pride and self-esteem. But things have changed. Nothing is static in this world and life is all about change. What we, my husband and I, have to tell our children and our grandchildren is that no matter what happens in the future with racial intolerance again so rife, they must stand up for their beliefs and principles and remember above all else, that they are proud Aboriginal Australian citizens. This is their country and they will survive.

'Just you and the paper and the pen' an interview with Angeline O'Neill

AO: Your first novel, Bulmurn, *is fascinating and it's been very well received! Why do you think this is?*

Well, I think it's well received because it's written along the lines of the truth. It's oral history that's been passed down by my father and by other people around me. Yeah, basically it's the truth. I mean, the truth … maybe it hurts, but in the long run the truth always prevails. So I've been taught to believe.

Nobody else'd ever written about these Nyoongar people; their life and the takeover of the land by the early settlers. I mean, people forgot about the feelings of the Nyoongar people and what they had to bear. That's why I wrote *Bulmurn*. I wanted it to be not only for my own people but for all people to enjoy it and to read about history; how it was from a Nyoongar's point of view. Basically, that's what the whole thing's about. It's presenting our side of those early days and how history made through colonialism affected us.

AO: You say that you've never been influenced by any other Aboriginal writers …

No. That's true … I think that at that stage I did read *Wild Cat Falling* and I think I read one other story about an Aboriginal person from the Kimberley area. Basically, I just picked up pieces here and in the news or whatever, you know? But now in later years I find out that *Wild Cat Falling* by Mudrooroo … well, he isn't an Aboriginal person. So, then, I feel good about that because in actual fact I wasn't influenced by any Aboriginal writer whatsoever.

The ability or gift that I have within me didn't actually come forth until I was well into my forties. Before that, I'd always thought that I'd write something, but I never ever pushed myself to write something like this. I think, too, that I probably didn't have the confidence in my own ability to do it, mainly because I only had a Year Seven education and I thought, 'Gee, how the hell am I going to write a book when I only have this limited education?' But I overcame all those odds and ended up writing *Bulmurn*. Yeah, and I did it all on my own, too, you know? Sure I've had advice here and there, but nobody can write a book for you. You're the only person who can write the book really. This is what I always told myself; you're the only one who can do it so you've gotta do it, you're the only one who can write it so you've gotta write it. I think by using that philosophy, that's how I overcame the odds.

Stories like Bulmurn's are the kind of stories, Dreamtime stories, that are told about Aboriginal people in the early days. They actually fought against the early day settlers. Also we had characters that were in amongst the ranks of the Nyoongar people and had these mystical powers and were able to use them in the way I describe in *Bulmurn*. So, Bulmurn is a real person. I mean, sure we can say he's fiction, but the thing is that those characters were real, even in my time. They had mystical powers.

See, these are the kinds of things. You'd have some police'd come out and they'd be chasing someone like Bulmurn and the black trackers'd be after him and all of a sudden he'd disappear and there'd be a blackboy sitting right in front of them and the black trackers'd always wonder, 'Is that him or isn't that him?' And of course, the troopers, they'd think, 'Oh well it's only a blackboy'. But the thing is, when they'd go away, the black trackers weren't sure and of course, the culture they were taught was that it was only a figment of their imagination anyhow. So these were the mystical things, the powers, that came to enhance the reputation of people like Bulmurn as being a Merlin, if you like, with these magical powers. So I think that Merlin must've learnt from the Nyoongar people anyhow — all his magic stuff!

AO: Bulmurn is certainly mysterious yet strangely appealing and the ending of the novel is well-suited to his particular character. Could you comment on why you chose to end the novel in this way?

Well, it comes back to our religion, I think. Not only did the people on Rottnest Island need something to lift them, to give them hope, but also we in the present day need to enhance our own religion and beliefs and that kind of thing, to let other people know that those are our beliefs — the way that Bulmurn was able to do those things. (One thing I've got to say is that, when I talk about *Bulmurn*, I always try to keep the ending out of it, because otherwise people look for that clout at the end, whereas when they just read it it's a surprise … So I usually never talk about the finish, otherwise you've never read the book and yet you've 'read' the ending of it, you know what I mean?) But, yeah the thing is that the religious beliefs of the Nyoongar people are all the way through the story. You can look at one passage there where the troopers say, 'God is on our side' and then Bulmurn says, 'Yes, but it's all right for me. The spirits of the Dreamtime are pleased,' and Mar, the wind, blows around him and Babbangwin, the lightning, strikes and Mulga, the thunder, makes the noise. So there's the depiction of the two religions, how they collided. One looks more natural whereas the other is a spiritual being that nobody's ever seen or heard; it's only a figment of what's in your mind, of what you want it to be. But Bulmurn's beliefs, what he knew was there, those spiritual beings, were something that he felt and that he could hear and that's the difference. This is where our religions differ somewhat. Ours is more governed, I think, by what we know about things.

AO: How important is history to you as a writer?

Very important, because people need to know about history and we need to know what happened to us as well. There are some of our people who really don't know what some of our other people suffered, because they were in a different situation. For instance, when the takeover occurred, then they developed Rottnest Island as a penal island for the patriotic warriors who actually were fighting the early day colonists for the land. I mean, the writing of the history is that the Nyoongar men succumbed; they just didn't care about the land, and that's a lot of bull, because they did care about the land — otherwise they wouldn't have had Rottnest as a penal island!

Every time they sent warriors out there they always said that they were thieves, thieves who speared the stock and they didn't put it down to the massacres and the many skirmishes that the whites had with the patriotic Nyoongar people. So they were sent out there and what they did was they graded the prisoners [and sent them to] certain places: some were sent to Carrolup, down south there near Katanning, and then others were sent to Moore

River Settlement. These were the ones who were considered to be not quite as dangerous as the ones who were out on Rottnest Island. Then, along came the 'fruit', if you like, the result of white seed going into black ground. I mean, the brown tide came and of course, the white fathers sent all these half-caste kids into these settlements. So what you had was a brown camp and a black camp — you had a division within those places. But people knew what was happening. They were united in such a way that colour created no barrier for them. They could identify their blood lines and skin groupings and so on.

Then along came the missionaries and they wanted a piece of the action too, so what they did was set up missions here and there; down south were the Baptists, centred around Perth were mainly the Roman Catholics and the Church of England. Then you had the Jehovah's Witnesses, Seventh Day Adventists and you got the lesser churches even further out. They all created missions in those areas and they became religious-controlled slave camps. I went into Moore River Settlement. I went in there and I can just about quote the Bible as good as any preacher. I mean, if he wanted to quote from the Bible I'd heard it all before and probably could say it word for word with him. I mean this is how much we were brainwashed into believing that religion was about Jesus and God and we weren't learning about Mar, the wind, and Babbangwin, the lightning, and Mulga, the thunder, and about the Jenarks and the Wargyll and Bujara, the Mother, the earth, you know what I mean? Those things were taken away from us so we couldn't learn those and then down south what they did was they stole our language. They wouldn't let us speak the language and anyone who was caught speaking the language, they were jailed. Usually in the missions they had the boob, what they called the boob. (I don't know where the word comes from.) Anyhow, 'boob' was the word for the jail. Yeah, everybody was scared of the gaol; a lot of people died in it and people were being hung outside it. There's a place there near Moore River Settlement that's never talked about much, but if you'd like to go back through the archives you'd find that the place was called Chalk Cliff. There was one tree on it and it used to have a limb sticking out and they used to put them on the edge of the cliff and swing themem out there and let them hang there. Every time someone was hanged they were left there for two or three weeks as a lesson to the blackfellas, as the whitefellas put it.

The descendants of the early day settlers may say, 'We didn't do it. It happened a long time ago. We weren't there. We never did it.' But I ask them a question, how did they get here? Yeah, how did they get here? And they have the cheek to call other people 'boat people'! What were they? We have Aboriginal critics out there, people who criticise the Aboriginal people; they don't realise that without Aboriginal land they wouldn't be in the position of wealth that they enjoy today. They wouldn't have the gold they get out of the land. They wouldn't have natural resources like water, like gas and coal and diamonds and all the other minerals they're getting. Not only that, but also the wheat that they're growing, and, I mean, it's our land that they're growing it on and this is why they don't want to share it with us. The thing is, there were no treaties signed whatever, so we do have the right to claim ownership of this land. They've said, 'Well, prove who you are and where you come from.' So at the end of the day, if we can't prove that we come from a certain place, then we have no claim to this land. So I can see that with land rights a lot of people are going to miss out if they can't prove where they come from. In their own land they will end up being paupers and they will never be compensated. And yet we are the owners.

AO: Did you have these issues in mind when you were writing Bulmurn?

Yes! That's right. These are the kind of things that the present day white Australians are denying us. But I've got to say in fairness to them that only fifteen per cent were against the referendum to give us citizenship rights. (That's only happened in my lifetime, in 1967, and that's not long ago.) So there are fair-minded people out there, but the reasonable people are being undermined by people like Pauline Hanson and Howard Sattler, Graham Campbell and David Etheridge, Ross Lightfoot and others like that, you know. I would like to ask Pauline Hanson who owns the sea and the land she takes her fish and chips from?!

AO: You must have had a lot of support from your family and from the Nyoongar community in general when you were writing Bulmurn. *Would you like to comment on that?*

Yeah. Funnily enough, I never really received that kind of support. Mainly because … a Nyoongar person writing something was unheard of because of our oral history. I think my family thought, 'Yeah, he's writing this now, but sooner or later he'll give up, come back and join us and we'll get on with life.' I think a lot of Aboriginal people around there, well, they didn't know too much about what I was doing unless I told them. [If] I started talking about what I was doing a lot of them would walk away because they were ... bored with me talking about something I was writing, something they couldn't see. So I guess, in a sense, I really haven't had too much support in a way that, well, everyone would like to get. I think that when you're writing something you're really on your own; you and the paper and pen, just you and the pen and paper. At the end of the day, when you finish whatever you're writing, then you need a critic or two to read the manuscript. I found that that was pretty good.

AO: How important did you see Bulmurn *being as a way of expressing and sharing Nyoongar culture?*

I think that when people read *Bulmurn* they can almost track his trail around the metropolitan area and out towards Toodyay, along the Darling Ranges and down to Boyagin Rock and then they can come back to Perth and they can almost follow the jail coach right down to Fremantle and come down High Street and over to the Round House Gaol. Then they can follow him out in a boat over to Rottnest Island. Those trails and the names of those places are very important to highlight the fact that Aboriginal people did live around here and that the land was owned by the Mooro, the Beeliar and the Beelu people.

Yeah, I think *Bulmurn*'s a pretty good book. I'm putting in a plug for myself, but I don't think I've read a book that's equal to *Bulmurn* at this stage. But that's only me. I'm biased.

AO: The issue of Aboriginal identity has always been very important and it is particularly so at the moment. Would you like to make some comment on how and when you think a person is entitled to call himself or herself 'Aboriginal'?

That's a hard question. I mean, we have a lot of people who don't even look like Aboriginal people claiming that they are. They've got more European features than they have Aboriginal ones. But people do know that they have an Aboriginal background, so they allow them to claim that heritage. So, you know, the

Aboriginal identity has been with them. People who know them can go back into their Aboriginal past. See what I mean?

Well, there are differences, I suppose, in the way each case presents itself, but identity is something that's there. I say this straight out. I can't be kind to people who pretend, as I said to you, because of the rape and pillaging and plundering of Aboriginal land and religion and culture that has taken place over the years since colonialism was introduced to this country. They're still trying to take everything we've got; trying to steal the last bit of culture we possess by pretending that they're Aboriginal people and writing about our culture. Really, they're imposters. I mean, that's the only way you can describe them. They're the Judases of this country because they're stealing our last bit of religion that we have and turning it to their advantage to get recognition. Wanda Koolmatrie could never have got that recognition if he didn't have the name 'Koolmatrie'. In actual fact we find out that he's a white man and not a woman! Colin Johnson's in the same category. In my view, he's an imposter ... See, I've got to say this and I'm a writer (I'm not sayin' it through sour grapes either), but they take away the theme of what Aboriginal writers are about. I mean, they get recognised and we're battling. True Aboriginal people are battling. Here's these bastards out there pretending that they're us!

Elizabeth Durack's a different kettle of fish, I s'pose. But the thing is that she had no right to paint under the alias of an Aboriginal male. She's a female. I don't know why she did it (and maybe she had good motives), but the fact is that she was an imposter. There's no excuse for it — Elizabeth Durack should've known better. Yes.

AO: Would you like to comment on the position of Aboriginal people in the broader community and how they can improve their situation?

I think we're always trying to improve our situation but the government doesn't listen to what we're talking about. What they're trying to do is come up with the answers themselves. They can't leave it to the Nyoongar people to work out and to help themselves. Personally, I believe that all Aboriginal money should be given to Aboriginal people to allocate wherever they want it to go. The government should help them in all areas, especially in housing. A lot of Aboriginal people are homeless and yet all this money is poured in. Where's it going? At the end of the day what I believe is happening is that when Aboriginal money is put into Homeswest funding, when the people vacate the place and they move somewhere else, then Homeswest houses a white Australian or somebody with an ethnic background or Asian background. So they give the housing to other groups. See what I mean? All right, a lot of Aboriginal families might move and go back to their home towns. But there are still a lot of Aboriginal families on the waiting list and what Homeswest is doing is putting other than Aboriginal people in those houses. That's wrong. That's stealing. It's like our land — they take it from us and they don't want to give anything back. In this case, they give something and then they take it back. That's black money that should be ours! Can you see what I'm getting at?

AO: So how are you going to improve the situation?

Well, we've set up what we call the Aboriginal commission of elders, set it up throughout the state. What we're trying to do is link up with the Premier and the cabinet so that when we do have our meetings we can have sessions with the main ministers. We need to talk about things; health, housing, money, whatever. You know what I mean? (People hate us using the word 'money'. They hate us asking for money, 'cause they reckon we get all the handouts under the sun and this is false! We get very little.) They did give us one per cent of Western Australian revenue at one stage, but then they even made legislation to take that from us.

AO: What do you think are the major issues facing Aboriginal people today?

Equal rights, equal opportunity, equal housing, better health, better education. Everything equal, it's got to be equal. If we don't have equality the same as other Australians enjoy, then we'll always be the underdog and we'll always be the poor relations of the Australian nation. I think that the major ingredient to give us back our self-respect is land rights, but the High Court is making decisions in favour of the Nyoongar people and the white Australians are saying, 'That's not right. The High Court's wrong.' So what's the High Court? I'd like to think it shouldn't be tampered with. They shouldn't be able to make legislation to overrule the High Court decisions. It's supposed to be the highest court in the land, yet they're able to turn it around to retain their assets.

I think we do get bitter and some days are worse than other days, but we've got to live in this place. We can't change it over night. See, we had to wait years before the Mabo decision happened. We had to wait two centuries before we were recognised as Australian people! All these things we've passed through have taken time.

Who is Stone Age?

I was talking to a friend
The other fine day
I commented on many things
And then she had her say.

'Aboriginal people
Are coming out of the stone age'
She finally said to me.
'Why is it that
White man's view is always
Taken as truth!
Who are they to label?'

Two hundred years ago
We had an affluent society
We knew our place
In the scheme of things.
And then 'they' came to this fair land
To rape, pillage and plunder.
They tore the sacred land apart
and made the stock exchange instead
Their sacred site and wonder.

They used only the intellect
And in their rapacious greed
They pitted science against religion.
They change the laws every year
For some new fancy, whim.

So who is stone age now, my friend.
Is it white man who is prehistoric?
He cannot find the answers yet
Because he only lives in
Rhetoric.

Jillawee and Jilga

The sun was setting quickly over the hill as darkness approached. The wiljas that the desert people had made earlier in the day out of gum tree branches, interwoven now provided, shelter for the long, cold night that lay ahead. The fires also now provided light for the people, as the smoke bushes and saltbushes shimmered in the low flat country of the desert. The family consisting of twenty waited for the evening meal. A whole marloo (kangaroo) was lying on gum leaves after coming out of the ground, and it was cooked to perfection. The meat was broken after it cooled, and divided out for the tribe. They squatted, eating their meal around one huge fire. There were smaller fires outside the shelters. The meal was plain, roasted witchetty grubs in the ashes of the fire and lovely bush bread made from seeds of the desert, similar to our wheat of today. The desert women had pounded the seeds on flat rocks earlier in the day and now the bush bread was sweet and cooked. The children's eyes danced over the fire, teeth pearly white, glowing over the embers of the fire. After the meal was eaten the cooked kangaroo leg was hung on a tree to feed anyone passing in the night. The rest of the cooked kangaroo was given out and wrapped in leaves for the tribe to take with them on their journey tomorrow.

Jillawee and Jilga stirred as the sun started to warm their bodies in their shelter.

'Buggala, get up,' said Jillawee to his wife Jilga. 'We have a long journey today to reach the Dividing Ranges, home of the Water Snake, by tomorrow afternoon. So it will mean walking all night. There will be all the tribes from all over the desert there in Wonumbee, Snake Dreaming country. Jillawee reached for the coolamon (water dish) to go to the rockholes in the hills for fresh sweet water to drink. When he returned with the water Jilga had a drink and the tribe all got up and walked Indian file through the desert.

Nothing is said for hours as walking is all they do, rhythmically. The women are gracefully striding over the sand, luggage balanced on their heads, their babies in slings on their backs. The men folk are carrying spears and hunting sticks.

Sun directly over them now, and this means rest time. They stop for a camp under the big desert sheoaks. The cooked kangaroo and bush bread is eaten and the water is drunk. Later in the afternoon the wind birds arrive. The desert people know the sound of these birds and it means travelling time again. All up in Indian file once more for the long journey all night following the stars, and yes it will be a moonlit night, ideal for Walkabout. Late tomorrow afternoon they will reach their destination, where the Great Dividing Ranges will be Home for the next three days, where much healing will take place. Red ochre will be rubbed all over their bodies. Lots of fun, laughter and language. The six skin groups of the desert — the Boo-roong-oo, the Bunugu, the Nilungu, the Yi-bu-rrgu, the Thaa-oodoo, the G-ree-mud-du — will all sit in their groups for three days to celebrate the Remembrance Time of the Water Snake Dreaming. Many shelters will be erected and dancing, stories, songs and paintings will take place. Yes, family is important in the desert way of life. This is what this story is all about.

Trilogy

PART 1: IN THE BAG

It took three hours before Scrooge finished his business with the department of social security. He walked out with his head hung down, almost dawdling. Robert and Darryl, who were sitting in the car, knew instantly that he never got his money.

'What happened?' yelled Robert.

'I gotta wait till tomorrow,' said Scrooge.

That evening while cooking tea around the fire in the back yard, Darryl suggested a fishing trip if the weather stayed as calm as it had been. Robert, who was always negative, couldn't help mentioning other possibilities, such as breaking down, getting bogged or getting caught for trespassing. He preferred to stay in town. Funnily enough, Robert had a dream two days before about catching some 'wild' fish, and had second thoughts as to whether to go or not. He knew Scrooge was apathetic about what he did for the day as long as he had a good drink of beer.

The three cousins were up at the crack of dawn and off down town to get things organised. Darryl did most of the organising as he had done it a thousand times before. Scrooge handed over the bucks for fuel and tackle and Robert complained about this being a waste of money. After loading up the badly dented HQ Holden they set off for Bremer Bay. After a half hour of travelling, Robert asks, 'What time ya reckon we'll get there?'

'Ooor, 'bout dinner time,' replied Darryl.

By the time they reach Bremer Bay, Scrooge and Robert were half pissed, and Darryl couldn't wait to stop driving so he too could have a beer.

'I reckon we should camp along the river,' he said, 'then we can go sea water fishing in the morning.'

'What we gunna eat tonight?' asks Robert.

'We'll put the net out, should get enough for supper,' Darryl says assuredly.

The night was a feast of bream, beer and bullshit. It was a night of laughs and although it was cold, the alcohol took the edge off the chill. Darryl got up early to retrieve the net and boil the billy. After breakfast, it was a nine mile drive to one of Darryl's favourite fishing spots. Upon arrival he suggests, 'We need to catch some crabs for groper bait.'

Robert and Scrooge, who were extremely hung over, reluctantly searched for crabs.

'I don't know why we come groper fishing for. We got enough fish in the net.'

'We'll be right,' comforted Scrooge, taking another drink from a beer bottle refilled with Moselle. 'Here fix your head up,' he advised, pushing the bottle in front of him.

'Yeah, give's a go,' replied Robert reaching for the bottle.

Darryl got busy catching as many crabs as possible. He knew Robert and Scrooge wouldn't get many. They were too busy drinking. By the time Darryl decided he had enough crabs and started searching for a groper hole, the sun was almost in full view. 'Burly up first,' said Darryl, reaching for the home-made burly. 'Then we'll wait for a half an hour.'

'I might try over here,' says Robert, picking up a line and some crabs. After two crabs lost in two casts, Robert was convinced this was all a waste of time, but he persisted.

Suddenly he felt a small nibble. 'Hey, I gotta bite,' said Robert in a most casual way. 'It feels like a bream.' Then there was a huge yank on the line and it ran through Robert's hands. He tried to grip the line, only succeeding in burning the nylon into his palms.

'Darryl, Darryl,' he cried. 'Quick, I've got a big one.' Darryl looked up then jogged over, thinking Robert was over-reacting.

As Darryl grabbed hold of the line, he knew instantly this fish was bigger than usual. Flashbacks from stories told to him as a kid coursed through his mind. The one that stood out most was about how smart gropers were. How they dart down to find a hole or ledge to snuggle into. Two possible consequences are, that coral might cut the line, or the fish will drown. If the fish drowns you have a fifty-fifty chance of getting him out safely. So Darryl knew he had to pull the fish in fast, as the groper would

195

have a head start while Robert was in control of him.

'He's a bloody big one all right,' he gasped, straining to pull the line in. Eventually they caught a glimpse of the big blue figure in the water.

'I don't bloody believe it,' said Scrooge, running to get the gaff. After fighting with the fish for no less than half an hour, both Darryl and fish were exhausted. At last Darryl pulled him to the water's edge where Scrooge hooked the gaff into the fish's gills.

'Gottcha,' yelled Scrooge as he eagerly awaited Darryl who had run down to the water's edge. With the fish flipping and flapping towards lifeless exhaustion, the two men pulled it up onto the rocks.

'Far out, man,' says Robert. 'This is unreal. I've never seen a bigger fish in my life.'

'Me neither,' replies Darryl. 'It's gunna be heavy carrying this back.'

'We'll take turns,' says Robert, bending down to pick up the tail. 'Oor, nah man, this is too heavy.'

'The only way is to cut it into three and we all carry a piece each,' said Darryl. 'It'll be a shame, 'cause I wanted to show them other fellas back in town. I'll show 'em the head.'

The walk back was three times harder than the walk there. The only comforting thing was the thought of showing the relations and friends what they had caught. The drive back home was dominated by talk on how they landed this big fish. Robert wanted some of the credit for it being caught on his line, and Scrooge campaigned that his swift actions with the gaff played a large part in the capture. Darryl, humbly, and not wanting to buy into the argument, was content knowing the fish was in the bag.

PART 2: BULLSEYE

It's been nearly a month now since Rob put anything to eat in his fridge. Plenty of beer. But that didn't last long. He really wanted to go kangaroo shooting, but without a gun and car this was difficult.

Jeffery then pulls into the driveway in his Toyota Landcruiser. 'Hey, what's happening bro?' he says with a friendly smile.

'Not much. Watcha up to?' replies Rob, who is envious of his younger brother's car and money. He knew Jeff worked for it and didn't drink much, only on weekends. He was also very tight with his money.

'Aw, not much,' said Jeff, opening the door to get out. 'You got any kangaroo meat?'

'Nah, nothing,' said Rob.

'You wanna go shooting?' asked Jeff

'Yeah, no worries,' said Rob, jumping up excitedly. He found a pair of his cleanest dirty socks and put his shoes on.

'I reckon we pick Mulla up. He's got a 243,' said Jeff.

'Aw, not that know-all,' mumbles Rob.

After putting petrol in the car they drove around to Mulla's house. Their oldest brother loves shooting. He would stop whatever he was doing, no matter how important, to go shooting. It's been nearly two weeks since Mulla last went shooting. A long time for him.

As the men are travelling, a beer can flies out the window every five or six kilometres.

'Can't be far now, hey?' asks Jeff, looking over at Mulla.

'Nah, not far now. Just up here,' he replies, swallowing the last half a can in three gulps, then tossing it out the window to join the other empties on the side of the road, many of them also flung by him on his numerous expeditions. After an hour of travelling, Jeff starts to get restless. 'I reckon there are plenty of kangaroos in that bush over there,' he said, slowing the car down.

'Well, let's check it out,' said Rob, reaching for the 243.

'Hey, I'm using that,' said Jeff, stopping the car. 'Here Mulla, you wanna drive?'

Mulla, who is half drunk, has always wanted to drive Jeff's car and only needs to be asked once. He drives down a bush track which begins to narrow as a result of protruding branches and bushes.

'Don't scratch my car,' said Jeff, with his eyes darting around looking for a live target.

'She'll be right,' assures Mulla, easing his foot off the accelerator.

'There's a kangaroo over there,' screams Rob, loading the .22 semi-automatic rifle. Just as the car stops, Jeff fires from the 243. Bang!

'Aw, ya missed by a mile,' said Mulla, watching what was an easy target bounce into the horizon and out of sight. A little further down the track Mulla spots another roo. 'Here, give me that gun Rob, you can't shoot,' he said, grabbing the gun before Rob could respond.

'How you gunna shoot'n drive at the same time?' asked Rob.

'Like this,' said Mulla, stopping suddenly and firing two shots at the target and missing both. He passed the gun back to Rob saying, 'Nah, that gun's fucked.'

'Bullshit, there's nothing wrong with that gun,' said Jeff. 'I've got more kangaroos with that gun than you've ever seen.'

'Yeah, right,' said Mulla.

Rob then saw a kangaroo hopping about one hundred and fifty yards away. 'Slow down,' he said, pointing the rifle towards the kangaroo. 'Slow down.'

'Nah, he's not gunna stop,' said Jeff who was also ready with the 243. Rob aims for an instant, then fires. Bang, Bang, Bang. Then the kangaroo tumbles into the dirt, kicking and trying to get up.

'What a fuckin' fluke,' said Mulla, who by now has bought the four-wheel-drive to a standstill.

'That gun must be fucked,' joked Jeff.

'Bullshit,' assured Rob, before getting out with a jack handle and running towards the now crippled kangaroo. Whack, whack, whack. The iron smashes into the kangaroo's head, relieving it of pain and stress. He drags it by the tail over to the car.

'Where'd ya hit him?' asked Jeff.

'In the leg,' replied Rob, lifting the roo into the back and feeling proud of himself. With that roo in the back they continued in search of more.

Another eight kilometres down the track they see a group of kangaroos in a paddock about three hundred yards away. Jeff quickly gets out and leans across the bonnet, aiming at one of the kangaroos. Bang!

'Aw, ya missed,' said Mulla, getting in before Jeff blamed the gun. 'Ya missed again.'

The kangaroos remain, despite their obvious suspicion. Rob leaned the .22 out the window and took aim.

'Ya won't reach that far with that gun,' said Mulla. Meanwhile, Jeff missed another two shots with the 243, a rifle designed to reach distant targets. Rob fired, and to his astonishment, the kangaroo that he aimed for jumped and started hopping. The other kangaroos, although alerted, remain stationary for the time being. After five bounces, the kangaroo fell to the ground.

'What happened?' asked Rob.

'Don't know; which one you aim for?' asked Mulla.

'That one,' replied Rob.

By now the other kangaroos hop into a small piece of remnant bush. 'Nah, there must be something wrong with that kangaroo,' said Jeff.

'Yeah, that gun couldn't reach that far,' said Mulla.

They drove to where the roo was lying on the ground without any sign of life. Upon inspection, they discovered a hole with a spot of blood on its chest area.

'You must've hit him in the heart. Hey man, I didn't know you could shoot,' said Mulla.

'It must've been me,' Jeff said, knowing full well he didn't aim for this one.

'Bullshit, man, you was shooting way over their heads,' said Rob, who, despite his disbelief, is cocky.

They drove for another twenty kilometres and saw nothing, so returned home.

PART 3: RAMPAGE

It was nine o'clock at night when Chooky knocked on Jamie's door. Jamie reluctantly crawled out of bed to answer the thundering bang.

'W-w-watcha d-doin'?' asked Chooky.

'Bloody sleeping. What, you looking for a reviver?' inquires Jamie.

'N-n-nah. You seen R-Rob-Robbie?' asked Chooky.

'Yeah, he's in the end room,' says Jamie as he walks towards the toilet. 'Go wake him up, he's got a packet of smokes.'

After waking Robbie, the three young men discuss possibilities for the night, ending a lengthy discussion with the conclusion that whatever they do they need money. Jamie, who is always proactive, suggests they break into the local hotel in search of whisky and cigarettes. Chooky, who has never had much experience in this type of activity is in two minds. He wants the commodities, but is terrified of being caught. 'N-nah man, the a-al- alarms will g- go off,' he stutters.

Eventually, Jamie talks Chooky into an agreement. Robbie has never needed much persuasion when it comes to getting a drink. It was a long dry wait until the pub closes and the publican was asleep, so Robbie asked Jamie to buy a couple of bottles for the waiting time.

'Yeah, that'll be a good chance to case the storeroom. Let's go,' said Jamie.

When the men arrived at the pub, Jamie pointed at an old doorway that had been blocked off by chip board. 'See that, that's how we get in.' The trio purchased six bottles of beer and a packet of smokes. 'Two bottles each, make it last,' jokes Jamie, looking at the old doorway.

As the men sat in a dark bushy spot sipping their beer, Jamie runs through the plan. 'It's piss easy, man,' he says, as Chooky's sips get bigger.

Come 12.30am, an hour and a half after the pub shut, the six bottles were long gone and Jamie was jimmying the skirting from around the blocked door.

'This should come off pretty easy,' assures Jamie. Creak, snap, smash.

'Y-you're ma-making too much noi-noise,' whispers Chooky, who is clearly having second thoughts. It wasn't long before Jamie created an opening and they were crawling towards the storeroom. 'Make sure yous keep down low,' he warns.

'What shall we take?' asks Robbie.

'Grab some whisky bottles and some cartons of UDLs. I'll grab some smokes,' says Jamie, crawling towards the counter. As Jamie reaches up for the carton of Winfield Red, he unknowingly triggers the alarm that's heard only in the owner's bedroom.

As he crawls back towards the other two he notices a light come on. Knowing instantly that the owner is awake, Jamie stood up and ran to where Robbie and Chooky were sorting out what drinks to take. 'He's coming. Grab something and run,' commands Jamie, quickly picking up a box containing twelve bottles of scotch.

'F-fu-fuck this,' said Chooky as he runs without carrying anything.

'Grab something, fuck ya, Chook,' commands Robbie in a high

pitched whisper, scuffling towards the opening where Jamie and Chooky have disappeared.

'Chooky Brown, I heard your name you little black bastard. Don't think you've got away, ya thieving little prick,' yelled Kevin, the tall, well-built publican. Watching a figure dissolve into the darkness, Kevin is unsure whether to give chase and leave his hotel vulnerable to further raids. He decides to leave it up to his good friend, the town constable. He almost felt a sense of blame for putting off blocking the door with bricks since he bought the place nine years ago.

Meanwhile, the brothers gather after running three hundred metres in panic, particularly Chook, who by now is a nervous wreck. 'He knows my name, you big-mouth jerk,' said Chooky, looking at Robbie in a most disgusted way.

'Oh well, we got a good drink anyway,' replies Robbie.

'Nah, stick ya drink, I'll-I'll go t-to gaol,' answered Chooky, taking a large mouthful of scotch.

'You won't go to gaol,' said Jamie unconvincingly.

'Nah, I'm buggered,' sighs Chooky.

'Why didn't ya grab something, ya little shitty arse?' asked Robbie.

'You get fucked you. I'm sick of you,' yelled Chooky, jumping up into a fighter's stance.

'Settle down you two monkeys,' advised Jamie. 'Or I'll smash you both.'

For the next three hours the men sat and talked about other breaks they've done in the past. Jamie mentions a safe he stole up in Perth.

'You blokes wanna go to Perth? See Aunty Marge an' that?' asked Jamie.

'How? We got no car,' replies Robbie.

'Steal one; I'll steal it,' said Jamie.

'Nah man, you're going off,' said Robbie, not sure if Jamie is serious.

'Come on man. We'll get caught tomorrow, they know Chooky; let's go while we can,' pleads Jamie. Chooky needed a little persuasion then finally agreed.

'Well, you go and get it and meet us over at the wheat bins,' suggests Robbie. They disperse with Jamie heading off up the dark street and Robbie and Chooky walking along a familiar bush track through thick scrub towards the wheat bins. Upon each of their shoulders rattled a box containing bottles of whisky.

A short time later Jamie arrives at the wheat bins in a well-used one-tonne ute. 'Aw, nah, he got old Alf's car. Why didn't ya get someone else's car instead of this poor old bastard's?' asks Robbie as he opens the door to let Chooky in first.

'Bugger him, the old bungy man,' replied Jamie.

'L-let-let's just pi-piss off,' said Chooky.

After stealing petrol from a nearby farm they drove to Perth. With the help of a few relations and a couple of hangers-on, they finished twenty-four bottles of whisky in three days. The stolen car was parked at the back of Aunty Marge's. Jamie told her it was Robbie's. The CIB have been around to get it. They also asked Aunty Marge questions about it. She told them what she knew. When Jamie returned to retrieve the car he certainly copped an earful from Aunty Marge.

Disappointed and depressed, coming off alcohol and dope, Jamie decides to steal another car that night, then talks Robbie and Chooky into coming on a ride to Port Hedland to visit a cousin. A rampage more like it. That's exactly what it was.

Lenny's Story

There is this bloke who is one of those persons who leaves a mark on your heart whether good or bad. He'll do things that you will think he's not capable of. He'll out-talk you if you are willing to have a conversation with him. This fella is slightly intellectually handicapped, but you would never know unless you talk to him. His name is Lenny Indich. Sometimes he stands around in public places and when he sees a police car he tries to hide and drops his head. When he does that, the police get suspicious, so that makes them stop, and then they'll go question him about a break-in and take him to the police station. They'll never let him go until one of the family gets in touch with the police.

Long time ago, back in the 1950s, his old parents used to work on farms, clearing and burning off. They used to bulldoze the trees down. What the bulldozer couldn't get, the old people gathered. They put the rest of the wood that was left in a heap. Everyone used to do that. They would burn the wood. Lenny was reared up in an era where he was part of what was going on. His parents took care of him most of the time. His sister May was always there to help her parents look after him. When Lenny was ten years old, he started to light fires. Where there's grass around he'll throw a match to it and he'll stand there and watch, but if someone spots him, he'll take off.

Lenny's parents moved around a lot. They went to work on farms around New Norcia when Lenny was about eight years old. In about 1955 when Lenny was ten the family moved to North Fremantle. They lived in a State Housing Commission home in those days. His father used to work with Fremantle wharfies, and his foreman was Paddy Troy. If he was in trouble, Paddy Troy would always help him out. Lenny would go down to the wharf with Colin, his brother, to do some fishing. If there wasn't any fish at North Fremantle, they would take the ferry across to Fremantle. And they would pay five pence to go across.

A bloke at the beach used to hire out rubber mattresses which were blown up. Lenny and Colin used to ride the waves for hours and hours. It was their favourite entertainment to go down to the beach. They also went down to Harvest Road, which was where all the kids went. Out there they had a diving board, which Lenny always got on. He used to stand there and look around to see if anyone was watching him, then he would do a big bombie and make a big splash.

When the ferry boat went past, all the kids used to swim out. Some of them would take a bicycle pump with them which they would fill with water and squirt the passengers. Sometimes when the fishing boats were getting repaired, the kids would climb on the pole, and when they started up the engines, the kids would jump into the water, twirling behind the propeller which would pull them along with it.

The family lived at John Street, North Fremantle, next to the football and hockey ground. Across from the football was the Swan River where there were boats tied up. One day Lenny took a boat and rowed across the river. He was paddling as fast as he could. Everyone was trying to catch him, but he was too fast for them. He made it across the river, and left the boat and walked away. Lenny was about twelve years old.

There was a caretaker named Jack Streeter who knew Lenny very well. Lenny was a bit of a nuisance around there. There was a sign at the oval which said, 'No Riding Across the Oval'. It didn't do Lenny much good because he couldn't read. That old Jack Streeter used to shout at him and chase him, but Lenny used to look around and keep pedalling and the old fella couldn't catch him. Sometimes Lenny used to go missing from home and his parents used to tell Colin to go look for him. He would get on his bike and would go all over town. Lenny would go to different places, the shop or down the river. He would go off any time of the day, it didn't bother him what time it was.

Lenny's parents tried to send him to a special school. The first day the bus came to pick him up, he didn't say much when he came home. On the third day he went missing at school. The teachers were looking for him, and then they found him underneath the building. After that he didn't go back to school.

He used to get up early in the morning and get up to his tricks;

wherever there was smoke, he wasn't too far away. Colin's parents used to say, 'Go over and look for him,' and sure enough he would be hiding not too far away. He got up to lots of mischief when he was little. He hasn't changed much. If you leave him on his own he gets himself in trouble with the law.

Lenny went to the country to live with his sister May for about twelve months. His sister used to take him for a holiday to the city to meet his mother and father and brothers. All his friends were glad to see him again. They asked him where he had been, and he told them that he had been in the country. And they all went down to the shops to play on the pinball machine and listen to the jukebox. Lenny's favourite singer was Elvis Presley and still is.

Every pension day Lenny used to steal wine and smokes from his parents. His mother used to poke him with a walking stick, for stealing from them. On Saturday mornings his mother and father used to go to Fremantle. Lenny used to go to the cinemas, and when the movies finished he would wait for them.

Lenny had four brothers and one sister, and he was the youngest. Three of his brothers are now deceased. Lenny's sister, May, had five sons. The two youngest boys grew up with Lenny, and he used to boss them around. May's second eldest son used to take Lenny for a while to help his mother out.

Lenny used to go to Perth early in the morning on the bus, and do his rounds. Firstly he would go to the hospital and hang around there for hours. At about twelve, he would go to the soup kitchen and have his lunch. And he would catch the train to Fremantle and spend the afternoon there. Later on he would catch the train back to Perth and get on the bus to Karrinup. Sometimes he would fight some kids on the bus, and his sister would get a call from the police about a complaint about Lenny's behaviour.

We are writing this story about Lenny because he always got into trouble with the law since he was a little boy. He is intellectually handicapped but he has a sense of direction, and never gets lost. He gets into trouble and gets put into prison. When he was little, he was picked up often by the police and put into Graylands. He has been in and out of Graylands and at one stage he went missing for a very long time. He just walked out one day and went to Fremantle and met some people he knew. They were drinking and went on a ship, and Lenny ended up in Sydney.

He was over there for two years. We didn't know where he was. When we went to visit him at Graylands, he wasn't there. We asked the people in Graylands Hospital but they didn't know where he was or what had happened to him. We asked all around but the people didn't know. Two months later, someone told us they saw him get on the ship. We didn't know where the ship was going.

About two years later we got a letter from a Hostel in Redfern saying they had a bloke named Lenny Indich, and asked us if he was related to us. He keep telling them he had a brother named Colin who lives in Medina, Perth and works for the Shire of Kwinana. So they put him on the train and sent him back home. When he arrived he was drunk. When we asked him what happened, he just shrugged his shoulders and said he'd been away.

He's a character. He's all in one. He thinks he knows everything. He said he's been in the army and he tells everybody he's been in the war in 1952, but he was only a kid then. He also said he was in the navy and that he was a policeman too. He goes to a telephone box. He doesn't put any money in; he just dials a number and talks to himself. People could be waiting to ring up. He looks around and sees the people and he talks and talks.

The Miracle

It was spud digging time again. The Aboriginal workers had gathered at the south-west township of Waroona for the start of the season. They came by the cartload, they came by passenger train, paying their fares. Others simply packed their swags and jumped the goods train. A lucky few managed to get lifts with their wadjella bosses on the back of farm trucks. In return, they helped to keep an eye on the stock or produce on the journey to the markets in Perth. Whatever their mode of transport, most of them arrived in time for the spud digging season in the Drakesbrook district on the Perth to Bunbury railway line just south of Pinjarra.

Waroona at that time represented the northernmost sector of the potato-growing area. It extended from this small town to Harvey, Benger, Brunswick and on down through Roelands and Burekup to Marybrook and Busselton along the south-west coastal strip. This was because Waroona was also the northernmost sector where irrigation channels were built to carry water from the catchment drains in the hills to irrigate the lowlands to the west of the Darling Ranges. The irrigation channels directed and regulated the flow of the water to the various potato-growing areas in the region.

Irrigation allowed for two potato-growing seasons. The first started when the seed potatoes were sown in January and February each year and ended when they were harvested in April and May, before the winter rains. The second season started in June or July and ended some time between October and December, depending on how wet the winter had been and how far north you were. Waroona usually harvested earlier than the other areas, and the diggers worked their way south as the potatoes ripened and the ground dried out.

During the April–May harvest, the Aboriginal people would

have plenty of money around Easter time. Many of them were Christians, both Anglican and Roman Catholic, and were anxious to attend church services and mass at the local churches, and to observe the ritual of fasting on Good Friday. These religious rituals were strictly adhered to by Catholic and non-Catholics alike. For those who did not fast, fish was the food for Easter.

Because it was difficult to make food last over the Easter break, the practical aspects of fasting all day Friday were not lost on those who practised this Christian ritual. As well as it being good for them to be seen as good Christians, strong in their beliefs and the teachings of their respective churches, it also helped them to stretch their food supplies over the break. This was also true of the Christmas festival.

The local Aboriginal families were known to most of the church congregation and were well respected by the wadjellas. When asked for information on other Aboriginal workers, their word was accepted and their opinions valued.

Apart from these religious festivals, the annual Royal Agricultural Society Show and occasional gymkhanas provided the social and cultural events which helped to add a rich diversity to the traditional aspects of their own culture, which they still practised. They shared their good fortune with their families. Their spiritual beliefs were still observed and talked about as they shared the oral history of their people.

Their respect for regional differences was observed and put into practice when camping, and this year was no different. Families had congregated at the designated camping area and, according to traditional custom, those Nyoongahs who came from towns south of Waroona pitched their tents in the southerly position, the local Nyoongahs took the central camping area, and those who came from the north and north-east of the township camped in the north-north-easterly aspects. The eastern areas were taken by the families who travelled down from Collie and other townships east of the Darling Scarp, and any Nyoongahs who lived west of the town took the western positions. There were variations to this rule; for example, if somebody arrived from elsewhere who had been born into the local Nyoongah community and had moved away, they might take a central position with their families, no matter which direction they came from.

At this time, it was the first potato dig of the year and Easter was looming on the religious calendar. The Nyoongahs had arrived and pitched their camps on the Biddairs' property on the edge of town, although most of the townspeople didn't know it because a vacant strip of land and a belt of trees and thick scrub created a barrier which screened the camp from the town. A small creek, which was part of the irrigation system, provided constant running water for the camp and kept the trees and scrub growing in thick abundance, hiding a huge log which had fallen across the creek. It was this log the Nyoongahs used as a means to gain access to the camp from the town and the railway station without having to go the long way around via the road out of the township, or by going slightly south of the camp to cross the creek at the sluice. It also gave the Nyoongahs fair warning of anyone approaching the camp. They were given time to get the smaller kids and allow the older kids to flee along the creek. The women were also able to clear the camps of any signs of gambling or gebba because, at that time, Nyoongahs were not allowed to drink or purchase alcohol from the local hotel. However, some of the Italian men who made their own wine, or rotgut as the Nyoongahs called it, sold a bottle or two to some of the Nyoongah men they knew, or gave it as payment for their instead of money. They also gave them potatoes, pumpkins and plenty of other vegetables and fruit.

That year the camp was close to the township, but the Nyoongahs felt comfortable because the screen of trees and scrub would ensure that their camp and its proximity remained unnoticed. The only wadjellas who knew of the camp were the 'Big Biddair'; a Mister Sampson, who owned a big property on the edge of town and who was a man of substance in the district; the local monaitch [police], because at that time the movement of Aboriginal people was strictly monitored and controlled; the local priests, because the war to win their souls was still being waged between the two dominant churches, and the school teachers, because the kids still had to go to school.

Potato digging at that time was hard yakka. Modern equipment, such as potato-harvesting machines, was not in existence. Tractors and trucks were the main forms of machinery used on a few farms. Even so, most of the poorer farmers relied on the horse, the plough, the cart and manpower. Generally, the potato growers knew the regular spud diggers and their families who came every year. Indeed, many of the 'gun' spud diggers had arrived early in January without their families to find work planting the seed potatoes. By doing this, they secured the promise of employment when the potatoes were ready to be harvested.

The day before the dig, the Big Biddair drove the tractor over to the camp to see if the diggers were there and to tell them that they were to begin the dig early next morning on the biggest, number two, paddock. It would have to be forks and spades, because the soil was too soggy and wet in places for the tractor to cross, and the risk of getting bogged was too great for the rows to be ploughed.

Next morning before sunrise, the spud diggers arrived at the number two paddock. The Biddair divided the rows between them. The paddock was approximately seven acres in area and, by the look of it, would yield a bumper crop, top tonnage to the acre. This was verified as the guns went to work forking the rows across the length of the paddock, from east to west. The Biddair watched as he waited for a few of the last stragglers to be allocated their section of the dig, to sign or put their mark in the book of payment, and also to get twine and bag needles, so that the bags could be sealed once full. They were told to leave the twine and bag needles on the trailer at knock-off time, or with old Lew, a local elder employed with the Biddair.

Having recorded the names of the workers, the Biddair sat for a while, watching as they took up their forks and shovels and turned the rich, dark soil, exposing the new potatoes. There were supposed to be four teams of four men, although one team had only three. As he watched the guns and their teams establish a rhythmic working pattern to the dig, he noticed that each team had a number of youths. In many cases there were two adult males to two youths.

All of the guns and their sidekicks would commence the digging, forking the soil over, moving along each side of the row. After a certain distance, one of the adult men and his helper would stop and sort the potatoes into roughly graded piles of first, second and third grade, and rejects, which were potatoes that were deformed or had been cut in half by a shovel or pierced by a fork. The other adult would bag the potatoes, stand the bags up and sew the top up with twine, leaving each end of the bag pointed so that whoever loaded the bags onto the trailer could get a good grip on them. At an agreed-upon time, the two guns would swap places so that their young sidekicks could learn the skills of digging with either fork or shovel, grading and sorting, or bagging and sewing. The leader of the team, usually the older man, would stop and check the work of the youths.

By doing the work in this way, the oldies and the gun spud diggers passed their skills on to the younger men, ensuring that there was always a skilled spud digger in the family, which in turn ensured that their families always had work and food and the ability to earn a living during the spud-digging season. Even the women and children were able to earn a few shillings by going over the rows, picking up the rejects.

Before the Biddair drove back to the house, he walked over to the first team, a group of local men, and spoke to the elder, old Lew, who nodded and went to speak to the next group of diggers. As they watched him approach, the men called a smoko for ten minutes. As Lew reached the next team of diggers, their leader, old Bob, nodded and said, 'Winjie, Ngoon, what's up?'

Old Lew stood for a while as he rolled a smoke and said, 'The boss will be back mid-afternoon to load the spuds and cart them to the shed for grading, and to separate the seed potatoes for the next crop.' Looking back along the rows of spuds, he continued, 'The Biddair said we could take a few spuds for our families, also a pumpkin each, and a few tomatoes and cucumbers. He also said to get some rockmelons and watermelons, for the coolungas.'

'Is he always this good to the workers?' asked old Bob.

'Yeah,' replied old Lew. 'He's always been this way, for as long as I can remember working for him.'

Old Lew continued along the section of allotted rows to tell each group of diggers what the Biddair had said about their right to take some vegies and melons home for their families. Upon returning to his own section, old Lew noticed the weather changing; clouds were gathering in the west. 'Could get a shower or two tonight,' he said to his team of diggers.

'Yeah, probably get twice as cold overnight, this time of year,' said his brother, John.

'Better get on with the digging then. Wanna get this paddock done by this afternoon,' said old Lew as he forked the soil over, exposing the new potatoes.

Later that afternoon, after most of the bagged potatoes were loaded and taken to the shed, the men called knock-off time.

211

Most of them elected to walk back to camp by way of the creek, gathering wood for the campfires to cook their food and for warmth. That evening after tea the men sat down, yarning and enjoying a smoke around the big open fire in the middle of the camp. 'Jesus, it's cold!' said Bill, old Lew's eldest son. 'Next time I get paid, I'm gunna buy a big coat for myself!'

Johnny Smith laughed. 'God, what I'd give for a good drink of gebba; that would warm us up!'

'Yeah, whisky, boys. That's the drink to warm you up!' said Henry, old Bob's eldest son.

Ray Cox looked at his cousin Dennis. 'Hey, Coorda, where's your bunji woman? You shoulda brung her with you, man. She coulda went to old Tony's and got some gebba for us!'

'Aw, she gone over to Narrogin to see her people, mate!' Dennis replied.

Johnny looked up and laughed. 'Need a whole bloody barrel full to keep us fellas warm,' he said as he threw another log on the fire. 'I hope it's fine by tomorrow. We'll probably start on the second paddock by mid-morning if we getta early start!'

Next day at knock-off time, the women and children met their menfolk at the edge of the paddock, where the irrigation channel intersected with the creek. All of the blokes joined their family groups and went looking for firewood. Some went south and some went north along the creek almost to the Biddair's house where they crossed over and moved back towards the camp, down the road running alongside the railway line. As they walked along, they picked up empty cool drink bottles, pieces of copper wire and lead, some coal, as well as wood. Apart from the coal and wood, the other items could be sold, although they kept some of the lead and copper wire which would be useful items for fishing for marron as well as freshwater catfish, or cobblers as they were known.

When the group neared the railway station, the women and older kids crossed the line to go to the shops to buy bread and meat. The single blokes also crossed the line to go to the fish and chip shop to buy tobacco, cigarette papers and matches, as well as tailor-made cigarettes. The older people, married men and younger children continued on to the camp with the wood and coal, to start the fires.

After the women and children had settled down that evening, the men, as usual, sat around the fire, smoking, yarning and catching up on the news from other towns throughout the state where they had friends and family connections. Some of the single and married men from the other camps came over to share and strengthen the social bond between men, and to strengthen family ties, their work ties, their culture and their Nyoongah identity.

Old Lew chuckled, saying, 'I saw the reverend Father Kelly when I went around to see the Biddair this afternoon. He's expecting us to go to the midnight mass, this Good Friday.'

'He's got Buckley's!' said Lew's brother, John. 'I'm goin' bush!'

'I'm gunna get my woman; it's too cold here by myself!' said Dennis. 'So I won't be here.'

'Aw, I dunno, easy way to get a mouthful of gebba,' said Lew as he looked around the group by the fire.

'Yeah, I heard Jesus can turn water into wine,' said young Joe, old Lew's grandson. 'Pity he's not here now. We could ask him to turn this water into gebba for us, unna?'

'Nah,' said Joe's cousin, Peter. 'He'd get chucked in gaol, 'cause Nyoongahs not allowed to have gebba, unna, Pop?' he said as he turned to his grandfather for confirmation. The elder men burst out laughing.

'Jesus,' said old Lew's brother Ben. 'That's a good one. I wonder what them wadjellas would do 'bout that?'

'It'd still be a miracle though. Probably two miracles — turning water into wine, and us Nyoongahs being allowed to drink it, unna!' said Paul, another of Joe's cousins.

'You not allowed to drink gebba-ngooninj anyway, Pauly. You only a kid!' said Peter as he poked the fire with a stick.

'I'm older than all of you,' said Joe. 'But I'm too young to drink gebba, unna, Pop?'

'Yes, and you keep it that way!' said old Lew.

The fire was burning brightly and throwing out plenty of heat. The older men sat in comfortable silence, staring at the live coals and the little blue flames dancing in the heart of the heat. They heard the whistle of the train in the distance and looked up.

'That sounds like the passenger train from Perth,' said old Bob as he looked around the campfire. 'Where's Bill and Ray?'

'Dunno!' chorused the young teenagers. 'But we're not waiting for them, we're off to bed. See you oldies in the morning. G'night!'

As the youths departed, old Lew and his brothers, old John

and Ben, and his cousin, old Bob, sat yarning with their sons, Henry, Dennis and Johnno. They heard the passenger train blow its whistle as it drew away and headed south toward Bunbury. As the quietness descended once more, they heard footsteps coming through the bush, then the squeaking of the fence wires, some heavy breathing, and swearing.

'Sounds like they're coming by way of the stops. Must be carrying something, otherwise they'd come over the log,' said old Lew.

'Must be someone who got off the train. Probably carryin' their luggage,' mused old Ben.

'Yes,' said Dennis, as he stood up to go down to the creek to relieve himself.

They heard the noise getting closer, puffing and blowing, and loud voices swearing and arguing. Suddenly, two dark shapes loomed up alongside the creek by way of the sluice stops south of the camp. They appeared to be bent over, as if pulling or pushing something.

'Who's that?' said old Lew and Ben together, as they stood up, peering into the darkness. Next minute, something rolled into the circle of light. They jumped out of the way as a barrel came to rest at their feet, followed by the two missing men, Bill and Ray.

'Jesus Christ! You pair of stupid bastards!' said Johnno. 'What the fuck have you got here? What've you done?'

'God, you fellas done for now!' said Henry. 'Monaitch gunna be after you for bloody sure, now. You gunna be sitting in goal for Easter, you pair of mugs!'

'Keep your voices down, you'll wake the kids,' said John. 'The missus will get shitty!'

'Yeah, right! My missus won't be too happy about that, either,' said Henry. 'It'll take a bloody miracle to save you now!'

At that moment, the clouds parted and moonlight bathed the camp area in brightness. The import of what Bill and Ray had done sank in.

'Shit! Whatta we gunna do with it? We can't bloody well drink it all tonight!' said Henry as they all stood there, looking at each other and at the barrel of wine.

'Jesus Christ, you pair of fuckin' stupid bastards! When I said we needed a bloody barrel of gebba to warm us up, I didn't mean for you to go and steal one!' said Johnno, glaring at Bill and Ray. 'What did you do, break into the pub?'

'Nah,' said Ray. 'When we were walking back from the fish shop we had to wait for the goods train to finish shunting and pass through. While we were waiting, Bill saw Guiseppe from Brunswick, so we went over to have a yarn with him while he was unloading stuff from the goods shed onto the truck.'

'Yeah,' said Henry. 'Bill can speak Italian, unna?'

'That's right. They don't call him the Bloody Black Ding from Southern Italy for nothing,' said Ray.

'Yeah, me an' Guiseppe grew up together down at Roelands,' said Bill. 'He likes me because I fixed him up with a wife.'

'Who?' asked Ray.

'My sister,' said Bill. 'But she's white like a wadjella and his people don't know she's a Nyoongah. They think she's a wadjella. She speaks fluent Italian, too, and they think she's very clever and that Guiseppe's very lucky. They got three kids now.'

'Yeah, how's my grannies?' asked old Lew.

'Guiseppe said they okay, Pop!' said Bill.

'Why don't you go and see them?' asked old Bob.

'Nah!' said old Lew. 'Kathy got her life to live, now she's settled down. Giuseppe is good to her and the kids, and he helps us find work when he can. He gives us a drink of wine, too, but we don't get drunk though. They're living over at Hamel now, for a while. Does Giuseppe know about this barrel?'

'No,' said Bill. 'He didn't see us slip it off the railway truck and put it in the culvert near the shed. Besides, that lot was goin' to Bunbury, so they won't miss it until when they unload after Easter. He just took the beer and wine barrels and some foodstuffs to put in the hotel coolroom.'

'Yeah, when the goods train finally finished shunting, the passenger train passed through, so we had to wait for both trains to leave before we could carry the barrel over the railway line and roll it down here,' said Ray.

At that moment, Dennis returned. He saw four blokes standing around the fire. 'What's up?' he asked them.

'Want a livener?' asked Bill.

'What, you got some gebba?' asked Dennis.

'Yeah. A whole bloody barrel full of it!' said Johnno.

'God struth!' said Dennis. 'That's a lot of gebba to get rid of! How you gunna do that? Better not wait until after Easter, or even tomorrow. Better empty it right now!'

The five of them looked around the camp area by the light of the fire. 'Got to empty it out of the barrel and put it in something else,' said John as he handed a mug of gebba to each of the other four blokes. Then they set about finding all the other containers they could lay their hands on.

It was in the early hours of the morning when their task was finished. They had filled up all the canvas waterbags, except one which was left to hold clean drinking water, then they filled up the billy-cans, big and small, the camp oven and several pots. Most of the empty bottles were filled, sealed with corks, tied with long lengths of twine, put in the creek and anchored with the rocks that lay on the bottom of the creek.

The barrel they took back over the road, right opposite the railway station, where there was a clearing which had a wide expanse of sand. A few stumps, some berrin bushes and gum suckers lined the edge of the clearing and as the moon began its descent into the western rim of the clearing, it cast deep shadows over the sand. Bill and John took a shovel and dug a deep hole right in the middle of the clearing, which was almost all in shadow. They put the barrel in the hole and put all of the sand back on top of it, then swept the area clean to remove any sign of disturbance. Then they backed out of the clearing until they reached the fence, crossed it and continued on until they reached the grassed and leafy entrance to the place where the big log crossed over the creek.

Over the next few days, several things occurred which were to have a far-reaching effect on the lives of the people in the camp. Firstly, early in the morning, just after the men had finished clearing away the incriminating evidence, young Joe emerged, sleepy-eyed, from the lean-to and made his way down to the creek, downstream from the camp, to have a coomp. On the way back, he grabbed a tin mug and made his way to the nearest waterbag to get a drink. He poured the water out of the waterbag. It was still dark, so he couldn't see the colour of the liquid. He quaffed his thirst then went back to bed. He vaguely remembered that the water tasted different, it warmed him, but he turned over in his bed and slept soundly until about six o'clock.

When he woke up, he lay for awhile, puzzling about something. 'The water! That's it!' he thought. He got up quickly and went to get another drink of water from the small waterbag which was hanging from the tent pole where it had been earlier, in the darkness of the morning. He gulped it down. The water was cool and sweet, but it was not wine! It was water! 'It's a miracle!' he thought to himself. 'The water turned into wine, then it turned back into water!'

Young Joe was very quiet for the rest of the day. Indeed, he was very thoughtful for the rest of the Easter period. He even went to church throughout the Easter break, beginning with Good Friday. On Easter Monday, he expressed a wish to join the church and become an altar-boy. Later, he would like to study to become a priest. When he was teased about it by his cousins, he simply said, 'I believe in miracles.' He also found an ally in his grandmother, for she also stated her belief in miracles. However, her source of faith was arrived at differently.

That Easter Sunday, as old Granny was preparing the meal, she had made sure that she did exactly as the menfolk had instructed, and had not touched the little waterbags, the billy-cans or the camp oven. It was thus the Monaitch found her on Saturday morning early, cooking breakfast. She had onions, chops and sausages frying in the pan, bread toasting by the open fire and the big enamel billy-can sitting by the fire, full of freshly made tea.

'Good morning, Granny. Where's Lew and the boys?' asked the Monaitch.

'Hullo, Sergeant. Lew and the boys have gone out to Hamel, to the spud-digging on Mr Sampson's property. Why? What have they done?'

The Monaitch didn't answer. He just strode over to the big waterbag and turned the tap on and tasted it. It was water. He turned and tipped up the little waterbag by the tent pole. It, too, held only water. Nonplussed, the Monaitch stood there, scrutinising the camp area. The kids were playing mud pies on the banks of the creek, the bigger kids were swimming in the clear pool above the sluice gates. The smell of cooked onions floated on the air with the smoke from the campfire. The camp oven had a big cooked damper sitting on its slightly skewed lid. Old Granny was busy. The camp looked normal. Nothing was out of place. The Monaitch looked puzzled, but nodded to Granny and her daughter Hilda as he turned away and retraced his steps over the creek by the sluice gates towards the town. Later that day he returned to speak to the men and some of the other families who were camped by the west and north sides of the area.

By Easter Sunday, the gebba had all but gone. The camp was back to normal. 'Just as well,' thought Granny as she busied herself getting ready to walk to church with young Joseph. He'd asked her yesterday if she believed in miracles and she had said yes. He'd told her about the water turning into wine early in the morning on Good Friday, and that it was a sign for him from the Lord.

Granny didn't tell him that Bill had come back for the bag with the wine and had substituted the bag filled with cool, clear water in its place while he was asleep. Nor did she tell him that her belief in miracles stemmed from the fact that the blokes hadn't been caught. No one knew where the barrel of wine had disappeared to. As far as the Monaitch could ascertain, there was no trace of it in the Nyoongahs' camp. Nor did the men or women show any sign of drunkenness. The kids didn't know about the theft, they were too busy having a good time.

As for Joe and the other youths, they marvelled at the fact that their old grannies didn't complain about the cold and their aching old bones. It was a miracle which they attributed to the good food. Joe often thought and prayed about the miracle of the water turning into wine. Old Granny prayed daily, thanking God, Mother Mary and all the Saints for the miracles. Yes, Easter was truly a time of miracles and mysteries.

Amen.

Grand Masters

When I was a child my family lived in the small country town of Waroona, in the south-west of Western Australia. We were very poor, not able to afford much in the way of toys and leisure-time activities, so I spent a lot of time reading about knights in shining armour, riding around on horses, attacking castles and saving damsels in distress.

As a child I took many of the ideas I gained from reading into the games I invented or helped to invent and, along with my sister, cousins and friends, played lengthy and eloquent games of love and war, chivalry and heroism. In a country town in the early nineteen-sixties there wasn't a lot else to do, so we all became dramatic actors at a very early age. We dressed up as best we could for our roles and, of course, the texts, voices and accents were followed as closely as our unreliable juvenile memories would allow.

Whole days would pass this way, especially during school holidays, until my father arrived home from work. Then the dramatic scenes and equipment would be dismantled in favour of a game of cricket in the back yard. Our house had an outside laundry, bathroom and dunny, separated from the main house by a strip of asphalt that was about twice as wide as a regular cricket pitch. Because this area was relatively flat and smooth it was used as the pitch. The wickets consisted of a tin drum or piece of board propped up against the back stairs of the house. As we could seldom afford to buy a proper cricket bat, Dad would cut one out of a fence picket or any other suitable piece of wood he could find, and we used a tennis ball instead of a cricket ball. Our whole family, and sometimes most of the neighbourhood kids, became involved in these games, and sometimes we staged our own test matches in the back yard.

Dad was the umpire and sole arbiter of decisions, as well as being a player. He was very good at the game, so nobody ever disputed his decisions. Dad was also one of the stalwarts of the local cricket club and played religiously every Saturday during summer. I'm not really sure where Dad first picked up his cricket skills, but he knew things about the game back then that I've since only heard from coaches during my playing career, or from vastly experienced commentators on the modern-day game.

Dad was a swing bowler and was just above medium pace, but to an eight-year-old he seemed mighty quick! He always bowled slowly to us kids, but as we got better, he started to bowl quicker. My sister, who is a year older than me, copied Dad and became a lethal fast bowler. She used to play cricket with the boys at school, and terrorised them. I'm sure she ruined many a budding cricket career with her deadly inswingers. My mother was more guileful, and bowled a tidy combination of wrist and finger spin which she had learned from Dad.

I took to the long run-up from a very early age and modelled myself on the great Dennis Lillee, even though I'm black and he's white, I'm left-handed and he used his right! So there I was, this skinny little kid, pushing off the picket fence, ducking under the clothes line, charging in to try and knock his Dad over. Sometimes Dad would bunt a catch back, but not until he had scored his half-century or had seen me execute properly one of the many technical instructions he used to build into our game. Similarly, when I was batting Dad would explain technical aspects of stroke play and I am sure he bowled balls that were designed for me to play particular shots until I had perfected them, although he rarely let me outscore him. I never realised it until much later on in my life, but Dad was probably the best coach I ever had, because he made the game fun for me, he patiently and thoroughly explained any technical aspect that I might question, and he tolerated with great humour all of my juvenile tantrums. Dad was never a pushy or authoritarian coach, or father, for that matter. Cricket was a game to him, and he believed that the first element of ANY game is enjoyment. As soon as one loses one's enjoyment of a game it becomes a task, and nobody likes to work for fun.

Dad also liked a beer, and I can remember many times when he would come home from the local pub, three-parts pissed and full of good cheer. He'd sit at the kitchen table and eat a meal that had dried up and wrinkled from waiting in the oven for him to get home, after which he'd say, 'Grab the bat, Tom. Let's see your shots.' He had a routine, on those occasions. He'd call the shots and I'd play them to an imaginary bowler. If I didn't play straight, or my foot work was lazy, he'd tell me what I did wrong and show me how to do it properly. I probably lost a lot of sleep playing kitchen cricket, but it didn't matter one little bit to me. Dad was my hero and any time spent with him was quality time.

Of course, things weren't always so perfect. Dad sometimes came home so drunk that we would have to cart him inside and put him to bed. There were other times when he would be very aggressive, particularly towards Mum, and would try to physically and verbally brow-beat Mum, my sister and me. I remember once when Dad gave Mum a thick lip. He was very contrite afterwards, once he had sobered up, but Mum had a sore face for days. Another time, Mum got jacked off with Dad and sconed him with the solid metal shaft of one of his golf clubs — stopped him in his tracks, I can tell you!

One of the things Dad couldn't teach me was strategy. Because our little playing area was so confined, I had no idea of field placings, or of bowling on one side of the wicket, or bowling to a set field. Those elements of my game came later, after I started playing competitively. My first inklings of strategy came when my mother befriended a Dutch woman whose family had moved into the town. The lady's name was Dora van Aalst, and I think she must have been a great beauty when she was young because even though she was middle-aged when I knew her I could see the residue of that beauty even then.

Dora had three children. Theo, her eldest son, was an adult and had little to do with us kids. Rudi, the second son, was a couple of years older than me and I thought he was the cleverest boy in the world. He was constantly making things with his hands, like a parachute, using a handkerchief, some string and a six-inch bolt, or a wood-turning lathe which he converted, with his father's help, from an old electric sewing machine, and on which he turned out beautiful pieces of furniture. His games were even more inventive and realistic than my earlier ones had been, because he would make all of the props, as true-to-life as possible. He also had a great collection of toy soldiers with which he played elaborate war games. Beatrix, his sister, was the same age as my sister and they became good mates. Everyone called her 'Trixie', and I used to daydream about us falling madly in love and running away from home together. Trixie had inherited her mother's beauty, you see.

However, it was Dora's husband, Kees (pronounced 'Case'), who fascinated me most of all. Kees van Aalst was an invalid, and every time I saw him he was in a wheelchair. I used to think that invalids were useless and had no quality of life until I met Kees. Even though he was an invalid, he had a trade, as an electrician, and was a capable gardener. But the thing about Kees that I came to respect most of all was his ability at chess. The first thing I saw whenever we visited the van Aalsts was Kees's chessboard set up in the lounge room of their house. It was a work of art, this chessboard, made of dark, European wood with the marquetry panel on the top made of dark brown and honey-coloured wood and highly polished. The pieces themselves were ornate, hand-carved pieces, made of the same two types of wood as the marquetry squares on the board, although they were much darker because of the constant handling by Kees and other players. There was a stop-clock fixed to each side of the base of the board, and it was set up on a low table covered by a dark velvet tablecloth, and was always ready in case Kees got a challenge.

The finishing touch to this chessboard was a small brass plaque which was inscribed with the words *Kees van Aalst, Gross Meester*, which translated to 'Grand Master' in English. On this board, I had the honour of learning to play chess, first of all by watching Kees teaching my mother, and then by being taught by him myself. Under his tutelage, I grew familiar with all of the pieces, their strengths and weaknesses. I discovered that, by using the pieces in unison, I could eliminate or cover weaknesses and force or lure less skilled opponents into errors which would leave them vulnerable.

I began to find that I could apply the strategies Kees taught me on the chessboard to the war games Rudi and I played. When I mentioned this to Kees, he told me a little about the history of the game. Although it was widely claimed as a European invention, the Chinese had apparently been using boards to plan strategy for their elaborate and highly stylised wars for a thousand years before the game was first seen in Europe. The Mongols, Kees said, had brought the war-boards west with them when they invaded Europe in the early medieval period, so they were well tried and tested prior to the game becoming Europeanised. One of Genghis Khan's grandsons, Kublai, had breached the Great Wall and occupied one of the northern Chinese provinces, where he had seen the boards in use, and he subsequently adopted the practice himself, according to Kees.

Once I learned the rudiments of chess, my mother and I began a fierce competition for supremacy. We were fairly evenly matched and we were very much alike in our thinking, so the contests were always close and often became a battle of wills, more than skills. Dad was never really interested and my sister didn't have the patience to think her moves through, but one of Mum's sisters also played, so there was often a three-cornered contest.

Neither Mum nor I were ever good enough to hold a candle to Kees, though. It was a matter of great professional pride to him that he had never been beaten on his home board, nor was he ever beaten in Australia, either face-to-face or by correspondence. It was a pity Dad never took to chess, because I think he might have gotten close to Kees. They were similar in temperament, cautious and thoughtful in the way they approached problems and challenges, and had the same quirky sense of humour. I'd like to have seen that match-up.

Like all good things, however, my chess-playing days were numbered. One Saturday in summer, I accompanied Dad to a cricket match at Yarloop, and our team was short of a player. As I was wearing sand shoes, a white T-shirt and pale shorts, I was drafted to fill in. I might have been eleven or twelve years old at the time. I batted at number eleven and I remember being so nervous that my thigh muscles felt like they were cramping as I walked out to the wicket. The bowler was a left-hander from Yarloop named Gordon Bancroft, and he bowled everything pitched well up outside off stump. I only remember playing four shots, although when I walked off it felt like I'd batted for a week. Three of the shots scored, all of them through the covers — two twos and a single. The fourth was a little wider outside off stump and I imperiously drove it through to the wicket keeper, who caught it, then apologised for having done so. The bowler completed his follow-through, kept coming and patted me on the head, saying, 'Well batted, young fellow!' They were like that, down in the country where I grew up.

I don't remember the result of the game, but I was hooked thereafter. I started training with the men from then on, and by the time I left home to go to Boarding School in Year Ten, I was a regular member of the side. With my father providing the coaching, I blossomed as an all-rounder, batting in the middle order and bowling big, loopy inswingers. I also began to notice how many of the strategies and attacks I had learned on a chessboard could be translated without much difficulty onto the cricket field. In particular, I was intrigued at how particular fields were set for particular bowlers, for example, strong off-side fields for outswing bowlers, or employing close-in catching fielders when the spinners were turning the ball, or making a field placement several overs in advance of executing a planned move.

As I matured I got better and better at the game, and I grew to love it more and more. While it held most of the cerebral aspects of chess, I loved the fact that I could contribute to the physical achievements of the side on the day, in the field. There came a time when my long, loping run-up was more than warranted because I could bowl very fast, and I progressed up the batting order to number one.

Those glory days are past, now, and I don't really miss them, but I still play the game for the sheer love of it. I haven't played chess seriously since my school days, but I reckon I could pick it up again quickly enough. Although I really enjoyed learning and playing chess, I personally think cricket is the ultimate game, because you get to execute your moves physically, on a much grander scale than on a chessboard. I can understand why my father, having played cricket long before he ever saw a chessboard, didn't take to chess at all — he was already playing the game in three dimensions. I still sometimes wonder, though, how old Kees van Aalst would have gone at cricket. I reckon he'd have more than held his own!

Passing Through

As we drove into the small mining town a willy-willy hurtled its red dust spiral across the flats of sparse grey mulga and saltbush. Here and there the afternoon sun glinted in the scattered stones of white quartz, more white against the red earth. The willy-willy picked up balls of prickle bush and bits of paper, hurling them around in a dry fury. It fizzled out just as mysteriously as it had begun. I shivered slightly, recalling somewhere from my childhood that a willy-willy was the spirit of a dead person. I had been to this town before, years ago when I was small. Now it had shrunk to a few dusty boarded-up old hotels and shops. In the distance, rows of white transportable miners' quarters could be seen against a backdrop of gleaming steel towers that caught the last of the afternoon sun.

The only sign of occupancy in the town was the old service station with its neon sign that announced '24 H urs ervic' in a flickering ethereal blue. We were hot and tired from the last long stretch. A cold drink was all we needed, fill the tank, and we'd be off on the last leg of our journey to see Aunty Aida. Charlie wheeled in over the crunch of gravel, hitting a few potholes gone rock hard since the last rains. Puffs of red dust caught up with us as we pulled into the petrol pump. We both got out and stretched, saddle sore and slightly irritable. Our kids, Peter, nine, and Sean, seven, were squabbling in the back seat.

'Come on you two, stop the fighting and off to the toilet. We'll get a drink in a minute.' I felt a little guilty at being so cross with them, after all, the trip was long and we didn't have too much further to travel now.

As Charlie filled the tank, I felt eyes upon me. Turning I saw two old men sitting beneath a tumble-down trellised rotunda on the median strip of the wide street. A memory of the very same rotunda flashed through my mind. It was grand then, coated regularly with whitewash, rough to the touch. As a child I had swung round and round the central post while waiting for Mum to get the stores from the co-op. Where was the co-op?

The old men sat, shaded. I peered across.

'G'day,' I called to them. They both tipped their heads towards me and touched their hats. I smiled back and looked away; I did not want to embarrass them by staring. They were the only sign of life around, as far as I could see.

'Let's go and have a yarn,' I said to Charlie. 'I need to stretch my legs a bit. What about you?'

'Yeah, but not too long. I want to get there before dark, you know.'

Once Charlie begins a trip he wants to travel non-stop. Trips for him revolve around how we are making time, how long the tank of petrol will last and at what rate the car is using petrol. No scenic tours for Charlie. No siree! Get in, get going, get there! That's Charlie.

I strolled over to the old chaps, stopping a little way back. Perhaps they didn't want to talk to anyone. Both wore hats, one grey and the other khaki, both dusty and sweat-stained around the band. Although it was hot, they both wore old suit coats and white shirts buttoned to the neck, with trousers tied up with twine and red-dusty white sandshoes, no laces. 'G'day,' I said again. Once again they nodded, tipping the brim of their hats lightly. I shuffled a little, feeling a little foolish, put one hand on a hip while the other brushed back damp hair and looked around at nothing in particular.

'Hot today,' I ventured.

'Always 'ot 'ere,' the one with the grey hat said.

'True, true,' the other said. He seemed to be looking towards Charlie and the kids coming out of the service station. Charlie was telling the boys to stop and look to the left and look to the right before crossing the road. I grinned to myself. There wasn't a car within earshot, let alone sight. Good old Charlie, fussing again.

Charlie is a Koori, Melbourne born and bred, so he doesn't really appreciate this part of the country, although I'm sure he would if he could just stop and take the time to look around. Me, well, I was fostered out around about eight years of age, but this is the first time that I've been able to get back this way for years. The last time I came through on a bus we didn't stop, even though it was a busy little town. I wondered about the old chaps. Who were they and what in heaven's name were they doing in this ghost town?

Walking over to them I thrust out my hand. 'Margie,' I said, 'and this is my husband, Charlie. Charlie Rome, he's from the eastern states. And our boys, Peter and Sean.'

'Mum,' my youngest, Sean, whined. 'Let's go, I don't like it here and the toilet's real funny. I'm not using a toilet that's just a seat with a big hole in the ground!'

I shooshed him, not wanting my kids sounding like whinging city slickers. I shook the old proffered hands, cool and dry. Charlie tried to poke a hand out, unsuccessfully juggling cans of drink.

'Bert Nanding,' the grey-hatted fellow murmured, 'and this is my Uncle Sam.'

I could see now that Uncle Sam was the older of the two, though it was hard to gauge Bert's age. They both rose slightly and tipped their hats, sitting down again in unison. Nothing was said for a few minutes and the kids and Charlie were getting fidgety. I began to feel a little embarrassed, fiddling with my hair and straightening my tee shirt. I looked up the road in the direction we were to head.

'Goin' far?' Bert asked softly.

'Just up to the next town,' Charlie answered before I could. 'That's if this woman doesn't take up too much of your time. Wanna get there by dark.' Already the afternoon shadows had begun to lengthen.

'Plenty time,' Uncle Sam said, not looking in our direction.

The realisation that he was blind hit me. I looked at him more closely. His eyes were whitened by cataracts. His face was covered in a fine growth of white whiskers, and strands of white hair stuck out from under the hat. Both had skin an ancient deep, deep brown.

We all sipped the ice cold cans. I held mine to my face, savouring the cool. Charlie kept one eye on his watch and the other on the boys. Five minutes or so of silence had passed and I began to think that I had imposed, perhaps the two old chaps hadn't even wanted company.

It had suddenly occurred to me that we weren't being very hospitable, so I thrust my drink towards them. 'Want a drink?' They both shook their heads.

'Git one later,' Bert said.

'True, true,' nodded Uncle Sam.

'Live around here?' The minute I had said it I realised what a ridiculous question it was.

'Born 'n' bred,' Bert replied.

'True, true. Born 'n' bred,' Uncle Sam confirmed, nodding slowly.

A few more minutes of silence passed. Charlie made off to stop the boys throwing stones at the old tin hut across the road. I was about to say goodbye when Uncle Sam said, 'Where your people come from?'

'Oh, I was fostered out when I was little to some wadjellas, you know, wajbullas. Down south, near Albany. But my grandfather, he was from up this way, he's gone now, poor old fulla. But that's where we're going now, to see his sister, Aunty Aida. You might know her.'

'Yes, we know your people, but we don't see anyone much now, 'less they're passin' through. Good people, good woman, your aunty. Never see anyone go without.'

'True, true,' Uncle Sam concluded.

'Them fullas don't know 'bout it,' Uncle Sam stated. I thought he was referring to my aunty's generosity.

'What's that, Uncle?'

''Bout the gold,' Uncle Sam said. He had lowered his voice conspiringly, though there was no one else in sight. 'Them fullas,' he said contemptuously. 'Them fullas,' and pointed his lips and chin towards the distant mining camp. 'I seen it when I was a youngster, 'bout thirteen. Big seam of quartz full up with it. I been blind for years but I can still see it shinin' in the sun.'

Bert interjected. 'Uncle knows, but he won't tell anybody. I tol' 'im you gotta go out there and peg it or somebody will find it with them detectors. They jump in the four wheel drives and go for miles. Course 'e can't see, so maybe 'e'll take me there one day, tell me the way.'

I wondered why we were being told this. It sounded as though Uncle Sam didn't tell just anybody this story. I wanted to know more.

'So ... Uncle ... when you gunna go and find it? Somebody might beat you to it.'

'True, true. But I been thinking lately. Betta go out there. Maybe big rains this winter an' we'll get bogged. 'Aven't seen a flood for a while now. Flood time this year … might be.'

Charlie was beginning to get impatient. 'Margie, we gotta get going soon. Besides, I don't like this place either.' He had lowered his voice so as not to appear disrespectful. I couldn't believe how jittery he was. More so than usual.

'Wait a while, Charlie. Uncle, that gold. Far from here?'

He jutted his jaw to somewhere about east. I looked off in that direction. The mulga flats went far to the horizon. An unruly squabble of galahs were settling in for the night a little way over.

'Rough country. Should be all right with a good motor, but.'

My mind began to race. 'Charlie, maybe we could take Bert and Uncle?' I ventured.

'Margie don't even think about it. We got no time. Could take days. No, at least not at this time.' He softened his words a little, then hustled the boys back to the car. We'd only stopped for half an hour or so, but it seemed an age. I was hooked, not wanting to leave, yet realising we couldn't go bush, just like that. Or could we?

'Bert, your family around?' I asked.

'Nah. Just me an' Uncle. We both bachelors. But I tell you something. We find that gold we'll 'ave plenty 'lations!' He pushed his hat back to scratch his head, laughing.

'True, true,' Uncle Sam agreed, smiling. He raised an arm with palm oustretched. 'Yep … I can see it shinin' in the sun. Only tell my people 'bout it. Don't tell wajbullas. They hear 'bout it and ask me. I say no. Only stories. Nothing, no gold. Only stories.'

Charlie yelled from the car that we had to hurry up, that we had to get there before midnight.

'Look, Uncle,' I turned back to the old men, 'maybe we can see you on the way back, and me and Charlie could take you there soon, make arrangements … we're only staying at Aunty Aida's for a couple of days then we'll be passing back through. We'll check where you might be at the service station.'

Charlie yelled for me to hurry, the car was idling. I dashed across, turning and yelling back to them, 'See you in a coupla days!' They dipped their heads slightly and touched their hats.

I thought I heard Bert say, 'Righto, much obliged.'

Charlie revved up the car and roared off spraying gravel and dust. I turned back to peer out the back window as we travelled up the road.

'That's funny, Charlie. I can't see them. They must've gone to get that drink.'

'How can you see anything through this West Aussie bulldust?' Charlie retorted. 'Speaking of not seeing anything, Margie, there was nobody serving in the shop. I rang the bell a few times to pay for the petrol and drinks. Couldn't see anybody about so I just left the money under the bell on the counter. A very dusty counter too. They were probably out the back or something. Time doesn't mean much in the bush. Though you'd reckon they'd smarten up their act for the mining camp business. Anyway I got the creeps back there, that's why I wanted to get going.'

'What do you mean, Charlie? Those old fellows probably don't get to have a yarn much anymore, and that gold story, it's got to be true. That's the trouble with you, you don't take enough time to find out about people and things. I think we should try and help 'em out somehow.'

It darkened as we travelled on and the boys fell asleep after exhausting their repertoire of school songs. Charlie concentrated on the road for roos. I laid my head back on the headrest thinking about the hard life old Bert and Uncle Sam must have had. Surely the least we could do was help them find that gold so they could end their days comfortably, and it'd be fun for us. Who knows? We might be able to go shares. We'd talk to Aunty Aida, she'd know about it, surely.

'Charlie, we'll talk about that story with Aunty Aida, all right?'

'Margie, it's probably just one of those stories, love, don't get excited about it, okay? It'd be nice though, wouldn't it? To see them two old blokes get something from what is their land anyway.' That was all we said the whole last stretch. I dozed off to be woken by Charlie touching me gently on the arm telling me we were nearly there.

Aunty's house was all lit up and full of cousins, nephews and nieces waiting for us. Peter and Sean were bouncing around with energy pent up from the long trip. After hugs and kisses and greetings all round, Aunty served a big pot of kangaroo stew with bread and butter. We washed it down with large mugs of milky sweet tea, just as I knew it somewhere in my childhood memory. We settled the kids down, as it was late and we wanted to have a quiet chat to Aunty before camping down.

'Aunty, we met two old blokes, Bert and Sam … Narnding … I think they said, back at the last stop. We had a good yarn, and Uncle Sam told us about a reef he wants to go back to find … to

230

peg it. Seen it when he was a boy, he said. Have you heard anything about this story, Aunty?'

Charlie was looking resigned at my insistence at following up on the story. Aunty was quiet.

'Who you say you saw, girl?'

'Bert and Sam … Narnding.' I looked at Aunty. Her face was as pale as pale.

'Don't talk silly, Margie. Them two old fullas passed away years ago. Lookin' for a reef, they were, and we 'ad the worst floods we could remember that year. They got washed away from their camp in the middle of the night, or so people say. Couldn't find them poor fullas. Looked everywhere. You musta been talkin' to somebody else. Besides, that petrol station been closed for a year or more, now.'

Charlie and I locked eyes, a shiver raced through me. I grabbed his hand. He said nothing.

Charlie and I didn't mention that incident to anyone else but Aunty. Just the three of us silently shared that strange afternoon. We saw on the television news a few weeks after we got home that the very same little deserted town we passed through had recorded some of the heaviest flooding in thirty years. That was some time ago. Still, I dream of a rain-washed reef; the sparkling white quartz ablaze with gold in late afternoon sun, and two smiling old men.

The Royal Show

The girls from the Aboriginal hostel were so excited at going to the Royal Show. Some were going for the first time.

They had all come to Perth to go to high school in the city and now it was Show time. For weeks they had worried and wondered about what they would wear and now here they were, all decked out in their best dresses and eagerly looking around them while deciding where to go and what to do.

Some wanted to see the displays in the exhibition halls while others wanted to go at once to side-show alley, where all the rides and stalls were. Finally they decided to split into two groups and wander around the show grounds looking at all the different games to play, shows to see and things to buy.

Maisie, who was one of the older girls, was chosen to lead one group and Patsy was to lead the other. While Patsy and her group wanted to go to side-show alley first, Maisie's group decided to go to the halls where the displays were.

Their supervisor, Mrs Greenhalgh, who was in charge of them at the hostel, had told the girls to stick together in groups, to look out for each other and to be back at the hostel before dark. With Maisie was Beryl, Alice, Lizzie, Fay, Rosie and Susie. They were the quieter girls who didn't want to spend their hard-earned pocket money all at once. They much preferred to see the displays and the animals before tackling the wonders of side-show alley. It was still early in the day and if they could wait until the afternoon, they could buy their lunch and have all the rest of their money to spend how they wanted to.

After wandering through the exhibition halls, looking at all the articles on display such as the flowers, needlework, cooking and the rest of the exhibits people had sent in from all over the state, they made their way over to the side shows. They had bought hot dogs and lemonade for their lunch and felt they could now buy showbags and anything else that took their fancy.

Some of the younger girls bought kewpie dolls, while others won small furry animals on the open-mouthed clowns, the dart games or the shooting gallery where you got the chance to shoot at moving targets.

There were so many people milling around and lining up for rides on the ferris wheel, the octopus, the merry-go-round, bumper cars and other rides that at times some of the girls lost sight of Maisie and the rest of their group.

Alice, Susie and Fay became separated from Maisie and the rest when they decided to go on the ghost train. The three girls screamed and screamed all the while. They dodged creepy crawlies that touched their arms, and ducked low at the shape of a ghost coming towards them. They yelled their heads off at the skeletons dangling from the roof of the train and swatted bats that flew towards them from out of nowhere. By the end of the ride, they were exhausted with yelling and glad to get out of that spooky place.

After regaining their breath, Alice, Fay and Susie looked around and couldn't see the bigger girls anywhere, so they decided to wander further up the alley to see what was on offer there. They passed a stall selling fairy floss and each bought a packet. Further up they saw Maisie in the distance and headed over to her and Beryl, Lizzie and Rosie, who were looking up in front of a tent, giggling their heads off.

In front of the girls was a boxing tent with loudspeakers blaring. On a high platform just outside the tent was a sturdy plank where some young men were standing in their boxer's shorts. One was beating on a drum in time to the spruiker's spiel about the expertise of all the boxers. By the time Fay, Alice and Susie had arrived, a big crowd of people was gathered. Some young men were jeering in the crowd and heckling the spruiker, saying that his men couldn't fight anything and were a lot of sissies. The spruiker was answering them back and daring them to go into the tent and have a go. Words flew back and forth as the crowd grew. The excitement was tangible as tempers flared and challenges were flung left and right.

Yet the girls were still giggling amid all the insults and the younger girls wondered what was so funny for the bigger girls to be laughing like that. Maisie and the others would look up at the boxers who were prancing around in very colourful shorts on the plank, the makeshift stage. Most of the men were Aborigines and Maisie and the older girls were flirting outrageously with some of them. When the men would shadow-box on stage, they would look at the girls and grin cheeky grins as much as to say, 'Look at me, I'm solid, eh?'

The girls would laugh hilariously and move closer to the plank for a better look. What the boxers did not know was that the girls were looking up their wide-legged boxer shorts and getting a good view of what was underneath. Some didn't even wear underpants and the girls could see their plums under the brightly coloured shorts.

But soon, a couple of the boxers cottoned on to what was going on with the girls, they were so embarrassed and quickly closed their legs. When some of the boxers shook their fists at the girls and promised to get them after the show, Maisie and the older girls knew the game was up and they made a hasty exit from the boxing tent.

They ran away looking back and laughing at those fighters, knowing very well that they would never see them again. The older girls laughed all the way to the railway station and back to the hostel. They all declared later that it was one of the best Royal Shows they ever had the chance to see.

The Disappointment

I had a somewhat hard life, the way I see it. I have my family of fourteen and there is my mother and father who I do not see much because I was brought up in missions in this state of WA.

I was born in Carnarvon on an Aboriginal Reserve in 1957. I have a twin brother. We both had a hard time, but I am telling this story about how I see my life then and now.

To me, life back then was the best of times because things were simple. I could understand the simple things like running around and having fun, getting into a lot of things that were a no-no. Boy, when it was a no-no with mum and dad, look out! Out would come the strap and I knew it was time to run and run. I did, till I came home for a feed and sleep. I hit the roof when dad hit my bottom. I think my bottom was black and blue. He hit the living daylights out of me. I ran to my Pop to hide but that was no good at all for I knew deep down I was wrong.

The most disappointing time in my life was when I was taken away by the Native Welfare. I did not see my mother or father until Christmas time, and I was very lucky to get to see them at all. I went to seven different missions in my young life. To me it was very hard to cope with. They took me away from my mum, dad, and my brothers and sisters. I only knew them when I was young. I thought I did mum and dad wrong, but that was not it at all. I found out later in my life that it was good in a way for me to go to some other place. But they ripped me from my family and I thought I would never see them again.

I'm now a young man. Back then, in the 1970s, I got to know both my mother and father when I was in my teens. I knew in my heart who they were and I know that I will always love both and nothing in my life will ever take that away from me.

I never get things right. I got on the wrong side of the law and ever since then, that's all I've been doing, running from the law. I blamed my family for what I have become. I did not blame myself. Everyone but me. Why did I do things that were not my fault, only the other guy's? I have been in and out of boys' homes. I blamed my family until I got a little older, in my early twenties. Now I know gaol; I found it hard. It was the end of my life. When they locked the cell door on me I cried to myself. I knew this was the end for me. The outside world I will see no more. I am still behind bars. What a disappointment I am to myself and my family.

Helpless

I am sitting in a world of four walls, helpless, waiting for news I do not like to hear. The news that families do not want to hear and that's bad news, news of loved ones; something has gone wrong or even worse. I feel helpless in a place where you can never do anything to help your family and loved ones.

This is hard on me because I am doing time. I know that I have let my loved ones down and I'm not there to help them when they need me the most. I can't help at all with these four walls keeping me in. I feel helpless in a world of high wire which keeps me in and keeps them out. They only come in on weekends or on days when you don't like to hear what they have to tell you. If they can't come in, a phone call can bring a man to his knees and make him cry to himself in his cell. And think. But all you can think of is nothing. Your mind runs in top gear and you get nowhere. I know because I am on that road of helplessness and I know what it can do to a man in this place. It's a very lonely road.

I have had mates come up to me and shake my hand. In this place your mates can do little for you but they try to help. All you want is to be alone in your cell and think of the good times you had with the loved one you have lost. You wish, 'if only I was out, could this have been different or what?'

Your mind runs around and around. You can't stop drinking coffee or tea and smoking a packet of cigarettes in a night, looking out of your window with bars and looking at the fence, wishing that you were on the other side. But you know that you are helpless because you put yourself in this place of helplessness. But you know that your mates are there to see you through this time of your bad news. Without them what have you got? Nothing. I thank them for being there in this world of emptiness.

To You from Me

Dark was the day you left me,
my sorrow would overcome,
for you broke my spirit,
the spirit that set me free.

So here am I,
in your prison cell,
doing what you think best,
what you think best for me.

Why have you left me all so sudden?
can't you see that I'm in sorrow?
do you not care for me?
for forgiveness is in my heart,
what have I done for you to forgive me?

Long were the days that followed,
you were not to be seen,
for without your persecution,
sorrow would not be with me.
So to you I write these words,
in hope it will break the conspiracy,
that you would give me back my spirit,
and leave my mind at ease.

Forever is yet to come,
visions I have not seen,
but I have seen now,
and it does not please me.

Civilised is a word you brought with you,
you think it is for me,
but we come from different worlds,
will you ever see?

My Sea

Through the sea of forgetfulness
I wander to find distant old memories

Memories that burn when thought
as my feet do when touched by scorching sand

I shall not walk without the scorch
as the sand boils within me

My soles ache to find rest
as in the comfort of a soothing cool

Though I long to ponder through these memories
I know the consequences they clasp

As a man of desire I am yet a child
with no wisdom or understanding

If I could only shun these yearnings
my pain could be diminished

If I would not seek the sea of forgetfulness
I would find contentment in my present

I am troubled to see myself in years to pass
still pondering my mind for images I horde

If all the pain-felt thoughts I keep remain
I am lost and have not gained

Time of Change

I am an Aboriginal from the south-west of Western Australia and was born into the Nyoongah People. My parents are both Nyoongahs. My first memory is a very vague picture of me and some other children being taken for a ride (pardon the pun) in a vehicle, which was a blue coloured bus. I am still unsure of the validity of this first memory; all I can say is that it has never gone away. I believe this fateful day was 5 December 1960, and I and my fellow riders were being taken to a place where we, as wards of the State, were supposed to spend the rest of our time until we turned eighteen years of age. The full name of this place was the Saint Francis Xavier Pallotine Mission Wandering, or plain old Wandering Mission for short. This place is situated approximately two hundred kilometres from Perth going southward.

When I 'checked in' I was only three years old and when I finally went home to my mother I was about fifteen. I didn't leave officially, as was their plan. I left by my plan; I ran away. Three times, in fact, before I found out where my mother lived. The other two times I ran away, I didn't know where to go so I made my way, sheepishly, back to the Mission, to be given the usual chastisement of the day for those who transgressed, and no, it was not a verbal caning. I'm sure you can imagine, or know, what discipline they used in those times to encourage a change of heart.

I think clarification is needed here: I only ran away from Wandering Mission after I had been seconded to do my high school education at the Pallotine Mission in Rossmoyne, which is in Perth. It was here that I completed first and second year but whilst doing third year I began to get an overwhelming urge to be reunited with my mother. Mind you, I had often thought about this before but had pushed it out of my head believing that it was an impossibility. Where would I start? I hadn't the faintest. It seemed that as I grew older the need to be with my mother became stronger. Normally, at this stage one would be looking to leave home, but because of my situation it was the time to be returning home, whatever and wherever that was. So my mind was made up for sure this time; I needed to be with my family, at their home.

Something really weird happened a little while after I had made up my mind to go, even to this day I can't explain it. Maybe I was just overwhelmed at the time, I don't know, but somebody seemed to slip a piece of paper into my hand very secretly. This had an address on it. I still can't say whether I was conscious of the transaction at the time because I have never been able to clearly visualise the event.

To me this remains a mystery but I am thankful to that person, whoever it was. So if you are reading this, thanks.

I can honestly say that my Mission days were a constant, mixture of fun and sadness. I was an emotional wreck by the time I came out, I didn't know whether I was Arthur or Martha, so to speak. It was a real culture shock for me when I first made contact with my people. All those years in the Mission with a structured routine, each day knowing what you were required to do automatically, and then to come into a place where anything goes and usually did; (excessive) drinking, fighting, stealing, this really blew me away as I had never before witnessed this type of behaviour and I was scared, and I didn't know what to do. So I gathered that 'if you can't beat them, join them'. And so began a life of misery with the drink, drugs, crime and everything else that goes with this promiscuous lifestyle and I acted (at least outwardly) as if I didn't care what was going on. This show lasted for many years even after I settled down with a woman and had children. I used many, many strategies in my endeavours to straighten myself out but, alas, could not overcome the urges to live a carefree life with all its fun, although I suffered the consequences — physically, emotionally and mentally — for my actions. I would not or rather could not, quit. I was hook, line and sinkered but didn't want to admit it.

My story is exactly the same as many of the kids who grew up in the Mission system and then found themselves summarily detached from that comfortable system and struggling to understand this 'new' system called Freedom. We were brought up to be like the white man and then when we went home, we were told to behave like a black man. This really confused me so I just copied what my new-found peers were doing and most of this was of a rebellious nature. Naturally, like all kids, I wanted to fit in and did what the biggest and the loudest in our group wanted us to do. This led to a lot of heartache, not only for me but also for my mother.

Unless you have been in a similar situation you cannot fully appreciate the emotional confusion and degradation that many 'Mission kids' endured for many years after, and still endure in many cases. On a positive note I honestly believe the Mission (apart from a few other things) prepared me for the outside world by giving us daily chores and tasks to do. This commitment and familiarisation with work has always stayed with me and has ensured my own and my family's survival. Although I dislike work, like possibly 99.9 per cent of the population, the Mission, I believe, instilled in me the value of working, and work I have. I still remember that, for the boys, the Dairy was the most popular place of employment because, after we had finished hand-milking the cows and doing the other duties, we would sit down with a big, steaming enamel mug of fresh milk straight from the udder. To us children this was definitely the highlight of the day. For those who don't know, Wandering has always been the coldest place in Western Australia and I can vouch for that, but when we had those steaming, hot mugs in our little hands we were in seventh heaven, nothing else mattered. Then we were rudely jarred back to reality by the sound of the old bell alerting us to the fact that it was now time to go to classes. Never mind, the next day we'd do it all over again and maybe we'd get to eat a couple of fresh raw eggs, too lovely. So you see (for me at least), it wasn't all doom and gloom at this particular Mission. We had everything that we could want in terms of material comfort, but there was something that they could never give us, and this was the thing we needed the most; the love of our parents.

In my case, because I'd been taken away at such a young age, I could not remember what it was like to be with my parents but in my heart I knew that that was the place I desired to be, wherever that was. To be quite truthful, for me the novelty wore off very quickly after I returned home. I suppose there are many factors that contribute to this (a psychologist could have a field day identifying them). In fairness to my people I can say that I am grateful to have returned home to my own kind and do believe that they loved me dearly, but I feel there was a lack of support once a child had left the Mission. Basically you were thrown out the door and told to fend for yourself. I realise there was a lack of support services available back in those days, but I still believe there could have been a lot more consideration and after-care planning. It was this negligence that had a major impact upon many ex-Mission kids, myself included, and has severely affected every part of our lives and unfortunately, has extended to our children and their children.

After leaving the Mission I spent the next few years experimenting with many substances in an attempt to escape reality or cover the pain of the past, and when I could no longer live like this I spent many hours and years thinking about and putting into practice strategies that attempted to address my problems. I was not very successful and continued to slowly destroy myself whilst attempting to look as if I had everything under control. This miserable state continued for many years.

When all seemed lost I remembered what the Mission taught us, that there was a God who could and would help you if you cried out to him in times of trouble. At first I thought this was a bit silly, but as the pain increased I began to appreciate this option and finally made an impassioned plea to this invisible God. I was sick of my life and knew I needed to change it radically before time ran out for me. I had tried everything else so why not seek help from this so-called Creator. If he created me, he should look after me. I can now truthfully say that for me help came immediately and I could write pages and pages giving testimony to the many times God has revealed Himself to me in answer to my prayers. So as you can see, I am now a committed Christian who believes in the Lord Jesus Christ and believes that He offers peace and forgiveness to all who would call on Him and I am a true witness to this fact. My life now has meaning and purpose and I now truly possess the love that I so earnestly desired as a child and also as an adult. Many who know me are amazed and can testify to the radical change that has taken place in my life.

The Day I Call Round-up Time

As a child, I was brought up in a little town called Woodanilling in the lower part of Western Australia.

I lived with my grandparents, Mr and Mrs Tim Quartermaine, who owned a farm three miles out of town. We always had lots of food and we were very happy with our grandparents. Wherever they went, we were there. Grandad was an old bloke, but was still working for other farmers. My grandparents were the only ones my sister, Fay, and I had. We saw Mum on the farm once or twice, but when she left, we didn't really care because we had Grandad and Nan to look after us. We loved Mum but we knew she'd married Bill Cox and we didn't fit in with his way of life. As the years passed I got more and more attached to my grandparents. We used to go out with them while they worked. Clearing land and burning off so the land was ready to plough and seed.

One day as we were coming home from shopping, a man picked us up and said he was from the Native Welfare Department and started to talk to Pop and Nan. I looked at Nan and saw tears in her eyes. Pop was angry and started to argue with the man, who I now understand was a welfare officer. My sister and I grabbed onto Nan and Pop. We told them we'd never leave them. They were the only things we had going for us.

That night everyone was quiet as we sat around the open fire. Pop told us that the welfare officer had said that he and Nan were too old to look after us. As I watched Pop and Nan, tears flowed from their eyes. I put my arm around Pop and said, 'If they take me away from you, I'll run away and come home and look after you and Nan.'

The longer we talked of what was going to happen to us, the more I started to think, why was the Welfare taking us away from our home? At the time I was nine years old, but this stuck in my mind for days until Pop and Nan said we were going to Katanning, because the Welfare Department was taking us to court. They said we were not being looked after. As we neared Katanning I jumped off the cart and tried to run away but was caught. I started to think, what were they going to do with us? Were my sister and I going to be separated from one another? I said to my sister, 'Let's run away and if anything happens we'll always be together.' But Fay was older than me and said, 'I'll look after you, brother. We've got to fight this out together. If we lose Pop and Nan we have no one.'

So we walked into the courtroom and I saw this red-faced bastard staring at us. The police were there talking to Pop and Nan and said that they had to sit in the other seats away from us. I tried to hold onto Pop but was pushed away by a police officer. I tried to kick and punch, but was forced to sit down and see what was going to happen to us. Pop tried to argue with the Welfare and the police. Then I heard them say they were going to send Fay and Tom to Marribank Mission. Before I could run the police had hold of me and Fay. They led us to a VW van where the missionary was waiting to take us to the mission. Mr Brutone was the Superintendent at the time. As we took off, I said, 'I'll get you bastards for taking me and my sister away.' I was told by Mr Brutone that if I kept crying and saying things, I'd be given a flogging when we got to the mission.

Fay held me and said, 'Come on, brother. Be quiet and then they won't belt you.' The hate I felt toward the Welfare and police I held back inside my mind.

Finally, we arrived at the mission. There weren't many kids at this time. Fay was dropped off at the girls' dorm first. Then I was taken to where the boys lived at the top part of the mission. I was taken into the dormitory and told that I would be living here till I was eighteen years old.

As I said before, I was only nine years old at this time. The hate grew in my mind as the years passed. I ran away about ten times to go home to Pop and Nan's. They made me and cousin Peter undertake work before breakfast. Milking the cows by hand then chopping wood. After breakfast we had to clean the hall, wash up dishes, make our beds then go off to school. All this time I'd only seen Pop and Nan when I ran away. We didn't have shoes or boots to wear to work. Later I was suspended from school and made to work on the farm.

One day I came home from milking the cows and as I walked past the girls' dormitory, one of the girls said that Fay was crying. I became angry and ran to the dormitory where I was grabbed and thrown to the ground and sat upon by four of the mission men. Then I was dragged off into the office where I was flogged with a bellyband that is used on horse saddles. For the next week I could hardly sit or walk. I told the missionary who had flogged me, 'You can kill me, but if you hurt my sister I'll kill you all one by one.'

At this time I was fourteen years old. I tried to fight back the hate that was starting to get the best of me.

One day I saw Fay coming towards me with hands open. She said, 'Come here, brother, we have to stick together from now on. There's only me and you here.' Mum had died. We were taken to the funeral. We were leaving and Pop came to me and said, 'I wish you were allowed to come home and work on the farm. This is going to be yours one day.'

I looked at Pop. He looked tired and sick. I knew I was going to lose him some day. I hugged him and Nan. I said, 'I'll be there to help you Pop. We can do things together.'

We said goodbye that day, but I didn't think things would happen so fast. A week later I got a message that Pop was found dead on the farm. I became angry and ran away back to the old farm where I saw my relations drinking and saying how they would get the farm and Fay and myself would get nothing. Not that I cared, I just loved Nan and Pop. I was taken back to the mission, and I spoke to the Superintendent and told him, 'If I am going to be flogged you'll have to kill me.' The hate was growing inside me. I was let off and was told after the funeral that they were going to do something with me.

After the funeral was over, Fay was sent to Bridgetown to work. I was sent to Pingelly to work for a farmer named Mr Monks. I worked for twelve months. I came back to the mission where I was told my pay would be waiting for me. I was given two pounds ten shillings and a thirteen ounce cloth and dropped off in Katanning. I was left to get on the best way I could.

At the time I didn't know where to go so I headed to Woodanilling where Nan now lived in town because they had sold the farm. But by the time I arrived in Woodanilling the feelings between myself and my family grew into hate. I loved Nan; she was all I had now. I got odd jobs around town. I started to drink and fight with my people then got mixed up with the police. I left home and started running from town to town. Work, drink and fight. Then the day came when I was grabbed by the police in Perth. The officer was one of the ones from the court when I was sent to the mission. I could remember his face — Sergeant Traler. I said, 'Not this time, it's my turn.' I went blank. I was seventeen years old at the time. The memories of what the Welfare and the police did to Pop and Nan came racing back to me. Nothing could stop me. I was sent to Longmore Detention Centre and later let out. I roamed the Perth streets.

In my later years I spent a lot of time in prison, but not for serious offences. To me, if I had been left with my grandparents things would have been better, and the hate would not have been there towards police and welfare.

Many years have passed now, but the memories are still there. Today my job is that of a Support Officer here at Greenough Regional Prison where I've been given the chance to help others who have problems with the past. I know it is not easy to put things behind you, but by working with others who are having problems with police and other things, I can come to terms with myself. The only friends we have left are the ones we call 'Bro' or 'Sis'. While I was in a home and the mission it was hard for me to let out things that had happened to the other kids and me. We have to live with the past. No one else seems to care whether we last or what was done to us, and our old ones, who have been laid to rest, are a lot better off then we'll ever be.

I tell my kids about things like having no dole and no one to turn to. In those days you had to work or you got nothing. It was good in one way; you knew you had to work to survive or be sent to prison for sleeping in parks, no money and drunk. All those things happened to me and made it hard for me to trust the police and welfare. I've lost the things I once loved and looked forward to in life. Today I live for love and the ones who are in need. In prison I can show them support which I and others didn't have and try to break down some of the barriers that we are still facing in life today.

Let's say the Welfare has done the best for us, but they don't know what we went through: floggings and some were raped. But there wasn't anyone to listen to our problems. To me, it was round-up time for the welfare and police, so they could have fun breaking up families who cared for each other. I don't think memories of the past will ever leave me and many others till we are gone. Giving us money will never heal the feeling that I have in my heart for what I have lost.

My Christmas Holidays in Perth

My name is Stephen and for the past two years I've been living in Derby, Western Australia with my parents, my brother, and my sister. My family and I come from the Nyoongar people who belong to the south-west of the state. We moved up to Derby when my father got a job transfer.

Derby, in the Kimberley region of Western Australia, was a bit of a shock to me when I first arrived there. It is a small town and very hot and although I'd been there for holidays with my aunt and uncle, I didn't know how it was going to be living there permanently.

My first year in high school at Derby wasn't very good because I found it hard to settle down. I made some good friends, both boys and girls, but now I am on holidays in Perth with my family and so far it has been fun.

We travelled down by car from Derby, a very long trip. Although we had a few minor problems with the car, we still looked forward to arriving in Perth and seeing our relations again. After we had paid our visits to our people, we were free to go and enjoy our holidays. This sounded really good to us kids because we missed all the things the city had to offer which aren't available in Derby. After Christmas dinner, the whole family went fishing in Fremantle. My aunt nearly got pulled into the water by something large on her rod. She lost her hooks and bait and got such a fright that she shouted. We saw a seal swimming near us and all the people were looking at it and throwing their unused bait to it.

A couple of weeks later all my family went to Bunbury to spend the weekend and it was really great to see our mob again. On the way back to Perth, we stopped at Mandurah to find mussels under the Old Bridge and went crabbing in the estuary. That turned out to be a waste of time as we only caught about ten undersized crabs which we had to throw back otherwise my dad would have been fined.

The next week we had a barbecue at our Nan and Pop's place and caught up with the rest of our family. Now it is time to return to Derby because my parents have to work and us kids have to get ready for the coming school year. But it's been raining up north and there's been reports that a cyclone has caused flooding. I don't mind because we can spend a little bit more time in Perth. But soon, I suppose, the roads will be open and I won't have any excuse not to go back to Derby. Never mind, on the whole I had a good holiday and can't wait to return to Perth for the next Christmas holidays.

From God, the Devil and Me

When I was a very young child growing up in New Norcia Mission in the late 1950s and early 1960s, the priests, brothers and nuns used very cruel words to us Aboriginal children. Thinking back on it now, I remember being afraid of God. They used God as an executioner, like, for instance, if you commit a sin you will forever burn in the flames of Hell. Imagine saying that to a seven-year-old child. How the government in that era must have felt with their pompous attitude, not only to small Aboriginal children, but to adults also. For the sake of good common sense: why? Why did they do this to us? Did these people of good Christian values inherit the values of murderers, rapists, thieves and liars? Why, after committing such atrocities, did they tell themselves that God loves them and they will enter into the Kingdom of Heaven?

As a child, like I said, I was so afraid of God that I would welcome the thunder, lightning, hail and the darkest night rather than someone coming down from the heavens to send me to Hell. They made Hell such a ferocious and evil place. I think we kids have grown up rebelling against the same God who society says is kind, caring and loving. How many gods are there? Did the white people make this God up and make us Aboriginals bow and pray to him? I wonder if they prayed to him like we did. I think now, when I die and go to their heaven and see some of the people who banished us in our own country, I'll be asking that God for a transfer to wherever.

Hurting for my mother at the age of seven, I decided then and there I had to communicate with her and my father on a reserve somewhere in the bush. But how? It was impossible. That's when I grabbed a pencil and paper. With tears in my eyes I wrote a small poem to God, asking him to look after my Mum and Dad. Imagine a seven-year-old kid writing a poem to God, whom he was afraid of, but not afraid to ask God to help his mother and father; not to help the lonely and sad child in a mission where there were great big statues of Jesus, Mary and Joseph around, but two wonderful people who were also hurting for their small son.

When I was seven or eight, my friend had eight marbles and I, seven. I decided to get even with him and stole a couple of marbles off one of the other boys who, in turn, told the Brother on me. The Brother took me to his office and lectured me on stealing. He gave me three cuts on each hand and told me I wasn't going to amount to anything. I can still hear his words very clearly spinning inside my head: 'Taylor, you're never going to make it in life. When you get out of here, you are going to get a flagon of plonk, find yourself a shady tree and drink yourself to death.' Being so young, with tears in my eyes, my hands clasped in prayer, I nodded and said, 'Yes, Brother, I'm gunna do all those things when I grow up.' Little did I know that alcohol was to play a very important part in my life. Not only yesterday but, more importantly, today.

The reason why I agreed with the Brother at that time was that I thought that God was passing those words down to the Brother who in turn passed them on to me. What a stupid child I was! I still consider myself stupid today. In the mission, never mind how hard we tried, we were never complimented. Even after I got my first book out, which is called *Singer Songwriter* published by Magabala Books, when people were complimenting me, I just couldn't accept that they were talking to me. I was totally embarrassed or, as the Nyoongahs would say, choo, shame, shame. Even when I got my second book out, *Winds*, in late 1994, I had to have a belly full of alcohol in me to realise that I can actually write. Even now while writing this, I still have my doubts.

Maybe that Brother was right. Or maybe white society looked upon us Aboriginals as pissheads and we played the part to perfection. Like I said earlier, about my life while in the mission, alcohol was the foundation of my life. I was about nine when I was told I had to become an altar boy, which I thought was the greatest thing since Moses was found in the bullrushes. Wow, me, Taylor, the greatest fuck-up since the Hunchback of Notre Dame. I said Mass in Latin, but I wasn't allowed to talk in my own Aboriginal language. Deep down I thought, whilst being on the altar, I would be closer to God; try and make friends with him and try not to be afraid.

After learning everything there was to learn about serving on the altar, which I passed with flying colours, I was given my first assignment; serving at the Boy's House where we were all staying. Boy, was I nervous! I could feel the Nyoongah boys' eyes were upon me, just waiting for a fuck-up so they could laugh and tease me afterwards. But it was not to be. I came bursting through the clouds, but my knees were knocking and I was practically wetting myself on God's own altar. The priest was saying the Mass in Latin and I was assisting him in Latin. With the beautiful statues of Jesus, Mary and Joseph, also surrounded by the beautiful paintings of the angels, I was in the midst of so much beauty. I felt bad within myself, remembering the words of the brothers, nuns and priests: 'You are no good little black devils; you people will never amount to anything in your life.'

I lasted about a week at the Boys' House, serving mass, before being promoted to the big church which caters for all the Community in New Norcia; the white college boys, white college girls, Nyoongah girls of Saint Joseph's Orphanage and the Nyoongah boys of Saint Mary's Boys' Orphanage. It's still got me fucked today, why the blackfellas were classified as orphans. We had mums and dads but we were never allowed to see them or they were never encouraged to have contact with us.

I remember after I ran away from New Norcia, through the Nyoongah grapevine I found out that my mother was living in a reserve in Coolgardie. I hitchhiked there immediately from somewhere in WA. I arrived in Coolgardie, asked a few questions and was pointed in the direction where she was staying. It was two kilometres out of town and my heart was thumping. I hadn't seen my mother in ten years or more and was walking at a brisk pace. On approaching her — a small fair-skinned woman, her eyesight was a bit dimmed — I wanted to run to her, but looked at the conditions she and her people were living in. It was disgusting. A little humpy catered for five or six people including my mother. The reserve they were living on wasn't fit for human inhabitants. I wouldn't bury Hitler here, I thought; it would be too cruel.

As I got within talking distance of her, she asked, 'Who are you?' To me that was like a smack in the face.

'It's me, Alf, your son,' I cried, wiping the tears from my eyes.

'But they told me you were dead,' peering closer at my face.

'No, Mum, I'm very much alive,' grabbing her and hugging her. We both hugged each other and I felt our hearts beating as one, as tears streamed down our faces. She told me later on in life that she used to go to the Native Affairs and ask where I was. They used to say, 'G'on, get out of here; Alf Taylor is dead. He died in a mission somewhere.'

I mean, what the fuck could I say.

I promised myself, when I started this project, that it would be Alf Taylor the writer doing this, not the no-good little black devil. It's hard going back down that lonely road of childhood. It hurts real bad, never mind how old you are. Sometimes I wish I had no emotion. That's one of the reasons why alcohol plays a very important part in our community.

Getting back to my first taste of alcohol; it was through Mass that I encountered it. I awakened early, about 5.00am on a winter's morning, to go to the big church for one of the priests, walking there with just shorts and shirt on, no shoes. Those stones seemed to be sharper on a cold dewy morning and they enjoyed attacking cold, skinny feet as I crept along the cold, deserted street and, crossing the Great Northern Highway, headed into the warm sanctuary of the church. Shivering, I put on my red altar boy's robe and white vest, preparing the water and wine plus the holy bread for communion, then rushing to light the candles around the altar. It always fascinated me to look up at the ceiling, to look at all those beautiful paintings. Wandering around, admiring those paintings, head bent back, I sometimes would bump into the pews, or stub my cold toes, or walk with my hands out in front of me like a kid in a dark room. Then and there I wanted to paint like the great painters of Europe.

Realising the priest was not in yet, I hurried to the back of the church where the tomb of the Bishop Salvado was. Looking down on his tomb, there were thoughts of nothing in my head. I mean, here I was, nine years old, looking down at a tomb with a body or a skeleton in it. I wasn't afraid; I searched my head for something to say to him. Here was the remains of a man who came all the way from Spain to convert all the Aboriginals around Victoria Plains: my father, his father and, I guess, his father. There was nothing; I had only the images of those beautiful paintings in my head. Rushing back for a final preparation, I found the altar wine in the cupboard. Taking off the top, I smelt it. Hmmm, I thought, remembering the words that the brother said to me earlier on in my life. I took a mouthful. I coughed and spluttered and had another drink. Within a few minutes all the cold of New Norcia slowly ebbed out of my body. If wine can do this, to one so young, this is great, I thought. It beats all the gods, the Holy Communion, prayers, holidays, Easters, Christmas, ice-cream and lollies.

The priest came in, went to the altar and proceeded to say the Mass. I was nervous, slurring my words, and made quite a few mistakes. I was glad when the Mass was over. There were quite a few occurrences after that with the altar wine. If I was going to drink myself to death under a shady tree when I get out, I thought, why not be the little black devil and drink myself to death in God's House. no one gives a fuck any more. People were buying land, pushing the Nyoongahs out of sight of society. The further away the Nyoongah was from the towns the happier the town people were.

The thing that also fascinated me was how these Spanish brothers, nuns and priests dumped all their Spanish culture upon us Nyoongah kids. I wanted to be a matador when I grew up, killing the bull and giving the rose to the prettiest senorita in the audience. I thought that was very romantic.

The best thing in my young life at New Norcia was that I learned to read and write. To me, they were my weapons. I devoted so much of my time to reading and writing. I ignored the other subjects that were given to us, like arithmetic (ughh), social studies and history — another fucked-up subject I hated, but dare not express my opinion because I'd be flogged. We were told of Captain Cook fighting the natives to take control of their land. I used to look at the pictures of Captain Cook gallantly shooting the natives. I thought the natives were very bad people for not letting this Captain Cook take over their land. Little did I know at the time, those 'natives' were my own people. Those religious people really fucked our heads up. Another fascination, of course, was Mother England. If she farted, we, in Australia, would smell and wallow in it. They taught us so much about Mother England; I'm sure most of us Nyoongah kids said we were related to this great Captain Cook. (I hope no blackfellas skin me alive after reading this.)

I think, no, I'm sure, that writing helped stop me from going insane at a very tender age. I was too shamed to cry for my mum and dad in front of other kids. They would have teased the piss out of me. I know. I gave them just one opportunity. When I was eight or nine, it was a warm summer's evening and the Brother had all us kids around him. The holidays had just finished and a few of the lucky ones, not many, were delightfully telling stories of their mum and dad, about their holidays. I was sitting there listening to all their beautiful stories. Tears were welling up in my eyes; my young heart was aching. The hurt was so intense the floodgates burst open; I tried to stifle a sob, but too late. The sobs from my heart just exploded. The boys all went quiet, the Brother tried to console me and asked what was wrong. I just got up, took off to the toilet, locked the door and managed to quell my sobs. I let the tears run free from my face without making a sound. I managed to perfect the art of crying and not making a sound. The next day the kids called me sissy, girlie, sook and whatever names they could lay their tongues on. After that, even when the priest flogged me with a strap in front of the boys, I didn't cry; even if my legs and hands were stinging, no way.

I found a friend in the pencil whenever I went bush. I would take a piece of paper with me, get away on my own and write letters to my mum and dad or little poems to God asking him to look after them; that I love them with all my heart and I'll be good. The letters I wrote to them were two or three pages long and their addresses would be Paris, Rome or London; I think even New York. For a kid who was nine and very much afraid of God, writing this now, I think I've blown my chances of getting a one-way ticket to heaven. Well, actually, I don't give a fuck anymore. I mean, what I went through as a child and a man, the so-called hell would be a playground for me. Wouldn't it be great pissing on the flames of hell and the devil threatening, 'If you don't stop and behave, I'll send you back to some mission in Australia?' I'd probably say to him, 'Like fuck; I wanna stop here.'

What I also began to take an interest in was the girls. I knew that the Nyoongah girls were born different to us. There were some very pretty girls in the Girls' House; I think I fell in love with all the girls in my grade six or seven class. They all reminded me of the Virgin Mary, the Mother of Christ, the one I always prayed to. I know the ladies of that era are no longer the vibrant virgins of yesterday, but are the grandmothers — beautiful grandmothers — of today. I say this as an old grandfather. If only those girls knew then how us boys used to go

255

to extraordinary lengths to peek up their dresses and try to catch a glimpse of their bloomers. Even the young nuns at the time, they wore these great big flowing habits that covered them from head to toe. We couldn't peek up those things. Trying to undress a nun with your eyes at twelve years old was very frustrating; trying to strip layer after layer of clothing off. We didn't know what the nuns had under that habit. So we settled for the girls.

I remember writing about our school sports day, which I think my faction won and we all enjoyed. A week after that I wrote about it in our school paper and seeing my name in print at twelve years of age, I felt as though I'd just completed painting all those beautiful paintings on the ceiling of our church. Imagine me, Alfred Taylor: I went by that name many, many rains ago. I carried that story and everywhere I went I showed it off; to me it became a second skin. It was, 'Wow, fuckin' plus.'

****

I guess being put into New Norcia at such a young age has its advantages. We were put into classes of our age group at the Boys' House where all us Nyoongah boys were very competitive against each other, not only in classes but in sport — football and cricket — and even in our chores. I became a good reader and writer; someone else was good at sums; others, social studies; some, history and another boy was an expert at telling the time by the clock; most had a fair indication of when the monastery bell pealed across the hills and valleys of New Norcia, every hour. Thinking back now, if I had stayed with my family on a reserve, then I wouldn't be here now, sitting writing this. The kids from the late '50s and '60s from the reserves were encouraged not to go to school, not only by their parents but also by the white authorities. Can you imagine three or four little black kids waiting on the side of the road for a big bus full of white kids to pick them up to take them to school? I bet all the white kids gave them a joyous welcome. Even at school, as I was told later on, they were the butt of all jokes. The teachers responded to their needs by throwing them out of the school or locking them out. They were all classified dunces. Going to a public school with no lunch or, if they were lucky, damper and fat, there would be no glee for an Aboriginal child living on a reserve in a tin humpy, even though they had their families.

I had no mum and dad but a lot of little black brothers growing up together, even though all were hurting inside. That's what I see today; the real Aboriginal people are the ones who were taken away from their parents and the ones who lived in the slums in tin humpies on the reserves. Many born-again Christians have emerged from the reserves of the '60s and the '70s and I guess they were looking for a more powerful love than a reserve; not like us little black devils who had God thrust upon us, a God we were afraid of. I had to stumble blindly along life's righteous path only to find myself sitting in the front row of a church, any church; listening out of respect to some priest, pastor, minister or whatever telling us today how God died for our sins and how he loves us. Even today I am still confused, but like I said, if it wasn't for the pen I would have drunk myself to death. Lacking confidence (I'm still not sure of myself), forever apologising, angry and bitter, I would not have tried to converse or ended up hanging myself in a cell. May the pen lead me on.

****

I remember how we once lost a game of footy. We were playing a team of well-nourished, over-grown, young white men. Here we were, a bunch of under-nourished, skinny Nyoongah kids who tried our little hearts out and we got the biggest thumping that these white boys ever gave a team. When we got back to the mission, at tea time, the priest made all of us boys who played footy that day bend over in front of the other boys and receive two cuts each. And me, being the skinniest footy player amongst the lot, really felt the welts across my arse.

I felt at ease with Jesus around Christmas time in New Norcia because I'd look upon him as a little baby and often think to myself, I'm sure no baby could be so cruel and send us to hell. It was the holidays; we went either to Dongara or Lancelin if our mums and dads couldn't take us out. I really loved the holidays by the coast. We got to see real live white people too, and of course Jesus was still a baby. Within a few months Easter came around and again he was dying for our sins. Like I said, I always prayed to his mother Mary. I guess in a way she replaced my mother. It was around Easter — I had quite a few Easters in there — when I prayed to her asking her if I could take her son's place. I mean, I was the one who hung him on that cross so why shouldn't I be there instead of him? I thought that if I could take his place, then he wouldn't come down and send the other Nyoongah kids in the mission to hell. Like I said before; what a stupid child.

In some parts, my life is blank; I can't or wouldn't go back. I know I've done a lot of damage to my brain over the years through alcohol, pills and drugs. But when I got out in the middle '60s I tried to go back to the beginning. I know my father had one leg; he had an accident while loading coal on a steam train at Merredin. I loved him very much. I still think he and Mother are looking after me now, while writing this. But going back to my childhood, my early years are blank. It's like I woke up in a dream and found myself in New Norcia. Is it possible?

Question marks will follow me for the rest of my days. Even today I find there are things I can't answer. But I know there is a ray of unseen light that follows me. It directs me on my journey, guiding me to people of all kinds. I often say to people, I've been put on earth for a purpose. My life is meant to be. I should have died on numerous occasions through car accidents or being flogged by Nyoongahs. Wow and boy; did I get some kickings in drunken fights with Nyoongahs.

What intrigued me was that I didn't get to read and hear stories about Hitler until I left New Norcia. I was to a certain extent fascinated by his powers over his people. I hated the evil powers he wielded over the Jews and other minority groups. Thinking back, I could relate to those unfortunate people. I'm sure that the Australian government learned a lot from Hitler and his evil party through the rise of the Moore River Settlement or Mogumber, New Norcia, and countless other missions throughout Australia. The priests, nuns and brothers succumbed to the evil of the people who ruled them.

Another fascination of mine, whilst in New Norcia, was Michelangelo, the greatest sculptor, painter and poet of all times. I would visualise myself as him when I was growing up. Another was William Shakespeare. I mean he had so many beautiful words; they were floating inside my head, when I was a child. I sure was a dreamer and New Norcia gave it all to me.

Aboriginality confuses me today; I look upon blackfellas as those who drink in the park or square, picking up bumpers (cigarette ends thrown away), sleeping in the parks, squats. To me they are the real people, the underdogs that both black and white look upon as scum of society — not all the other blackfellas, but some. I hear some Aboriginal people, who never experienced the above, talk and laugh about it in an embarrassed way. I wallow in it. I guess I'm really lucky in a way. I can adapt to any situation at any given time; sitting, drinking a flagon with all the mob in a park or sipping champagne in Government House. Whatever challenge I am confronted with in life I give it my whole. Even waking up now, in the mornings, if I'm not pissed or stoned, I greet the day full on. With no money in my pocket I can achieve things I set out to do with ease. It's the complete opposite when I do have some cash on me. I'll start off with good intentions, but eventually wipe myself out before the day is done. There's only one way for me: give up alcohol. But being told so young, I think God will not forgive me if I give up alcohol and drugs. Anyway who is it for him to say; I mean, at some wedding somewhere in the Bible they all ran out of grog; he turned water into wine and eventually they all got pissed. We Nyoongahs like to drink on our own with our mob around us; it's usually the park or in the bush away from prying eyes. But us blackfellas, we bring ourselves undone when we get pissed. The men and women start fighting in the park where all white eyes are on the Aboriginal people, kids are screaming, mums and dads stuck into each other, even the 'fuck' words are bouncing off the clouds. The police are called and the troublemakers put in gaol; hopefully their wives and girlfriends will see them alive for the next time. Why can't they be like the white man; he takes his missus behind closed doors and beats the fuck out of her there. Oh well, we blackfellas have a long way to go in this society in learning the whitefellas way.

Amongst us Nyoongah people I feel that families fighting against each other is very disturbing. My old brother-in-law, rest his soul, once told me that when two Nyoongahs had a fight, after their fight, they then shook hands and made friends in front of the whole tribe. Not anymore. There's brother against brother, sister against sister, nephews, nieces, cousins, uncles, aunties, and fucking friends who're dumb enough to join in any clan. Why the fuck are these Nyoongahs insisting on hurting each other? Aboriginal and non-Aboriginal people talk about reconciliation, but first the Aboriginal people must learn to live in peace with each other, before accepting a white man into their confidence. But the more I look and see, there are a lot more Aboriginals who are finding it more comfortable to accept the non-indigenous people than to accept their own indigenous people. I just hope one day our indigenous people show the world that we are one and that we are fighting for democracy; that this is our land, not the gallant Mr James Cook's land.

I think I was about twelve or thirteen when my father died, apparently in Allawah Grove in Perth. I was washing dishes and the other kids were doing their chores when this priest walked in and said, 'Taylor, your father has just died; if you don't do those dishes properly you are going to get a belting.' All the other kids scurried around like myself trying to do the chores without getting a flogging. The words that skimmed off my head were that my father had just died, but the words, 'If you don't do those dishes properly I'm going to flog you,' will be forever with me. I mean, for the sake of fucking Christianity, why couldn't that man come up to me and say, 'Look Taylor, your father has just died. I'll do everything in my power to see that you go down to your father's funeral.' No, I didn't even go down to my own father's funeral. I loved my father with his one leg and all. I think he died thinking I was already dead and hoping to catch up with me somewhere. Oh, for being an Aboriginal in that era! I guess you can say the same for today. I never really got to know my dad, but deep in my heart, when I'm sober and with a clear head, I know he watches over me. Farewell my father; I hope your spirit is free in your ancestral land. One day I will be joining you.

Quite a few years after I got out of New Norcia, I ran into a few school mates and decided to go to the pub to have a few beers. Sitting in the cool beer garden, we were talking about New Norcia. They decided I should write about it. Then I asked if they remembered the nights. They both uncomfortably said, 'Yeah.' I told them that when the Brother used to come and tell us to be quiet and turn the lights off in the dormitory, and when I thought everyone was asleep, I would be thinking of my mum and dad, somewhere out in the bush. The ache in my heart would be overwhelming; I would let the tears run. Not a sound escaped my lips, not even a whimper came free, as the tears ran down my face. Turning to my mates, I felt a lot of shame telling my personal story, but I was in for a pleasant surprise when they dropped their heads and very sheepishly said; 'Yeah, we used to do the same thing too.' Wow, I thought, imagine twenty-odd boys in a dormitory, their beds so close together you can reach out your hand and touch the bed alongside of you; here were twenty-odd boys or more, all quietly crying for their mums and dads, and not a sound coming forth. That really blew me away.

I mean, don't get me wrong; New Norcia wasn't all fire and brimstone. The things I loved best were when we used to go bush for a walk. On a beautiful spring day, running free through the bush, watching the birds fluttering through the leaves or sitting by a stream, watching a babbling brook hiss its white foam at you or tasting the sweet water from the fresh rains, putting your lips to a freshly formed stream or ducking your head in the sweet water, I felt I was cleansing myself in my mother's tears. To me the bush was heaven. Only wadjellas went to heaven; we Nyoongahs, when we died, came back as a bird or an animal, even as a newly formed brook to quench the thirst of other weary Nyoongah kids who had yet to travel the hills of Victoria Plains. To me the bush was my everything, my mother, my father. In the bush I could do no wrong; the fire of hell did not exist in our ancestors' own yard.

We used to go digging for bush tucker whenever we could because the food they used to send over from the Girls' House was deplorable. For breakfast we had sheep broth; no toast, a cup of black tea (I think) and that was it. For an up-and-coming young lad you'd expect better. But we being little Aboriginal kids at the time, even that was too good for us. One breakfast I got a plate full of sheep broth. Hungrily I scooped the broth out with my spoon and looking down into the plate I saw a sheep's eye floating there. I didn't give a shit. I was that hungry I ate all the broth and left the lonely sheep's eye in the plate. I reckon an old boar pig would vomit at the sight of the food we had to eat. Most times for lunch we had soup or broth. Sometimes when we had sheep brains they had some sort of little bugs inside. I remember one lunch we had sheep brains, again boiled. And I hated sheep brains. I looked around to see if any boys were looking at me; none, so I quickly blessed myself and prayed to Our Lady saying, 'Dear Our Lady forgive me for wasting this good food. Amen.' Blessing myself quickly, I slipped my hand inside the bowl and put the sheep's brains inside my shorts pocket and tipped the remaining broth into the bowl of the boy next to me, unseen, because sweets were given to the boys who finished all their sheep brain broth. The sweets were chocolate custard. Boy, was I looking forward to it. It looked like thick muddy water. A plate of thick muddy water was placed in front of me. The priest suspected something and walked over to our table. The boy next to me wasn't making it any easier for me, saying in a loud voice, 'Hey, diss not all mine; I only had a little bit left. Now my plate is full,' and looking directly at me. Slyly watching the priest approaching, I could feel the warm broth running down. Quickly crossing my legs over the sheep brains in my pocket made it worse. They squelched under the weight of my leg, and the broth just oozed down forming a puddle at my feet. I was praying pretty fast for death to claim me. Then a booming voice called out, 'Taylor, why didn't you go to the toilet, instead of sitting there and wetting yourself.' I stood up meekly and quietly. There was a great big wet patch over the front of my shorts. His face was red as boiled gilgie. Pulling his strap out he made me bend over. He still didn't connect that I had the brains in my pocket. The strap came into contact with my skinny arse. Standing up straight, feeling the welts climbing out of my arse, I winced; never cried. I ended up with three cuts and had to get outside. I walked out very slow rubbing the cheeks of my arse. Tears running down my face, I took a peek at my plate of muddy waters before I went out the door, finding a lonely spot away from everyone else. I had a good cry.

I honestly believe today that those religious people were right; what a stupid child, and into a stupid man he grew. Walking back down that lonely road of childhood I think, did I actually live through all that torment, sadness, loneliness, depression, hunger for love and food; physically flogged, racially tormented? And they say Christ had a terrible death. The only thing they didn't do to us was stick that spear under our rib cage and crucify us. I'm sure the idea was in their heads, but thank fuck they didn't do it.

After I got out of New Norcia I worked anywhere and anytime, all shit jobs, the jobs that were suited to my intelligence. Of course, having none, I ended up with some arsehole scraping jobs. Religion was the top priority in our lives and that was all we had learnt. Why couldn't they teach us something to qualify and assist us in real life society? What the fuck will you achieve philosophising and quoting the life of Christ and his disciples? I mean, the stupid fucking government in my time should have sent us to Europe in exchange for some of those poor Jews, not into missions here in Australia. I reckon I would have stood a better chance with Hitler than with these missionaries in Australia.

After giving away being a matador, many of us kids were footy and cricket mad; England and Australia were playing for the Ashes. I thought that Australia and England were first cousins, and England was far superior to their cousins. Also they, the white Australians that is, all come from Captain Cook. And we Nyoongah kids were told so much of the great Captain Cook by the nuns, we were a bit confused by the Captain Cook's team of England and the Captain Cook's team of Australia. So half of us barracked for England and the other half for Australia; I'm sure we were doing the right thing for the gallant Mr Cook.

After I got out of New Norcia in the early '60s, I was working with a group of wadjellas and I had not long run away from the place; I was about fifteen or sixteen. These wadjellas asked me where I came from. Without thinking, I said, 'England.' I thought Mr Cook would be proud of me, but these wadjellas walked away from me very unsure. I heard words of, 'I'm sure he's a nigger', or, 'He's a nigger orright'. I mean I was a very fair-skinned blackfella; the only thing that was obvious was my blackfella nose and forehead. My skin was white as theirs, if not whiter; I had them fucked. And I also had a country I can call my own, Mother England. And of course the Beatles were just emerging, and I was proud to be associated with Mother England, my home country. Some of those white Captain Cook Australians were so stupid you could stick a firecracker up their arse and light it; they would turn around to you and ask, 'Hey mate, what's that burning up my arse?'

All fair-skinned Aboriginals are now looked upon as whites (in my days all white skin Aboriginals were black). These multicultural people from other countries have really confused the Captain Cook Australians. The only Aboriginals they know now are the ones who are really black in skin colour, the ones who sit in the park or squares tinged with dark, and the tribal people from the bush. I wish Captain Cook was alive today. He would probably jet to Australia and I'd reckon, boy, would he kick some whitefellas' arses and some white women's arses. I wouldn't be surprised if he kicked a few blackfellas' arses too.

This republic debate that is going on today: to be quite honest, I would be neutral. I wouldn't vote on it at all. Don't ask me why. I guess reading what you've already read, just maybe the answer is in the story. I suppose it's like someone asking me on my death bed, 'Where do you want to go, heaven or hell?' I guess I would give the same answer. Or again, just maybe the answer is in the story. I'd like the reader to work it out. Yeah, I'd like to leave it up to the reader.

A Wasted Life

The stark sterile walls of the hospital room seemed to stand in silent testimony to my brother's wasted life. The single room, normally reserved for private patients covered by hospital insurance, portrayed nothing that came to mind when one conjured up images of rich, cosseted white people who could afford the best in nursing care. If a person of substance lay in this bed, besides all the lifesaving paraphernalia connected to the walls and above the bed, one would see vases of flowers on the bedside table and windowsill brightening up the room. Sweet fruit nectar or clear cold fresh water, so necessary for keeping the blood flowing through the pampered body, would sit within reach of the bed.

If the patient was too weak to drink without assistance, the nurses would be hovering close by to render aid. At a glance, you could tell that this was a very special patient who could afford the luxury of constant attention. Nursing staff would come in and out of the room, fluffing up pillows, straightening out the bedcover and enquiring about the patient's well-being. That patient would be getting the best care that money and medical attention could give.

My brother, however, was not placed in a private ward because he was either rich or famous. He was placed here because he was a nuisance to the other patients and an embarrassment to the staff. He was Aboriginal and suffered delirium tremens. Two points against him. His room was bare except for the bed which had iron rails on both sides so that he could not fall, a chair stuck in a corner near the window and a bedside trolley used to place the trays on at mealtimes or when the nurses came to give medical treatment. Only the barest necessities graced his room.

I felt so sad as I gazed at my poor brother, Lionel, lying in the hard hospital bed. He looked so small and wizened, curled up in the foetal position, as if he wanted to return to our mother's womb where he was shielded from the rigours of a harsh life. As I sat by his bedside and watched him sleeping in a drugged stupor, my mind wandered back to our childhood and the vagaries of life which condemned our people to a life of constant struggle.

It is not easy being an Aborigine in Australia. It has never been easy since the white people took away our culture and our language, made our people dependent on government handouts and white people's hand-me-downs. It is doubly hard being a Nyoongar because we have next to nothing of our culture left. The whites have taken it all away and we get the crumbs of their condescension. Mind you, many Nyoongars have learned over time that it is better to placate the whites by learning their culture and lifestyle but, in my brother's case, he has learned the negative aspects of white ways by his love for the alcohol and drugs which ravage his body.

When the drinking rights came in after the referendum of 1967, my brother was a young man with a rosy future ahead of him. He had his health and his mental faculties intact; he was a man's man, as the saying goes. He wanted to tackle the world, but instead he tackled the bottle, and lost.

Over the years, our parents begged him to give up the bottle and the drugs before they ruined his life altogether, but he would not listen to them. 'Aborigines are allowed to drink now, aren't they? I have my macho image to maintain. Women won't look at me if I don't drink. They want a man to show them a good time and be party-loving — a real hero. Don't worry about me, Mother dear, Father dear, I know what I'm doing.' Famous last words of my brother dear.

Later on he was introduced to the false security that drugs offered him and he embraced them with open arms. He had no strength of will to refuse.

As I sit here looking at my brother and thinking of the mess he made of his life, I wonder why it is that some Aborigines can overcome the depressed state whites put us in. Many strive, by sheer determination, to prevail against all odds. Many now live like whites, with jobs, money, houses and cars. What went so horribly wrong with my brother? What quirk of fate made him become a drunken, uncaring person whose only thought is to get booze and more booze? To drink until he is paralytic? To sleep, then wake up and look for more? I feel sad for my brother whose love of alcohol and drugs has befuddled his brain to the extent that he excludes all else from his mind.

We, my four brothers and sisters and I, have tried to get him treatment for his addictions. We've pleaded and begged him to help himself or get professional help, but he ignores our concerns for him and still lives in the past when it was okay to drink and make a fool of yourself and have people, outsiders, just laugh it off as a bad joke. People didn't care. It wasn't their brother killing himself over the misconceptions of drink and drugs.

I must go now, my brother. I have a husband and children waiting for me at home. I have tried to live the white people's way. Although there will always be racism shown towards Aborigines — our people — we must not let the whites' vices totally envelop our lives. We have to be strong. I am only sorry that your young life is nearly over before you had a chance to live it. Rest easy, I will see you tomorrow.

Interview with Christine Nicholls and Lee Cataldi, Broome, 19 July 1994

CN: Maybe you could talk a little bit about the language of the books Wandering Girl *and* Unna You Fullas *and where it comes from?*

The home was run by Germans. I was taken off Mum when I was little, and growing up with the Germans we didn't know any other way of life, not even our own Aboriginal culture, which was sad really, but we didn't know at the time about our own people and, as for speaking languages, we spoke a lot of German, because they taught us these German words. We thought that German language and their words were funny; we used to laugh at those nuns when they used to say things and try and teach us. So that's when my own little words came in, like unna and bullai. Unna is an expression you can use for happy or sad [also agreement or a question]. Bullai was the word for, 'Look out, nuns coming', or something like this, just a bit of a warning; you're up to something. When the teachers came, the white school teachers, all our language was much different then, because they tried to teach us. If we used bullai or something, they'd say, 'No that's not the proper English, you are not to use those words.' But even now we've got a little bit hurt by us not using it. We used it after school when they weren't around, because we related to one another with these words.

CN: Did they try to make you feel inferior through your use of language?

You see the white school teachers separated the dark ones from the fair ones and they said the fair ones they could concentrate on, and us dark ones, we sat in the dunce corner. So life went on down there with us just sitting there not being concentrated on much and the fair ones had all the go; they thought that they could get so far ahead with the fair children. I sat in what the teacher used to say was the dunce corner, you see. They never really included us in much of their teaching, only now and again. When I look back on it now, I thought that they probably just wanted to ridicule us, to get us dunce kids up in front of the class and ask us to do arithmetic, which we couldn't really do and things like that.

CN: *It would be hard for you.*

It was very hard, seeing your own mates getting separated from you. We started to think something must be wrong with us.

CN: *So you never really questioned them, you just thought it was you?*

No. In those days you couldn't say anything to the teachers or the nuns, because they were superior and if you ever spoke up and asked them something, they would think that you were being cheeky. And then you'd get punished, and rather than getting punished, we just had to take that and be done with it.

CN: *So getting back to the unna and bullai and all those words, did they come from your own parents' language group?*

My mum always says bullai and winyarn and that sort of thing. And the kids who came from homes brought that in. I was the only baby at the time and these kids who were coming in from their parents, they used to tell us about their mums and dads and all these words and things like that.

CN: *So what's your mother's language group?*

Well, sad to say, I don't really know, because my grandmother was taken off Liveringa [Station], by McClarty's. And my mother was born in Pinjarra and then taken to the Moore River settlement. So a lot of this language and culture was lost with our people. We don't know what area really because there were records written up, but not the true records. So I don't really know what my mother's language was; it would've been coming from my grandmother you see, but my grandmother's tribe was Nigana tribe, they called Nigana, and she came from Liveringa and was taken off then by McClarty's. He was a parliament bloke in those days, and my grandmother worked for him. That's where it is sad, we don't know our own language, you know, and

268

where we come from. It is all right growing up in a home, but when you get out, you don't know who you are, or where you're going to.

CN: *When Magabala Books came to edit* Wandering Girl, *did they leave it exactly as you wrote it?*

When I was writing I got the help of Jack Davis because at the time I was travelling and I was sending bits down to him and he edited it and sent it back. Then I took it down to Magabala Books and worked side by side with the editor, which was good. And that's how we got it out.

CN: *And what about* Unna *was it the same process or a bit different?*

Unna was the same. These stories are all true you see and thinking of the days when we were there and how we spoke to one another, that's what I wrote about. That's why we call it *Unna You Fellas.*

LC: *When you and the editor sat down with the book that you'd written, what did you do?*

Well, we went through it all, he didn't say much. There was a lot of discussion on the first one, like *Wandering Girl*, but he knew how I'd written and how I write, so he didn't say much really. I explained to him a few of the words that we used and we worked together on the name, *Unna*. There were other people on the Committee that wanted to change the name, but my editor and myself stopped with the word because unna was my, our way of talking at the time. And still is. I wanted to call it *Unna* and my editor said *Unna*. There were some others who didn't really want it.

CN: *What sort of titles did they have in mind?*

Um … Oh, there was all different sort of titles, like *Mission Bells* and all that sort of thing.

CN: Mission Bells?

I'm sick of mission bells. We were woken up with a bell every morning and went to bed with a bell, that sort of thing you know, and I said, 'No, that won't be appropriate.'

LC: There's much more editing now than there would have been, twenty years ago.

Mmm, that's right. And I mean I wouldn't mind training one day to be an editor to help our own people get their books out. And things like that. When I'd written *Wandering Girl*, my editor kept saying to me, 'This little part here you need to bring out a little bit more and that little part.' I didn't know; I'd never even heard of an editor, you know. I was getting quite angry, because I had to sit back and write this and write that again; it was getting on my nerves. But I didn't know this at the time you see, but now that I understand and know what goes on, I do it myself.

CN: What's your main hope in writing those books?

There are a lot of problems about that stem from the past. I won't forget the past, because I believe we don't live in the past any more, we live for the future. I sit and talk to people and they tell me their problems and things like that and I say to them, why don't you write, you might help somebody else who's going through the same thing. Sometimes it's hard when you've got nobody to turn to; if you sit down and read a book, that can get you out of that thing, like if you lived a similar life, like that person did.

CN: When you got out of the home did you go looking for your mother?

Well, that was after I left those people I worked for. Because you see when you're in a home it is all right, you're protected all those years, but when you get out, you're like a bird in a cage and when the door opens, where you go, you don't know. It is very hard coming out of that home, because you grow up with all these kids and if you had a fight with somebody you could always go and talk with someone else, but coming out of there, there was nobody. And those nuns always told us, 'Look up to white people,' not to back answer them or talk to them, and when I went out working my employers told me I was only there as a slave to do their work, and not to associate myself with them, their sort of crowd. And when they had visitors, I had to run and hide myself and wait until they went, you see, then do all the cleaning up. And when I look back on it now and look at my own kids, I think, really that would have been hard, because I wouldn't send my kids out like that, no way.

CN: *Have you ever seen them since then, those people?*

No, I've never seen them.

CN: *They've got so much to answer for haven't they?*

They have really, but I've got no hard feelings against them, because I thought that's the way they were, I mean it is their problem, not mine, if they're like that. You've just got to feel sorry for people like that. It is not only me who had this experience. Other people had it too, even white people. The idea now is not to feel sorry for yourself and think of the past; what's done is done, and it can't be helped, but we won't forget about it. You look towards the future. I'd like to aim my kids in the right direction. Love everybody, not this black and white business. And I don't want them to go through what I went through. Because I sit down and tell my kids a lot of things and then they listen to it.

CN: *I'm trying to think of some more questions about the language. It seems to me that the ways the girls talk in* Unna *is a really accurate way of talking.*

Really there was a lot of silent talk too, when those weren't nuns around, or even when the nuns were there. Or some girl would be shouting her mouth off and the nun would be there, trying to tell her, 'Shut up', something like that. Even up here today, when people see you they go like that [gestures], you know, like 'Where you going?' But in those days, when those nuns were there we had to be like statues. And when they weren't looking, we'd go like that [gestures]. Sometimes some of the kids had brothers there and they wanted to talk, boys and girls were separated you see. There would be a lot of silent 'talk' there.

CN: *Do you ever bump into the nuns?*

I went over once to see them when I was in Sydney, when I launched *Wandering Girl*, but they didn't say much to me. They were still the same; they took me down the chapel to say a few prayers and away I went. When I came back home, I rang them up to tell 'em that I arrived back safely and everything, and one of the nuns said, 'You know you told a lot of lies,' that sort of thing. And I said to this nun, 'You always brought us up not to

271

tell lies; if we told a lie we had to go to confession. I only speak the truth.' But she thought that I wouldn't remember. They said, 'Do you know who I am, because there were different ones?' and I said, 'Yeah, you were Mother Superior, you were Sister Gedes, you were the one in charge,' and 'You were this' and 'You were that.' 'Oh,' they said, 'you've got a good memory.' Well, you can't forget them. I knew in my heart that they didn't really like me writing.

CN: When the nun told you that she thought you wrote a whole lot of lies in Wandering Girl, *did she really believe that herself or had she convinced herself that the past didn't happen?*

Well those nuns were like that. They kept saying, 'You're too young,' because they told us they were angels, you see. And they never done nothing, but they were the first ones to confession every Saturday. This is what I couldn't understand, those nuns telling us they never done anything, but they were the first ones there, it was strange for us kids to see those nuns line up like that. They always used to drum it into our heads that they were angels.

LC: So what were they confessing?

God only knows. Perhaps they were just going to see the priest, I don't know.

CN: The priest was a bit of a hunk was he?

I don't know, because we never had thoughts like that in them days, you weren't allowed to, you weren't even allowed to sing the hit parades, otherwise you'd be finished; they were devil's songs they used to say. They were no good; all you had to sing was bloody *Waltzing Matilda* and all those sort of things. But I mean the Beatles and Elvis Presley and all them, we were just growing up in that time. And I mean they were really good songs, they were; we liked them but to the nuns they were evil. And we didn't even know about the birds and bees. When the girls' monthly first came round, the other girls told us we were dying and we thought we were dying too. One girl told us that when you get these monthlies you gotta give her all your meat, when we sat around for a meal. When I come to think of it now, she must've been having a good feed while we were starving.

Looking back on it now, I think she's a rotten girl. Making us give our best food away and we were, you know, you only get that every meal time, you don't get anything in between. You might get a piece of bread and dripping for morning tea or something like that. But then you're working all the time, after that, then you look forward to your meal.

CN: Do the nuns give themselves better food?

Oh they had better food, yeah. So did the priest and the brothers. When they had visitors at the mission they used to get cakes and biscuits. And this girl named Anna, that main character in my book, used to have to go down to the dining room, 'cos the dining room was a two-storeyed place. One of the girls had to lift me up, because I had to always report back as to how many biscuits and cakes were left. I used to have to say, 'Oh there's only one left,' and if I told them that there was none left, they'd drop me and they'd walk away. But if there was any left over, they'd be happy. Then we'd volunteer to come and clean up because we knew we were going to get cake. The kitchen was joined on to the dormitory — we used to go and help ourself at night. We shouldn't really do it, but we were stealing currants and things like that.

We were hungry at night. We went to bed early. We had meals about five o'clock, and you still had jobs after that and then went to bed. They had a store and they used to keep biscuits, those broken ones, and when I used to go and work in the kitchen, I used to head straight for the storeroom — you know, make out I'd be going to get an extra potato or something like that — and have a good feed when a nun wasn't there. Oh, we used to get caught quite a lot.

CN: So despite the fact that they kept their eye on you the whole time, you had quite a thriving secret … ?

Yes, mm. My cousin pinched these currants one night and someone went down and told the nuns that us girls were in the kitchen, but when the nun came and opened up the door, we were all sleeping. My cousin was sleeping and this nun come and pulled her by her ears, because you have to get out of bed by your ears or cheek. My cousin said, 'I never done it,' and the nun said, 'What's all these currants … ?' because they'd trailed the currants to her bed. She'd dropped them all rushing back, you see. Some of the girls were real — what do you call them? — sisters' pets. Had to go down and pimp on anyone. Used to get a hiding or be made to sit and darn socks till two in the morning in the old laundry.

We had our fun growing up with them. They were good times when you come to think of it. When I look back on it now those nuns, they must have been brave coming away from their homes. They must have been missing their families. But because they were so dedicated to the church, and they were doing a good job for God, you know, they'd put up with anything. I've got in one of my episodes in one of my books, this nun came from Switzerland. She was teaching us to yodel. Every Saturday afternoon was singing lesson and I used to hate that because Sunday was a big church day, you see, and all the visitors used to come. They used to dress us up in our tunics and our little white tops and our berets and away we'd go. Those nuns all stood at the back of you in church. If you wouldn't sing you'd get a poke in the back and then you'd get no Weeties. Because every Sunday was Weeties, you see, soaked in a big pot of milk. We used to look forward to Weeties because we never got that during the week. We only got dried bread mixed with sour milk, something like buttermilk. They said that's how they used to eat in Germany — it was healthy food, you know. Used to make me sick. And sauerkraut was our punishment — making bloody sauerkraut. And when I got here one day someone asked me if I liked sauerkraut. I said, 'Don't even mention it [laughs].' We were only little kids then and they had a big table like that [demonstrates] and we had to stand on blocks to reach the table and cut this bloody cabbage up, all week. It used to go on for days. Oh, it was horrible. But, I mean, even though we had those hard punishments, it was still fun, because we were all together. Looked on the funny side of things.

Waiting

As the steel gate closed behind me, the starkness of the room closed in on me, my mind racing in all directions. Looking up, his face told everything; fear, confusion, despair. Not knowing what the future will bring. As our hands touched, vibes of fear and pain filled my heart. His trembling hands were shaking as he lit his cigarette. While we talked he was not here, too worried and sick with fear. When we parted, the feeling he had came with me; sadness.

Long Park

It's pension morning and very quiet as I sit in Long Park. It's mid-morning now and people begin to move around rushing to and fro, cars zooming past. It starts to get noisy, then our Wongi mob start to come in, looking for the best spots to sit in the cool of the day. Long Park is central, it has everything you might need only a few steps away. There is the Red Rooster across the road, with public toilets on the side; there's the Woolworths store with a liquor store on the side. So we have a lovely place to sit all day and enjoy a yarn with our friends, with all the things we might need only a few steps away. Yeah, that's my sister up there and my uncle sitting right up the top and that mob over there are my cousins; we come here every day. But it's a special day today, it's pension day. It's now mid-afternoon and Long Park is nearly full. Everyone's telling stories. At the same time they seem to be past listening, but who cares? We are all having a good time.

Four Kilometres

The dog ran, his tail a long black banner, darting from bush to shrub, sniffing and snuffling, vacuuming the hidden exotic smells on the bases of trees, on the leaves of low bushes and sometimes he'd come to a dead halt to sniff a clump of unassuming grass. He added liberal squirts as he sniffed. He ranged far beyond or far behind the constant moving point that was the man, depending on the level of interest of each smell.

Grunting. Sweating. Wheezing. Dull pain. Bloody Digger, the mongrel. Why did I bring him? Should keep him on the lead but that would be a bigger hassle, with him towing me around and me choking him to get going. So much for the dog-training classes. I should have kept up the practice. Why isn't he naturally good like those other dogs that walk so nicely on their owner's lead? Stopping and staying quickly on 'Quiet' command. Not having to shout and scream at them. Christ, this is hard. My legs feel weak … legs of lead. Keep going! Soon the adrenaline will kick in! Think of something else instead of how my gob feels like a tub of clag glue and my nose is running and how godawful shitty running is. Shit, it is hard but at least I won't end up a big fat bastard like all my mates. It used to be easier once, a long time ago, another life ago when he was younger, fitter, played sports, when things were simple before he started working in his job.

At least it isn't too hot, the weather is just right. Early summer evenings are perfect; crisp weather, not sweltering, still light. Not too many people around walking their mutts. But still, not as good as night jogs. Running under the moon through the park section gave you a disembodied feeling. Running under the tall trees felt like another time and place. It was almost primal. Digger, a black hound, surging through the forest and we were going somewhere.

Of course he'd never tell his friends and colleagues about that special feeling. The blacks would probably think he was cartwarrah [mad] and the whites would probably think he was getting in touch with his earthy side, his spirituality, his 'indigenous self'. Actually it was too bad he couldn't bottle the experience and sell it to those desperado whites who were always looking for 'indigenous spirituality' from blackfellas. Their culture had short-changed them and they wanted a quick fix from indigenous people.

Their culture gave them freedom to choose from a hundred different shampoos in the shopping centres but left them isolated and emptier inside. It had done worse for blackfellas, though.

Those New Age types saw things differently. Having indigenous experiences and friends made them feel special and good, it proved their broadmindedness and 'in-touch-with-the-global-scene-ness'. Could dye that big mutt Digger brown (bleach him?), say that he was an unusually big dingo, and slap loin cloths on my white followers and have them run for a couple of clicks in the moonlight. Campfire … tea and damper … a bit of didge playing after the run. Then a few short stories and meditations to get in touch with the earth, universe or whatever. They'd love it, silly bastards. I'd charge them like a wounded bull and be rich! Except, I can't play the didge. Where would I take them? Along the South Perth foreshore? That'd look a sight. We'd all be arrested. And I'd feel like a bastard suckering them in even though they asked for it, always wanting your wisdom of the Indigenous Peoples, even though you're still trying to figure out where it is. Should go to the lost property office of Human Well-Being to get back my lost mystical Indigenality and I could divvy it up to give out to everyone.

Yes, night jogging was the best, but passing car headlights sometimes made you feel isolated and vulnerable. You couldn't see or know who was behind those glaring spotlights. It could be someone with strange devil-devil eyes like the Scottish terrier on Digger's cans of dog food, someone who might take the opportunity to run over a lone blackfella. Things like that still happened, even nowadays. More so, nowadays. Or it could be someone who'd take the opportunity to run over anybody or anything, if they could get away with it. Run over a white person, black person, dog or cat. Too many sicko psychos around nowadays.

He missed the secret freedom of the anonymity of running at

night. Gliding past the dark houses like a bodiless ghost (when he was fitter). Squares of warm light would fall from the windows of the houses, smells of cooking and the blue flickering of TV screens. Occasionally, something special; people sitting in the pools of light on front verandahs with family and friends, happy voices murmuring, soft buzz of laughter, clinking glasses and the clear chime of the cutlery. It made him feel that the world was as it should be and he felt a great contentment.

Late afternoon in mid-summer on rubbish collection day was the worst time, and should be avoided at all cost. Dark green wheely bins lurched in disorder on the verges. They squatted along the street like a motley rank of square plastic monsters, wheels sunken in the sand and tilting them awry; silent and smug, exuding simmering rank smells into the hot air. Sometimes the man ran onto the road to avoid the variety of stinks but traffic usually kept him and the dog on the pavement, so he would try to hold his breath but would always end up desperately sucking up the unfiltered stenches through gritted teeth. The dog loved it.

Alert! People up ahead! Have they got a dog? The image jolted up and down as he jogged; he focused on the hazy figures, straining for the sight of darting smaller shapes. None. Digger hated other dogs. He'd fight them all, whether they were huge rottweilers or small poodles. He took particular delight when dogs were locked behind the gates of their yards. He'd saunter past as they barked, watching them with a cocky dog grin and he would very deliberately piss on every shrub and post of their front yards. They'd go into barking frenzies, hurling themselves against their prison bars as he trotted off in jaunty nonchalance. The man sometimes swore at the dog but usually he smiled. Digger had a right to flaunt his freedom. Being cooped up all day, every day, wasn't the best life. The fact that he could show off in his fortunate moment made it even more satisfying.

He could go to the big parks for jogs but it was easier to run out straight from his home. Not having to drive anywhere or keep the dog on a lead was a bonus. Also it gave him his only opportunity to look at this neighbourhood. He knew all the houses on his jog route and there were several of special interest. Some served as markers for the distance he had jogged, others were interesting because of the people he saw fleetingly as he ran by. He would pound past inspecting gardens, feeling good about the new houses or ones undergoing renovation; it signified that the area was improving and his house would be worth more. He also felt good about the old dilapidated fibro houses with their dry long grass sandpits of front yards; his compared well; at least he wasn't that neglectful. Some houses or certain places had bad memories. There was a particular spot where Digger had been attacked by two bull-terriers.

Digger had just been a young dog running by, minding his own business and the two bastard mutts came flying out of a yard. Digger didn't have a chance, they had him down; one was at his throat, the other at his back legs. The man was screaming and yelling, so were the owners of the bull-terriers. He was going to lift Digger up by the tail because the vet had told him that was the way to immobilise dogs but the bully owners didn't do that too. The bloke owner was punching his dogs to loosen their grips. Finally the owners got their dogs off Digger. He called Digger away, grateful that it hadn't been worse. Both the man and the dog were bleeding from cuts and rips but Digger was alive. He ran home slowly behind the bloody pawprints of his dog, heavy with helplessness and guilt. During the attack, when he first reached Digger and the other dogs, before the owners got there, Digger had looked up at him from the fighting and thrashing, his throat clamped in a vice of flesh and teeth; had looked up at his master, his eyes desperate and frightened, begging for help. Next time, the man thought with grim determination, next time I am going to run in kicking, punching and biting myself. Next time I will defend my dog properly. Since then Digger hated all dogs on sight.

Thank God, I've nearly gone two kilometres. Here comes that house. Halfway there.

'Digger! Get away! Brainless mongrel! Get here, boy, here!' Why does that mongrel bastard always have to run into that yard? He must know or sense with canine intuition that blackfellas live there. The house was one of the significant markers on his circuit. He didn't know if the exact same family had always lived there because he only saw quick snapshots as he went by. But the house and people were familiar to him. There were always different people; relations, kids, daughters and friends visiting all the time. Once there was a youth drunk and prone on the front lawn. The mother came bustling out mortified with embarrassment to take him into the house.

One time, a group of young teenagers, looking at him with hard eyes, were walking abreast across the footpath, practising the challenging they would do up town in Northbridge. He ran through them, smiling, feeling like a dickhead, wishing that he could stop and tell them that he was one of them, that he was like them once. They knew, like he knew, but there wasn't the time or opportunity to make contact. Beyond the occasional mutual nod, no communication had taken place. Another time, a group of kids had been playing across the front lawn and footpath. They paused as Digger ran up. A new game! They screamed in mock terror, scrambling to safer parts of the yard. He said to them, 'It's okay, he's a good dog, he won't bite you.' They clustered forward trying to pat Digger and to find out more about this man and his dog.

A young boy cried out to the running man, 'Where are you going?'

'That way,' the man replied, indicating with a swing of his head and pout of his lips the onward direction of his run.

Previously the house was built of fibro and had been burned out. During his runs it had been demolished and rebuilt with brick, with Homeswest landscaped gardens. He felt sad, thinking that the Nyoongar family had left for good, but they or another very similar moved in during a jog on an autumn afternoon. It was like the houses of his childhood in his home town, filled with people like the people and relatives of his past. Now and here he was an intimate stranger running past what was and could be his life. Back home he would have known the names of that family and who they were related to. They would have known him. The sameness was there but the difference was there too. If there were glass walls between him and his current neighbours then there was a finer membrane between him and the people of that house. He probably could get through but he'd have to stop and pull down the barriers. And then they'd get through too. That could mean an entire range of good and bad things, just like at home. So he ran by always looking, sometimes with a yearning.

As he passed the block where that house was, he thought of work. There must be a simpler life beyond work in the Aboriginal industry. A familiar sinking feeling of despair nestled in his chest. There must be a life beyond the work and the life he lived now. It was so demanding yet so compelling, because it might make a difference. But the politics, the jealousies, within the mob and between others who had a stake … The need to watch your actions, watch what you say all the time, everywhere.

He could handle it. He loved fighting the system for his people and for what he thought the 'cause' was. He had learnt quickly that it wasn't really a united front. Oh, they would come together for a common national issue or rally and march for a significant topic. That type of gathering was a powerful unity. It seemed to happen less nowadays. Now the meetings were usually held to run other blackfellas or organisations down. There were always contentious issues and division between the mob everywhere; backstabbing and deliberate misunderstanding. He could handle the whites criticising him, running him down and loathing him, but it broke his heart every time when his own people did it.

Yes, it broke his heart every time his people ran him down or denounced him. It went with the turf of black leadership; the role of a tall poppy to be cut down regularly. Some tall poppies grew stronger and shorter from these spiteful prunings; others withered and died off. He fancied that he might be of the latter species, because he could not seem to grow a thick skin no matter how he tried.

When attacked, he consoled himself by recognising that this was part of his people's pain and rage, part of their internalised oppression spanning many generations and many government policies. It was part of the tremendous oppression and racism they suffered in their day-to-day lives, internalised and acted out on their own people. The real target of their anger was immune, unreachable, so they lashed out at each other.

He consoled himself that this was part of the process of achieving self-determination, that he shouldn't personalise it at all. He tried not to think vindictive, bitter thoughts about his critics and told himself that the most valuable lesson was never to allow himself to be like them. But it broke his heart every time it happened.

The acts were all different; some direct, others indirect, some public, others private. The most recent one was where he went to a fringe-dwelling community of a small outlying town, hosting a group of white professionals who had come from all over the country to find out how they could help indigenous people. The timetable got out of control; it escaped, and they arrived at the community lost and late. It was his fault, his responsibility. He should have bossed the group around more, shepherded them into the bus earlier, not allowed them to get lost on those dusty roads.

The cheerful bus had rolled into the community, passengers darting surreptitious glances of anticipation and apprehension, attempting to give an attitude of respectful unintrusiveness. But the community had waited too long. Some had left, giving up on the bus load of visitors; the community leader thundered out, rage bristling from him like black lightning. Apologies and explanations were not accepted; he shouted his anger and frustration at the man and the group.

The community leader had fought hard for his people for many years, since he was very young. He was a man with a fiery heart of steel and of invincible will. His way of fighting was with brutal anger and aggression. That kept them all at bay; the white system and the black rivals. That was the only way that worked for him. Underneath that fierce rage, the pain could be heard.

Three old woman sat roosting on the verandah, supporting actors in the drama, plump with spite like jealous cats full of cream of justified anger against these visitors and their black hosts who dared speak about Aboriginal issues without their endorsement. They believed that they had cornered the market of who had suffered the most racism, oppression and misery in the world. They were the grass roots community people who knew the real pain of being black. Who was he, this jumped-up coconut, bigshot government worker sitting in an Aboriginal position when he knew nothing, did nothing and was nothing. Had he ever bothered to come and see them? Furthermore, one of their daughters had gone through the system not needing the likes of him and his department, so what good was he anyway.

The man tried to answer rationally, politely, as hovering kids snickered at their aunties' audacious antics with this bigshot. He wondered vaguely where that famous daughter was now? Bright enough not to be working in the cause, probably. He took his serve of bitter medicine and left with the bus. Shattered with humiliation, anguished and full of dull anger and remorse. It was all part of the process.

He thought that if all the mob could put aside their jealousies, wounded pride, dislikes and competitiveness for resources and a place to speak, if they could come together with respect and trust towards each other, what an invincible force they could be. Social equity would be achieved in his lifetime. Although the groups all sat around and talked about unity, integrity, protocols, support and mercy: and human nature, which in the end made them hypocrites, their new words and thoughts provided more sophisticated cloaks for small-minded actions and jealousy.

And why should the mob be any different? They were a diverse group. The whites had so much diversity they made institutions of the different factions and called them political parties.

Still, for him, the cause had been different once.

Sometimes the vision that steeled his resolve and inflamed his soul was so far away; times forgotten in day-to-day, week-to-week business. He could remember clearly many years ago when he was younger and fresh, having a conversation with his son in the park where they used to feed the swans and throw the football around. He told his son about how they had to use their lives to make a difference to the way their people were, that they were luckier than most and that it was their responsibility to work for social justice. God, the words sound tired and clichéd. He remembered that particular incident because a woman had been eavesdropping nearby and had smiled at them. He felt embarrassed and corny at the time.

Now everything seems complicated and frustrating. Nothing is new. White colleagues and academics desperately hound your thoughts and words. Any conversation is seized upon and put into their frameworks and theories for understanding life, their religions for the right way of dealing with Aboriginal people. Even the black academics have started. 'Oh that's an emic and that's an etic explanation! What you are saying is totally postmodern. Foucault would probably say ...' They cast their throw-nets of theory onto your soul and all your thoughts and words are analysed, sorted and categorised as they emerge, pinned like butterflies onto a mounting board; part of something else, someone else.

Hah, what if he shouted out his frustration just once? What if he shouted out, 'Fuck off! Just fucking listen to me! Stop moving everything. Stop making me into a reflection, a piece of evidence to support your fucking theories!' What if he shouted and screamed instead of the usual objective, rational, intellectual debate? How would that go down? What would fucking Foucault think of that; how would that fit into a community development framework? Good community consultation, hey? The community said, 'Fuck off and jam your etics and emics.' No, they'd see it as his problem. They'd say he was stressing out, losing the way, had a chip on his shoulder, and they'd be really concerned and tell him that he needed a holiday. The blackfellas would tell him he needed to go back to his community and elders for spiritual healing. They'd wait with bated breath, fear and excitement to see if he would crash and burn, another sad casualty of Aboriginal leadership. And that would further prove the theories of stress and Aboriginal leadership. Hell, I'm really negative! Shouldn't take it out on the mob, they're all on our side.

Ahead, the dog came to a sudden halt near a lush clump of gerberas on the boundary of a garden. It shuffled about and struck the stiff, serious squatting position of a dog defecating. Eyes front and tail upright. The man increased his pace to pass the dog, looking around anxiously to see if anyone was watching, especially if anyone was home in the garden where the gerberas grew. He ran ahead with mixed emotions; shame, guilt and glee, at least that was one less he wouldn't have to find and bury in the back yard.

He heard the heavy pounding and sharp claw clicks racing to catch up. The dog slowed near the man again for random pissing and smelling of the environment, tongue lolling out like a slab of pink ham. The man noted with satisfaction that the dog was tiring. It didn't surge about with pent up energy now. Two brownie points; I've exercised the dog and I've exercised myself.

When work was really hard neither got exercised, and there was more guilt. The man had many guilts. Over the years he had slowly, painstakingly collected them. In the mornings he would wake up, feeling a little sick and tired, and there would be the guilts and other things like a darkness in the edge of his consciousness. He would check that they were there and push them back by thinking of all the urgent important things he had to do at work and then he would stumble out to get his first coffee of the day.

There were guilts about his marriage break-up, that his children weren't experiencing Aboriginal culture, that he wasn't experiencing Aboriginal culture, that he had not gone home for a long time now, that sometimes he avoided relations because they always wanted money, accommodation, taxi services and too much time he didn't have. Guilts: that he should do more gardening and fix up the house because it all looked like a pile of shit; that he should spend more time with his colleagues; that he should go to more community functions; that he should have more social days at his place (at least one); that he should have visitors stay over at least; that his parents were getting very old and he wasn't with them; that he wasn't one of the stolen generation; that his mother was; that maybe he hadn't suffered as much oppression as other Aboriginal people had; that he didn't speak his language; that he drank too much and didn't look after himself properly; that he didn't exercise his dog regularly; that he might be incompetent at work and at life.

****

He lived his life in a time of racism and injustice. He had experienced this first-hand himself, where a person's appearance, their racial origin, immediately designated them as second class human beings. It was a time when you were told in many subtle ways that to be acceptable was to live in one particular way, to think and behave in one way. Even if he could live, think and act in that way, there was nothing he could do to escape the prison of his racial stigma. Yet, underlying that was a profound conviction that he would not and could not 'fit in' even if his skin was white: his sense of who he was, who his forefathers were, would not allow any fitting in.

And he could never leave it behind. Different towns and places had different prejudices. When he was younger and started travelling with his job, he always was excited when he boarded planes. He was going to new and different places of potential adventures, his business and meetings were cutting edge and were meant to change things, and then, too, he used to make sure that he made time to explore new places where he attended his meetings and conferences.

Those different places were exciting then, however the small towns were sometimes awkward and uncomfortable for him. The people of small towns would occasionally behave with a familiar sense of impermeable distance and superiority towards him; they would stare with hard censuring eyes and frustrate his requests with stony politeness. He'd leave with feelings of vague confusion, belittlement and resentment, not wanting to make a fuss in a place where he didn't know the rules of the game.

Was it racial prejudice or not? The rules were different in different places. In his hometown and the city he lived in, he knew exactly what was going down and had a whole armoury of weapons and strategies for defence and retaliation. But in other places, when he went exploring, sometimes he was uncertain. He had figured out the game in his small town; it was a town where they knew you were black and if you lived there and didn't get out like he did, they always held your race against you, and no matter how nice they were, they always felt superior. No matter how hard you worked and tried to achieve, they always watched and waited for you to fail; to fall, to pick up the bottle and meet their expectations that you could only be true to your blood. He saw the way they treated his father … grudging respect but patronising. Thirty years of hard work and staying on the straight and narrow wouldn't cancel that perpetual expectation.

But that was then, when his young explorer's heart had looked for the secret wonders of the world. Now when he travelled, he knew that there would be no adventures or exciting incidents. He travelled frequently. He always caught the last plane in and first plane out of those different towns and cities. He knew the airports of those places like his own home. He attended to business in venues that could be in any city. Each meeting and conference was a transparency placed over the many last ones with little difference; the entire was a singular blurred image of similar big oval tables, with similar faces, similar pastel air-conditioned rooms, similar coffee facilities and the same bowls of mint sweets on the table in front of him near the jug of water. It had become the same rhetoric, same dynamics, same posturing, same games, and same lack of real tangible outcomes.

Afterwards he would go to similar clean shopping centres and buy at the same chain-store shops. Sometimes he woke up in those similar hotel beds and wondered where the fuck he was, what city he was in. Was what he was doing making any real difference?

Sometimes he felt stuck in a cross-cultural quagmire. His white friends would tell him he was stupid when he gave money grudgingly to distant relations on request. They said that he should just say no. They didn't understand that the obligation was built into his character. He was obliged, and he knew it wasn't always the money or favour in the transaction that was important; it was the transaction itself, an unspoken ritual that reinforced the network that he belonged to.

This realisation came to him one day when his cousin Gordon rang and asked that he pick up Gordon's eldest son at the airport and drive him to the train station. His diary was booked out so he refused. Gordon was resentful at the refusal, and he thought Gordon was inconsiderate and selfish; the kid could have easily gotten a taxi. After all he had been to Perth several times before; it wasn't like he had come straight from the bush. Then he realised: Gordon wanted his son to know his Uncle, wanted his son to know that he was important to his uncle, that they were family. The man postponed some of the important appointments, sent some people to others and rang Gordon back. Although the time he spent with his nephew was less than the time it took getting to the airport and back to work, it was the best couple of hours he had had for weeks.

His experience was of conditional and sometimes guarded acceptance by whites. His people could not choose whether to accept him or not; he was a part of them like a branch of a tree. The tree and the branch do not choose their relationship; they are part of the whole irrespective of personalities or appearances. All parts belong. When he was younger, some of his white friends had given conditional acceptance because they said he was 'different' and 'not like the others'. He didn't have the understandings then nor the words of rebuke. He had wanted their friendship and acceptance, wanted a life where he could be just another boy, so he kept a vague resentful silence. To them he was another boy, and it was easier to mentally cut him out as different and the exception than it was to put aside their own racial prejudice and stereotypes.

Nowadays, it was different. Racism was still there but things were changing and in some areas race was desirable. Very desirable. Now he saw incidents where white people saw Aboriginal people as exotic. Or as protégés, a black extension and expression of themselves in the social justice business. His professional life was a chain of these experiences, commencing when he first took up a designated black position.

Despite the great regard and respect he held for his first boss, he saw clearly that his role was that of the black apprentice. He would not have got the job and attention if he hadn't been black. He had been the delightful evidence of his boss's genuine commitment to indigenous self-determination. For years it was all fine and good until he finally challenged his boss. Really challenged him; not one of those tame, contained incidents of the permitted demonstration of assertion to prove that 'the-boy-can-think-for-himself' (even though he was taught everything he knew by someone special). It was a very serious issue at the time and he felt strongly about it. His boss did not agree, but the man asserted himself and all of a sudden it did not suit his boss's agenda. All of a sudden it was personalised as the man having a chip on his shoulder, of him being wrong. Except he was right. He moved to another more responsible job in the Department soon afterward, and became his own boss. He was still a friendly acquaintance of his former boss, who probably still claimed credit for the man's success, but a distance was forged between them of mutual hurt and betrayal. To the man it seemed that many white people were more comfortable with those who spoke their specific language, echoed their values and ways of doing things. Challenge and disagreement made them uneasy and they'd start looking for those mental escape holes such as the there-is-something-wrong-with-you power trip, or stress from work, misguided notions or the line that other Aboriginal people who have been 'consulted' feel differently. The man also wondered whether it was human nature in general; he figured that he probably became better friends with people who agreed with his ideas and he with theirs.

Nowadays there were more opportunities to have a voice and gain a position of significance. So because of his experience he had made a commitment to change the way things were. He thought that his efforts might make a difference so he took advantage of the opportunities for indigenous people to be heard at a national level. Nowadays, the determination that used to burn in his heart was burning him out. He sometimes went through periods of disillusionment and depression. He worried that he might become like some of his indigenous peers whose ambition had taken precedence over their original commitment. Or they might have had self-interest at heart from the beginning. He consoled himself that his commitment was for the right reasons.

Yet it seemed sometimes that even the opportunities were conditional. He got them because he was black and was only good for a black perspective. He wondered whether his white colleagues saw his skills and worth beyond the black perspective.

He wondered if they wondered, like he did, whether he could get a job outside the industry.

****

The man and the dog came to the road. It was a fairly busy road during the day. The man focused all his attention on the dog, he called the dog to him and swivelled his head from side to side checking for cars. He was always anxious when he came to crossing roads; he didn't trust the dog not to run out happily and blindly into danger.

A few months ago when he used to be confident at roadsides, he had the dog 'stay!' and 'sit!' and they would wait patiently for the traffic to clear. One day when they were out on their run, the dog did not have his lead on. For some unknown reason the dog had bounded up and run across the road into the hurtling cars. The man stood frozen in astonished horror and fear as a car smashed into the dog. The world slowed and became unreal; the man couldn't see the dog anymore, just the glass and plastic of the car's headlights flying into the air. As if in a vacuum he heard the screech of car tyres and the thud of his heart beat. Momentarily, until the dog moved, he thought, 'Digger's dead, Digger's dead.' A great sense of being out of control overwhelmed him in that instant. There was absolutely nothing he could do to change the unfolding event before him. It was like when he used to go out drinking with his mates when he was younger. They would get drunk and aggro, they would pick fights and suddenly the moment was there. Shouting, screaming; the first blows landed; people and tables would be scattering, then the men would run together arms and fists swinging, boots stamping and kicking, glasses smashing, blood and spittle spraying. Afterwards they would relive and reconstruct the event and boast about it. He was always amazed that they couldn't remember how out of control everything had been, how dangerous it could have been and he would feel disgusted and ashamed.

****

The man and dog ran across the road. People ahead. The running pair came towards the people, a family; mother, father and two children. The man readied his face to smile. As they drew closer, the family collectively tittered and clustered to one side. The father pulled his children behind him so that he was between his children and the runners. They passed the family. Digger gave them a quick courteous sniff mid-pace. The father glared disapproval at the passing dog, 'You should have your dog on a lead, you know. It's against the law to have a dog running loose.' He eyed the approaching man coldly.

The man ran past shrugging his shoulders and held his hands out, palms up. A mobile gesture of apology, he cast a look of regret at the family and was gone. 'Sanctimonious prick! As if poor Digger would ever bite anyone, especially kids! Hope it's his garden that Digger bogs in. Arsehole! What an over-reaction.' The man pondered how it was that some people saw his dog as dangerous. His dog was gentle and particularly sensitive-looking. A small yappy poodle would more likely bite someone than his dog would. People judged appearance too quickly. Maybe it was because the dog was with him; maybe they saw the dog as a wild, uncontrollable blackfella's dog. Poor Digger — even he suffered prejudice by virtue of who owned him.

****

'Cross!' The dog raced across the last road and zigzagged slowly across the pavement sniffing fenceposts and shrubs obligatorily. Then the dog surged ahead, usually fast, for his final block of the route. A satisfied sense of euphoria and relief radiated from the man. He was nearly home; the run was done and he was a great bloke. Next time he'd do ten kilometres instead of the usual four, he said to himself as he always did at the end of his runs. 'That was easy! Too deadly! What a ripper sportsman! What a ripper sportsdog! A great sportspair. Too bad they don't have competitions for couch-potato owners and sluggy dogs. Me and Digs would piss it in.' He rounded the corner to his house and two strange sights greeted him. Firstly, there was his neighbour, old noseybody Hazel watering her dust bowl of a front yard, craning her skinny pale neck stiff with suspicion over the low fence between their houses. The second was the beat-up dusty Landrover parked under the big gum of his verge. Three brown children were throwing Digger's deflated basketball around the front yard. The dog barked and ran, tail wagging frantically. The kids were laughing and yelling, 'Diggy-dog! Uncle John!' They attempted to run to him but the dog was everywhere, licking, tail-wagging, jumping up, barking.

Cousin Gordon and the family had come down for a visit. On a blanket on his verandah two adults lounge, the larger stands up and slouches over the railing. A wide grin beaming on his broad black face. John thinks, 'That Gordon gets fatter and blacker every time I see him!' He strolls slowly up the driveway; sweating and smiling, mobbed by kids and the dog. They are yelling, laughing, talking, throwing the ball, and grabbing the dog all at once.

He quickly calculates how much money he has started to save for a new side fence and figures it should be just enough to shout his mob for a week or so, and to buy the kids whatever they needed and wanted. He calls out, 'Gordon! Lizzie! Gordon you fat bastard! You better be prepared to come jogging with me every day, if you're planning to camp here!'

Gordon waves his hand dismissively, 'What for? I don't need to go looking for womens! That's only for would-be studs like you, cuz.' John laughs.

His heart feels light and glad as he opens his arms to embrace Lizzie with one arm and shake Gordon's hand with the other.

Welcome to the Real World

Man, the sun does look good goin' down across the water. Check out all the little crabs movin' along the sand. Funny little fellas, runnin' sideways 'n' all. Gradually my body's desire to stay standing is hi-jacked and Commander General Gravity takes over the controls of this low flying plane. It crashes. My body takes in air and sand as I slump in a crumpled heap. I exhale deeply. My breathing disturbs a few of the thousands of grains of shell and grit that cover the beach for miles. The wind screams and the waves pulse out an uneven beat.

****

'Sonny, wake up! You all right then?'

Argh! Who the bloody hell is this? Wakin' a man up from a decent night's sleep! Ought to be a bloody criminal offence. Get lost! (All this I mutter to myself.) Out loud I say, 'Piss off!'

'Well now, there ain't no need to get all uppity tight about it! Jus' tryin' to make sure you's all right.'

'Yeah, well I was fine until you came along and woke me up! I was just fine!'

'There be no need to speak like that, boy! Anyhow, you don't look all right to me, ain't had a wash in weeks. By the look of you, those cuts could do with some looking at. And where's your mama 'n' papa? They'd be proper ashamed to see you lookin' like this, I'm sure!'

My one-cell, non-existent brain started working overtime. This old bag should be good for gettin' somethin' out of, I thought, spying her afternoon's grocery shopping trying to escape the confines of the plastic shopping bags. Now my voice takes on a softer, more helpless, needy tone. The sort that suckers 'em right in, 'specially the old farts.

'Nup, my mother 'n' father couldn't give a stuff about me. Dad was always on the booze and Mum, well it didn't take long till she couldn't take it no more, grabbed the baby and left.' (Cool, that was a good one, ay!)

I slowly rolled over and lifted my head from the sand. Small pieces of shells were embedded in the now dry blood from the gashes in my face.

'You're in a bad way sonny. I ain't got much, but what I do got …' She reached into her bag, my eyes flickered over her, judging her and her strength. 'Here you go. Like I said, it ain't much, but you look like you could do with a little somethin."

Something was an apple and a half a bunch of grapes, which was more than I'd had for days. Besides, it didn't look like it'd be worth the effort to do her over and she reminded me of my mum …

'And laddie,' she began to say, but I never quite got to hear the rest. My head felt as if some idiot was practising their karate kicks on it. God knows I felt bad. Real bad.

The next time I woke was to something or someone brushing past my cheek. I don't know why it was that in particular that woke me, it was pretty soft and for the last however many days a Saddam Hussein type of guy could've come up to me and said, 'Excuse me, but we're planning to blow up the world today and you're lying on the detonator. Would you mind moving?' and I'd have said, 'No, no! Of course not. Please go ahead,' rolled over and slept on oblivious. I wonder if I'd been unconscious?

Anyhow, this disturber of the peace was a possum. A goddam friggin' possum. Scroungin' around for food scraps. Well, I didn't have any to spare.

I raised my hand to a fist, with the intention of hitting, but that wasn't enough to scare it. Either it was tame or too hungry to care. I yelled out and startled it enough to bring back its instincts and get it and its adrenalin going, going, gone.

I guess I dozed for a while. When I woke, it suddenly occurred to me that I wasn't on no beach no more. For a second I panicked and sat bolt upright. Excruciating pain seared through my side, causing me to gasp and my face to contort. Once again my body reunited with the ground. After listening and observing what little I could see, I surmised I was in a warehouse-type building. You know, like the ones you see in gangster movies. Exactly where was I? Well … There was cold, hard cement below me instead of sand. I could no longer hear the ocean, though my ears did pick up a dripping sound, echoing softly from some place far off. Water … My God! Water! I dragged myself along on my stomach, ignoring the pain ripping me to shreds.

I finally reached the source of the sound but bitter disappointment and frustration was all that greeted me. There was no way that this was water. God only knows what it was, but it stank and I certainly wasn't going to drink it. I still didn't know how I got into this place. I tried hard to remember but this was one gauge where the needle just wouldn't move. Probably stumbled in here half conscious one night, I dunno any more. Wherever I was and however I got here really didn't matter. It had done me okay so far. My next few chilling nights were spent huddled and curled up in the corner of a room on a mouldy rug. The moulded decayed furniture stacked at one end of the room was probably home to thousands of termites and would crumble at a mere touch.

The next time my eyes opened I felt a little closer to being alive than I did the day before. I scrounged for food and came up with little more than a few dry crusty bits of bread and half a packet of chips. Enough. That bloody possum came back in the late evening and no joke, proceeded to pick my pockets as I lay still. Bugger that for a joke! My hand flew through the air and on contact sent the fur eatin' body ricocheting through space. The wall was its stopping force and with a thump it landed. A whimper told me its landing gear wasn't too crash hot though. And why should I be ripped off by a possum? Had it helped me 'shop' for my food? Did it have the decency to ask if it could share my five course, four and a half star meal? Nooo. Survival of the fittest mate. Sorry, you die, I win, suck eggs!

****

Stumbling blindly through winter's fury, a storm lashing out at the world for all its unpleasantness, and with no mercy, I'm blown through a doorway. Three years later and I'm back in this place. Swell. You'd've thought I might've gone up in the world, but no, here I am. Still no better than before. Worse, if anything. This place is a heap. Should've been bulldozed ages ago. It reminds me of gangster movies and I'm half expecting someone to jump out of the shadows and blow my brains out of my nostrils. Unfortunately, no such luck.

I can't help feeling I'm not really on this planet and I'm not like this, I dunno what planet I'm on, but it ain't earth. Earth is a loving, caring place. Maybe some little green men in white coats'll come and take me away soon.

Out of the corner of my bloodshot eye, I see something and casually, not at all worried, slowly turn around. After all, what reason do I have for using my reflexes to survive? Maybe the gangsters and the little green men are going to gang up on me. I wish. In the corner of the room I spy none other than my friend, the professional pickpocket (the furry one that is). Stupid bloody possum's gone and parked its leg in a trap. Wonder how long it's been there. The rain has steadied to a slow pitter pat. The wind howls in defiance. The sight in the corner is a pitiful one. Stupid dumb possum. How pathetic can you get? Well, don't think I'm going to rescue you. What if I did? Then I'd only have to look after you and feed you. I'm semi-living proof that I'm incapable of that. Stuff you. You can stay there and bleed and shiver with cold. If that doesn't get you, starvation will. no one helped me, well, properly, so why should I help you? My retreating footsteps echo softly, dimmed by the sound of the intensifying downpour.

****

Why? Why do I give in? Bugger'd if I know why! But here I am in the middle of the goddam freezing night, prisoner of a guilty stupid conscience, forced to take action. Getting soaked to the bone trying to free some goddam stupid robber of a possum. Unbelievable. There. You're free. Now nick off, you stupid little shit.

I set the possum down and hope to high whatsime it'll make a move. High whatsime seems to have taken the day off. Angrily I yell skyward, 'Great. Thanks a whole bloody lot!'

The possum stands and I begin to walk away. But dumb as I am I make the mistake of looking back. It doesn't even take two steps before collapsing. Great! Now what?

I walk over and gingerly lift it up, holding it close to me, inside my jacket. That's human frigging nature for you. After plugging the bleeding and doing what I can, I attempt to return to my fitful slumber. The furry little something snuggles up between the crook of my arm and my chest. Conniving little bugger! I nod off into the land of dreaming where at least there life can have some meaning.

Great. Another day sprawls over the horizon. Oh, what joy. I look down. The fur ball sleeps on. Moving carefully I wrap my jacket around the ball of fluff and leave the bundle, its body rising and falling, in search of breakfast. A few odds and sods are breakfast. I leave my fur ball to sleep and crouch in a corner, out of the chilling wind.

My head pounds and to breathe is to breathe pain, not air. My nose is running and my throat feels like a gravel road scraped and churned by bulldozers. Right, you little shit, time to eat. I am sharing my pittance of a breakfast with a possum. Not another person, no, a possum. Carefully I pick up my bundle and lay it gently in my lap. How in the hell do you wake a possum? 'Rise and shine!' 'Good morning?' What? I stare at it for a long time ... wait. Something ain't right here. I stare longer ... no ... NO! Breathe you little shit! You're supposed to be breathing. Not dead! NO! God I can't even look after a poxy possum. No. You can't be dead! Breathe! I fed you, kept you warm, now you owe it to me to breathe. Please ... I break into sobs. Words come out in half-strangled cries. I curl up and hold my possum to me hoping, maybe, to put some warmth back into its gaunt little body. Tonight, my lullaby is my crying and my utter frustration, desperation, hatred and sadness.

****

'Mummy, Mummy! Look what I found! It's a man with a baby possum!' The child's voice quietens to a whisper. 'Should I wake him? He looks sad.'

'No, no dear, you go home. I won't be long.'

The little girl brightened and skipped off. The woman knelt beside him and felt for a pulse. It's funny how the absence of something can be more startling than its presence ...

297

Mini Poems

I've known her for six months.
I've known her all her life.
There she lies, contented in my arms.
Her skin of downy softness,
delicate whispered breaths
of slumbering tranquillity
escaping her tiny lips.

To feel the child within you,
moving, growing … becoming.
To know that you will shape
a person with all that
you do, all that you say.
Nothing you do will be forgotten,
it will play a part in the child's
life somewhere, consciously or
unconsciously.
A child's mind is always on record.

The Story of Joanne Gray

I was doing the dishes when the phone rang. I quickly dropped the dishcloth I was using to clean the plates, dried my hands on the tea towel and reached over the kitchen bench to answer the telephone.

'Oh, hi Jess,' said a familiar voice at the other end of the line, 'could you come over? I've got something to tell you. It's very important and I don't feel like saying anything over the phone.'

'Okay, I have to finish the dishes but I'll be right there,' I replied. We said 'bye and hung up.

I finished the dishes, then asked my mother if I could go over to Jo's house. It wasn't very far from where I lived and it usually took me about fifteen minutes to get there from my place. Although it was pretty hot, I didn't mind the walk. Besides it would give me a chance to think over the conversation I had just had with Jo. She sounded very upset and I wondered what was wrong.

I arrived at Jo's house and rang the doorbell. She opened the door to me herself and by my first glance at her, I knew that she had been crying.

'What's wrong, Jo?' I asked in alarm. It wasn't very often that I saw my friend crying. She was usually a happy-go-lucky kind of a girl. With my question, she started crying again. Through her sobs, she told me that her mother had just died of a heart attack and her father was at the hospital. He had rung up and told Jo's aunty who had come over to keep her company at home. Jo's aunty had told her and the other family members what had happened, but Jo had wanted to tell me herself. I started crying as well. Both Jo and I stood in the middle of the room, hugging each other and crying our hearts out. I felt so sorry for my best friend. What a rotten thing to have happened!

I stayed with Joanne for a while, talking to her and trying to comfort her. When her father arrived home from the hospital, I left and went back to my house where I told my mother the sad news. Nobody could believe it. It was all so sudden.

The funeral for Jo's mother was held a week later on the Friday. There were hundreds of people from all over the place, some even came from Perth, nearly 2600 kilometres away, to pay their last respects to Jo's mother. It was a very sad occasion.

When the funeral was over, I went back home with my own family. My mum had told me not to intrude too much on Jo's family's sorrow, but just to be there for her if she needed to talk.

That weekend was very quiet. I stayed home waiting to see if Jo would ring to talk about things, but she never did. I felt very sad for my friend. Sunday evening, I got my gear ready for school the next day, watched some television and then went to bed.

Jo was not at school, so at recess, I walked to her house to see if she was all right. When I got there her father told me that she had gone to the shops for a walk. I decided to go to the shop where we all hang out to see if I could find her. I only had ten minutes to get to the shop and back to school so decided to skip school until after lunch. I needed to see if my best friend was okay.

When I got to the shop, I saw Jo. Just as I was going to talk to her, I saw that she was with Meagan and Shaw-Nae. I was surprised because Jo hated them and never mixed with them before. They were always cutting classes and sometimes they even got drunk in the park with the grown-ups, if they could. They always teased the little kids and made them cry and they smoked anything they could get their hands on, cigarettes or dope, they didn't care. Surprisingly enough, Jo seemed to be hanging out with them and liking it. It was a surprise for me because when Jo was friends with me, we never mixed with these girls. Our mothers had told us they were 'bad eggs'.

As I went up to Jo to say hello to her, I saw her light up a cigarette. She didn't see me as she had her back to me. The next minute, I saw Shaw-Nae open up a can of beer and pass it to Jo. Again Jo took it and took a deep swallow of the rotten beer. I couldn't believe it! I could not believe it, for just two weeks ago, Jo was telling me how she hated it when people got drunk and how she hated the smell of dirty tobacco smoke. People who drank and smoked smelled really bad. Now all of a sudden, here was Jo, my best friend, drinking and smoking with those two girls she hated. To make matters worse, when I went up to her to talk to her, she turned her back on me and said I was a baby, that I didn't know anything and that I was a spoilsport, a wowser and a nerd. I told her she was an idiot for doing what she was doing and mixing up with those girls. I left her at the shop, laughing at me and calling me names.

I thought about Jo all the way back to school. I thought that she had turned to alcohol and cigarettes because it made her forget all about her mum dying. I didn't know what I could do to help her with her loss.

After school, I went to Jo's house to see if she was home, but on the way, I saw her at the Apex Park where she was sitting all alone under a tree.

'What's wrong?' I asked her, as I sat down on the dry grass next to her.

She burst out crying, 'I want my mum back. I miss her so terribly. I want my mum.'

'Jo, she's gone,' I answered. 'It will take you a while, a long while, if ever, to get over her death. Remember when I was eight and my dad died? It took me a long time to get over losing him and I still think about him all the time. I miss him so terribly sometimes, but I try to think of all the good times we had together, Dad, Mum and me and my brothers. I just think of all the good things my dad did for us and how much he loved us and we loved him. I feel better then and I know my dad is with me in spirit wherever I go and is watching over me and Mum and the boys. Just because he's not with us doesn't mean to say he's not looking after us. He's like our guardian angel, I suppose, making sure we're safe. Try to think of your mother like that. It'll make you feel better.' We sat under that tree talking for ages, at least two hours.

After a while I asked her if she wanted to come to my house. I was sure there would be some cool drink in the fridge and Mum wouldn't mind if we had some. She probably had some biscuits somewhere too. We got up from the tree and walked home.

The next day I didn't saw Jo at all. I went around to her place and asked her dad where she was and he told me she just said to him that she was going out.

Over the next few weeks I never saw Jo at all except for a couple of periods at school some days. She did not want to talk to me and it really hurt because she was my best friend and we used to be close.

One evening I walked around to her place hoping that I'd see her. I again asked her Dad where she was, but he didn't know and didn't seem to care much either. Then I remembered hearing through the grapevine that Shaw-Nae was having a party at her place and thought Jo might be there. I was going to go to Shaw-Nae's house to see Jo, but thought better of it because Mum wouldn't let me go. She didn't like me going to places where people drank. It made me wild sometimes to be treated like a child but, as Mum said, she had her reasons.

One day, after not seeing Jo for weeks, she came up to me when I was walking home from school. She was crying. At first I thought she was crying because of her mother, but I soon realised it wasn't when she started telling me about the party which happened weeks ago.

'I'm pregnant,' sobbed Jo. 'And I don't know what to do or how to tell my father.' She was only fifteen, the same age as me.

'Did that happen at the party?' I asked her.

Jo nodded, 'I think so. I was so drunk that I don't remember anything about it. I don't even know who the father is. What am I going to do?'

We couldn't discuss this business standing in the street, so I asked Jo if she wanted to come home with me.

I had my own room and it was best if we talked about what Jo was going to do in there. After telling Mum I was home, Jo and I made our way to my room where we sat on the bed and talked and talked of her problem. We decided she had to go to the doctor to see if she could have an abortion. Jo didn't want the baby and there was no way that I could change her mind on this matter. Besides, I could see the sense in her not wanting the baby. Jo didn't know the father and she got pregnant through rape, not through love.

We then decided it was too dear to have an abortion and would probably cost the world. Neither of us knew much about this subject and try as we may, we could not come up with a solution. In the end, we decided to talk to my mother. She could tell Jo's father and all together, we might come up with some sort of an idea of what would be best for her.

My mother told Jo that she would have to see a doctor straight away and she must let her father know. With this in mind, we went around to Jo's house, but her father wasn't at home and wouldn't be back for hours yet. So my mother told Jo that we'd go home and we would see her in the morning and tell her father then.

Next morning, something terrible happened. I was talking to Mum about Jo, when suddenly, there was a loud knock on our front door. I opened it and Jo fell into our lounge room.

I screamed out for Mum and shouted, 'Call an ambulance, quick.'

Mum took one look at Jo and at once called the ambulance, which arrived in a few minutes. Jo was rushed to hospital with the ambulance siren blaring. I went with her and while they took Jo to the emergency room, I sat in the waiting room, more worried than ever before. Later my mother came in and sat with me. Together we waited in silence to hear of any news of my friend.

Mum had gone to Jo's father's place to tell him about the emergency before she came to the hospital. When she had left there, he was getting ready to come to the hospital.

After what seemed a long time, the nurse came to see us. By this time Jo's father still hadn't arrived. We didn't know what was holding him up, he should have been here by now.

'Jessica, Mrs Hansen, Jo has suffered a drug overdose. She is okay but she has lost her baby,' said the nurse.

'She's lost her baby?' said Mum.

'Yes, Jo was two months pregnant,' replied the nurse. 'Has Mr Gray come yet?'

Just then, as we were going to go to Jo's place to fetch her father, he came running down the hall. 'What's wrong? Where is Jo? What's happened to her?' he cried breathlessly.

My mother explained everything to him, even telling him about the baby. Mr Gray was very confused and angry, but he couldn't wait to see Jo and to tell her that everything would be all right, that he loved her and wanted her to get well.

Jo's father got over his hurt and anger at his daughter's troubles and when she got out of hospital, he promised her he would never again let her face her mother's death without his support. Jo said she was never going to do anything so stupid again. Poor Jo! I felt so sorry for her and all that she had been through.

When Jo came home from hospital, she seemed to handle her

worries all right, until one day, she came to my house with a blood nose and black eyes. Alarmed, I asked her what had happened. She told me that she got into a fight with Shaw-Nae because they, Shaw-Nae and Meagan, wanted her to go drinking with them again. When Jo told them that she was not going to hang out with them anymore, they called her all sorts of names. In her misery, anger and frustration, Jo had lashed out at them in the only way she knew how.

She fought with those girls and was very glad she did, for never again would she let anybody coax or cajole her into doing something she knew was wrong. In a way, Jo was lashing out at herself for her own stupidity.

Fragments from Life

ABORIGINAL POLICE AID

Police Aid Number 13. A position in society. A place where I can feel proud of who I am. A job. One that pays well. I've come a long way from the days on the station. A position from which I can see my family through the good times and the bad. A place to feel proud of myself. But, also a place to feel shame for my role. The place of a police aid is in catch twenty-two. The place of in between black and white. A place where no one really wants to be. A coconut. Brown outside but white inside. Called that name by both sides of the fence. Don't they know I've been put here to help? To try and work out the problems of my people. Problems with coping in the white man's world. My position is not seen as good by all. I can only try and do my job.

A VICTIM OF GOVERNMENT POLICY

She was a lonely soul. A woman deprived of her five children. Those people had no bloody right to send her children away. Was it her fault that she gave birth to children with fair skin? They were her flesh and blood. How could those people take them away? Without knowing the hardships they had to endure. What gave them the right to interfere in her life? She would have survived quite well on her own. There was family willing to help her. How would those people like it if their children were stolen away while they were busy inside? They'd be jumping up and down and screaming from the roof tops about the injustice. Aboriginal people couldn't do that. They had no voice to scream out for help. They were the victims of the white society which imposed itself on them. Victims of government policy. Government people who thought they knew what Aboriginal people needed. Could they have known the great sadness which was to follow? Aboriginal people all over the country not knowing who they are. Aboriginal mothers all over the country not knowing where their children are. Some people got to go back and find their roots. Others weren't so lucky. She was left to mourn the loss of her children. She died before they were sent back.

RESPONSIBILITY

She is the stronghold of the family. As the youngest of five it seems so unfair to place so much pressure on her young shoulders. She too has a life to live. Family to cope with. The daily running of a household is work enough, with a four year old. The phone rings. She looks at it nervously, not wanting to touch it. Maybe it has happened. Maybe this is the phone call which will turn her life inside out. Lighting a cigarette she reaches for the phone. Relief. It isn't them.

THE LONE MAN

He's a loner. Always has been and always will be. A private person. He doesn't want to communicate much at all. In fact he's got an unlisted number. He doesn't like people knowing too much about his moves. The main reason why he lives out in the country is to avoid people's gaze. Away from the hustle of city life. One day it all became too much for him, so he packed up and left. He didn't tell too many people about his plans. He just up and left within a matter of hours. Rather a strange sort of bloke. Used to spend most of his time stroking his beard while looking past you. If you tried to strike up conversation he would remain still and silent. Many a man would shake his head and walk away. They were wasting their time. I guess he felt they were wasting his time too. His life and his time are his. Private. Too private to share or talk about.

DEFIANT

He's the one who goes against the grain. Always doing or saying something wrong. Crossing his friends when he leaves debts unpaid. Crossing strangers, and receiving black eyes. Crossing the law for daring to look them in the eye! A true free spirit. Old enough to know better. Skilful enough to keep everyone thinking. He likes to play games with your mind. Sometimes the conversation gets twisted around so much that you become confused by your own words. He takes particular delight in his ability to do that. His eyes are black pools. Piercing you, and daring you to challenge him.

LIFE IN A SMALL COUNTRY TOWN, ANYWHERE IN AUSTRALIA

Ah! Pension day. The best day of the week. A day in which you can go down town. Mix with the other people of the town. Maybe even score a few drinks from someone who has received their cheque. Me, I don't get that. The Social Security mob cut me off for cheating them. Something about cheating the system. How can a blackfella know they are cheating the system? They have a system to suit them and a system to suit us. What about the system we've had for many years? Doesn't that count? My family come to stay sometimes. I don't have to let the bloody world know what's going on in my family. My business is mine. Private. What they want to know from me. I don't care what they do with their lives. Who they have in their house is their own business. Why don't they just leave me to mine? Anyway, these little words aren't going to change anything. They cut me off and so now I got to survive in the best way I know how. Check out the rellies for a loan. Someone always comes through with something for me. I'll get by!

'Hey you guys!' His hands went to his mouth to whistle. They turned around to see who it was. Instantly their faces lit up. Can it really be him? They didn't expect to see him for some time.

'When did you get out, bro?' asked Jimmy.

'Did they let you out early?' asked another.

Ralph hung his head in shame. Although it was good to be back, he felt uneasy facing the old gang again. He hadn't forgotten the reason why he had to go away. They didn't know the pain and suffering he experienced while in that place. The place he didn't even want to give a name to. It held too many bad memories for him. Pacing like a caged animal. Eating, sleeping and rising to the sound of an unfriendly voice. Those people didn't want to know you. They had a job to do, and you were the job. Most of the guys in there were okay. There's a strong bond between men in a place like that. They all knew their time had to be done. Regardless of their guilt or innocence. He strongly believed his stay was unnecessary. He knew he had been framed for it. Why didn't anyone believe him when he pleaded innocent? The system had failed him. The bloody system had failed most of the guys inside. They didn't know why they were there. Some of them were stuck inside for life.

'Hey Ralph!' cried Warren. 'We'll go out on the town, just like the old days.'

Ralph turned away. He didn't want no night out. That is exactly the same way in which he found himself taken away and put inside.

'No more, boys,' he replied. 'I'm gunna take it easy for a while. Let's just sit and yarn for a while.'

Victim of Racism

I awoke in the hospital. I'm lucky to have woke up at all. Another blackfella like me didn't get to wake up. Louis Johnson. He was out on his birthday. Me, I was out hitch-hiking to the next town for my daughter's birthday. I didn't quite make it to the party. I'll admit that I was drunk at the time. A bottle of JD in my hand. That's not important though. The reason for this story is to let you know one of the untold stories of us Aborigines. Because someone didn't like the colour of my skin they thought they'd deal with me their way. They decided to swerve off the road where I was sitting. I woke up in the hospital and I was told that I was being sent to Perth. I've been here in the city for some time now. This place is called Shenton Park. Rehabilitation they call it. Don't know when I'll get to go back home for good. Hope it's soon. I'm getting homesick now. Bored laying around. I want to get back to my job. Anyway I can thank someone for looking after me that night. Someone from the other side was watching. I was luckier than Louis. They took his life. Me, they only took my leg.

I Remember

I remember Aunt Louise at Sister Kate's. Breaking my leg while she was on holiday, the measles, needles and pain, my little brother in a cot, playing with spiders, Christmas spiders' webs, sun showers, being told to be quiet, a lot, all of the time, loneliness, sad times, fun times, the train at the zoo, the merry-go-round, the paddock at the home, the cow's head at kindy, picking lillies and cow dung, Mr Ashton and the circus. I remember man on the moon. I remember going home. Dad and the station. Fun times down by the river. I remember being teased and told I thought I was white. I remember a lot of things. I remember to forget most of them.

Junkie Man

Junkie Man lowers his woozy head at a snail's pace. His half-spent cigarette burns his spindly fingers unnoticed. Extinguished by flesh, it drops to the gaudy worn carpet beneath stolen Air Nikes, making its home for a day or two, maybe three. The dull, neglected atmosphere of his home envies the party in his head. The smoky corner of his ground-floor bed-sit purposely hides a photograph of Mark and Sonia. His best enemies, his worst friends. They're smiling. They're always smiling. On odd occasions, Junkie Man sits in his narcotic trance and makes an effort to wonder whatever happened to them, then decides against it.

Junkie Girl pushes dry eyelids over sulky eyes. Cheekbones resembling jutting hips, hips resembling a drying carcass. Her usual suffocating thoughts are ambushed by heroin's slovenly soldiers. Happy to escape Wheel of Fortune. Happy she doesn't have to change the channel. Happy, happy, happy. She wishes she didn't feel like vomiting. Although the curtains are fully drawn, a crack of light persists on invading her privacy. She curses its fragmented intensity and her fragile stomach as they conspire against her in endless attacks. She concedes defeat and makes her way, reluctantly, toward the laundry sink only to catch her thoughtless bile halfway there.

When Junkie Man was called Mark he could trap butterflies using his taped-up lunch box and a sheet of A4 paper. He stole silvery kisses from their wings then marvelled at their frail, fluttering escapes. He smelt his father's breath in Santa's beard and hoped that the tooth fairy's strike would soon be over.

He could ride his bike of bits and pieces from his house to Nathaniel's in a sweaty record of four minutes twenty-seven seconds. He could muster boundless energy to run from the service station's monster hound, laughing all the way to

Hainsworth Avenue. He could ignore his parents' shouting through the entire length of *Planet of the Apes*. He spent concentrated hours attacking his home-grown enemies and defending his backyard picket castle in rain, hail, shine or moonlight. He initiated The Smoking Hut by being the first of his renegade friends to fully drag in a cigarette without coughing, then changed its name to The Shack of the Bloodshot Eye on the celebrated arrival of the first foil. He could drink guys two years older than him under the table, then leave with their girlfriends, bloating on ego and Jack Daniels. He did the 'drive-in snog' for forty-seven minutes on a sheepskin throne in his Kingswood Kingdom and could still recall, with great accuracy, any scene of *Rocky* for his wide-eyed subjects.

He dabbled in deals, tampered in temptation, reigned in reverence.

He was a Lord.

When Junkie Girl was called Sonia, she rode the wild horses of fantasy along glittering paths of emerald grass, until the morning sun whispered its orders to rise. She could make fairy music on her father's shoulders by gently coaxing the dripping chandelier orchestra into play. She hid under a pillow mountain for hours on end waiting for detection, only to fall asleep in its soft, solitary closeness. She woke wearing a sweat and a frown. She could swim the lake to freedom and loot Mr Flannigan's grapes for her rascal pixie friends to scoff them in barefooted abandonment. She would kiss her poppy's wrinkly eyes, hoping it would make him see again, then dance in swirls to Chopin and Mozart to test her hope-filled theory. She set fire to her liquid black hair to spare it from the ivory scissors' cruel intentions. She could whisper so softly that no one could hear her, then smile at her own cunning.

She could whisper so softly that no one could hear her.

She could whisper so softly.

No one could hear her.

Until she met Mark.

She was his Queen.

Only I Know

Phone rings
Relations and friends drop in
the door bell sounds
telegrams, flowers and more flowers.

Acquaintances arrive
everyone shares the pain
of your youthful and
sudden death.

Who cares
about flowers, cards,
words, poems and telegrams
I only want you back

To love, to laugh with
and laugh at, to tease
to be your mum
and to share your dreams.

Please don't tell me
that you know how I feel
and that you understand my pain.
Only I know.

The heart-ache, the torment,
the anguish, the pain,
the void can never
be filled.

My veins are dried up rivulets
my heart a jagged rocky beach
my mind a child's playground at midnight
empty and desolate.

VIVIENNE SAHANNA

God's Dreaming, Aboriginal Dreaming

Aboriginal Australians have survived some 40,000 or more years, and have had strict moral codes and laws by which to live, successfully, before 1778. Following almost two hundred and ten years of subjection, it was not until 1992 that Aboriginal peoples practising in Anglican churches around Australia were invited to have a say and be listened to when we spoke. It has been the Anglican Church's desire to work earnestly for reconciliation of all our churches and all our peoples, indigenous and non-indigenous alike. We who make up the National Aboriginal Anglican Council were nominated by our diocesan bishops.

A PERSONAL STORY

I was born at a Western Australian Government Settlement in the Moora District where the Anglicans had representatives or missionaries. My earliest Christian learning was from Mum and Dad who taught us the Lord's Prayer. They took turns each night, whether we lived in tents or tin shanties and bags or finally at our old place, a four-roomed house which was our mansion, on five acres of land which they purchased for twelve pounds seventeen shillings and four pence, in Pinjarra, Western Australia.

Mum was Roman Catholic and Dad was Anglican, but there was no friction between them. Most of us were christened Anglicans. Only two out of the ten were Roman Catholic. Now, as a woman I appreciate our parents teaching religion to us, as their Aboriginality was forcefully taken away from both of them.

They grew up in two different missions — Dad at Moore River Native Settlement, and Mum at New Norcia Roman Catholic orphanage for Aboriginal children. So, now you know where I'm coming from!

I propose to compare the two spiritual expressions with a view to finding common ground. I'd like to label these two diverse cultural practices God's Dreaming and Aboriginal Dreaming. Most cultures have a spiritual component which seeks to address or accept the inexplicable aspects of the unseen and the unknowable within their cultural boundaries. The rituals are merely the outward expression of a deep and abiding inner faith which strengthens and directs the purpose of life. So often it is only cultural differences that cause criticism and disbelief of the oral histories passed down by word of mouth of indigenous peoples the world over.

GOD'S DREAMING

The Bible tells the story of the creation of the world from a formless mass of water and darkness. In six days our Triune God created every living creature, plant life and Adam and Eve. God, the Father, Creator of the Universe just said, Let there be light — darkness was night and light was day. Let there be a dome between water in sky and the earth … Let there be land. The sea God ordered to come so far and no further. Let there be creatures of every kind — and it was so. Let there be plants, fish, birds — it was so and it was good.

But the masterpiece of God's creation was the human being, who was made in our own image. God took clay and formed with his own hands, all the organs and frames and genes. With God's own hands Adam was formed. God's Dreaming was the Garden of Eden, made so he could walk and talk in fellowship with Adam.

By God's Dreaming, reconciliation can proceed between God and man, and man and man.

Indigenous people have several names for the Creator Spirit of the world, for example, Wunjana of the Kimberley, Western Australia; Rainbow Serpent in Western Australia; Wargarl or water snake creator spirit god, in the south-west of Western Australia. In Aboriginal oral histories the Wargarl, or Rainbow Serpent, is manifested as a Creator God with wisdom and knowledge and promise of life because it is usually associated with rivers, lakes and waterholes.

Nearly every traditional group of Aborigines has special or particular names for how their lands were created. In their storytellings there are stories about creation, the great flood and the spiritual ownership of our land Australia. There are sacred sites which have great importance to indigenous Australians.

Today Aboriginal people are telling how they are re-learning their tribal language with the guidance of spirits, and so there is renewal and the reclaiming of power to speak languages long thought lost. This applies to dance and music also, especially in the southern parts of most of Australia. With the use of didgeridoo, clap sticks and the tapping of two boomerangs, traditional Aborigines sing and dance to the spirits belonging to their ancestors. We believe our old ones' spirits stay close to us and the land they were born in and lived in.

Unfortunately, there is a communication breakdown of the traditional way of our ancestors. Alcohol and drug abuses, TV, peer groups and disrespect for the elders are shown by both young males and females. The young people are not steeped in the original Laws and ways of our ancestors, and that can mean the loss of our ancestral Laws and languages, dance and music. The Laws were strict, and punishment was enforced by tribal elders, both men and women.

The dispossession of Aborigines by Europeans since 1788 may never be reversed. Non-Aborigines have taken from them the best pastoral lands and pushed the ancestral owners of today off their own tribal lands, further testing intertribal relationships and accelerating the disintegration of customs and Laws.

The greedy white people also want our precious minerals, and don't want to pay rent to the people who have ancestral claims to these lands. My opinion is that the Western Australian

Government and big mining companies promote greed and dispossession. The Government of Western Australia will not acknowledge the Supreme Court Justices of the Federal Government of Australia's decision on Terra Nullius; and this is a lie as big and as bad as the lie the snake told Eve in the Garden of Eden.

ABORIGINAL CHRISTIANITY

This could be the most profound but also the most difficult to touch on, as our ancestral history since 1788 has been one of dispossession, of denial of homeland territories of tribes of all indigenous Australians, and Tasmanians in particular. Even today our non-Aboriginal populations think we are unreasonable to keep on claiming land rights or at least wanting to receive royalties for the land which cannot be redeemed, by governments and businesses paying rent.

If anyone has read the book by John Harris, *One Blood*, they may feel the total degradation, the ineffectual position Aboriginal people were forced into by British firepower, diseases, poisons and, not least, by the criminals, felons and unwanted of Britain. Rape, killing by alcohol, and murder of proud Aborigines who did resist the white invasion has never stopped. (I must note here that up to the 1970s there had never been any acknowledgement in white school books of the resistance, gallantry and fierce pride our ancestors had.) The British strategy of divide and conquer was very effective. It was on 3 June 1992 when, finally, the best legal brains in the land overturned that misconception. In 1992 most of us rejoiced when the decision to nullify Terra Nullius was handed down in the highest court of our land. It acknowledged our spiritual claims of Australia and gave us hope. We have been denied and ignored too long.

I am an Aboriginal Christian woman and I have spoken to many ordained people who have done comparative studies of the biblical Hebrew God and faith, and the indigenous Australian creator, perpetuated by storytelling and traditional Laws. These people have told me that along with the many other cultural religions they have studied, Aboriginal spirituality and belief in their connections to all living and non-living things of their land, have close parallels to the laws God gave the Hebrews through Moses. As a Christian and an Aboriginal, therefore, I can appreciate that the Aboriginal Dreaming is, in part, complementary to the Christian view of God's will for man.

Martin Luther King Jr said: I have a dream that one day every valley shall be exalted, every hill and mountain shall be made low, the rough places will be made straight and the glory of the Lord shall be revealed and all shall see it together.

This is my hope. This is my faith.

Night Fighters

Night provides a security
warm round soft black cocoon
confession booth bed.

We can now speak of
the tumultuous years
with rational retrospective
calm.

Old comfortable tranquil
slippers
dangerous familiarity
my love.

As I turn to meld into
the curve of your spine
secure arc
a distant scream pierces
my peace
a low pitched hostility
penetrates.

Night Fighters

It took thirteen years
to come to this
yet still swiftly flowing dark
subterranean streams
run parallel
never merging
ever seeking a mutual
mouth
my love.

Who You

I'm forgetting
About the
Spear
Ignoring the
Boomerang
Walking past the
Didgeridoo
The old man
Sits
In the dust
And asks
Who You

Family and Friends

We are
Closer
To death
Through
Alcohol, drugs
And pills
Than
We are
To our
Own
Family and friends

Stockmen

I would love
To have been
A stockman
Riding the range
So bold
Sittin' around
A campfire
Sharin' a couple
Of yarns
Drinkin'
A hundred stubbies
And still
Round up
The herd

Or yodellin'
An' a strummin'
A Slim Dusty
Song or two.
But
As you know
I sit
In the park
With a flagon
Waitin' for
The police
To
Round us up
And herd
Us in

Road to Nowhere

This feeling
Of
Pain, sorrow
And joy
Attacking
All at once
I'll never get to know
What's inside
My head

The things
You done
And the
Things you said
Leave me
In the
Higher sky
Sometimes in
The
Deepest sea

I've got
To find
The right
Road to nowhere
No one is
To blame
The laughter
In my head
Is still
The same

No one is
To blame
Wish my
Head
Will clear
And find
The right
Road
To nowhere

Death in custody
No one
Cares
Anymore
Same as before
I wish
Someone
Will turn
On the lights
So dark
In here
I can't
Find the door

For the Aboriginals

Be proud of your colour and colours,
We are the ones who stand tall,
White might hurt you with words and weapons,
But we got our spirits, wisdom and peace.
They got WAR.

When Love is on Your Side

When love is on your side, be free
So you will never be afraid of hatred
Show that you are proud of yourself
So the whole world knows you're here
And to stay.

Humans Say

Humans say we are a different colour
But everyone look inside you
And understand what you're feeling
Say to you:
Bleed the same blood
Have the same insides
Why don't we have the same feelings for each other
Tell me that!

Storm

The satin curtain of the night was drawn back last night
As the distant thunder rolled in.
Everything was still, waiting.
The flashing, forked lightning shattered the night.
The fireworks were spectacular,
Illuminating the city of different shapes.
The lightning filled the sky,
The rain started to fall,
First the tap, tap of big drops,
To the downpour of an endless drone
Of millions of raindrops,
Filling the gutters that overflowed.
Roads became rivers sparkling
As the lightning flashed.
The trees and flowers shook their heads
All clean and fresh
As they relaxed to the sound of the distant thunder
Rolling on.

Glossary
of Western Australian Aboriginal Words

Arcyumpalpa	desert oak tree
Bambaru	the blind one
Biddair	white boss
Bin	been
Bunji	lover, bunji woman or bunji man
Bullai	look out as in 'look out someone's coming'
Cadgebut	a thorny acacia tree
Cartwarrah	mad
Choo/Djoo	shame, big shame
Chunyart	twenty-eight parrot, rosella
Coolbardi/Koolbardi	magpie
Culunga(s)/Koolung(s)	child/children
Coomarl/Koomal	possum
Coomp	pass urine/relieve oneself
Coorda	brother
Coorr	bushtail wallaby
Cunmanggu	bush potato
Didj/Didge	didgeridoo/didjeridu
Gebba/Gebba-Ngooniny	wine, usually cheap red wine, plonk
Gnuk	little frog
Gududjara	area around the Rudall River
Japani man	Japanese man
Jerda	birds (generic)
Jigalong	Aboriginal community (Yamitji people)
Kanyjamurra	yams, like sweet potatoes
Kaarder	long-tail goanna
Kongi/Kongk	uncle
Koorlung	boy
Magarra-gudany	having a tail, devilman

Marbu	flesh-eating being like an ogre
Mamon	clever man, shaman
Mardu/Martu	Western Desert people
Marrugu	son-in-law
Mata	sweet potatoes
Mayi	small damper (Western Desert area)
Milalbo	millet
Minyarra	wild onions
Monaitch/munatj	policeman
Mubbarn Man	clever man/shaman
Murrandus	goanna
Ngarrdi	devil
Ngidiung	white person
Ngoon/gnoony	brother, brother cousin
Nguba(s)	spouse(s)
Ngunjy	self, I
Nyangumartu	language around the Port Hedland area
Nyingarn	porcupine
Nyoongar, Nyoongah, Noongar, Nyungar	Aboriginal man of the Bibbulmun people of the south-west of Western Australia. It has come to be generally used for all Aboriginal people of the south-west of Western Australia.
Palpinpa	cork tree
Pirrkiri	a carved stick like a wooden knife
Rainbow Serpent	Creator of Bibbulmun world, south-west mythical being from the Dreamtime
Umari	mother-in-law
Unna	question, agreement, support what is being said, pass comment
Waddies	clubs
Wadjellas, Wadjelas, Wadjullas	white people
Wagyl, Wargyll, Wogari	snake, keeper of the freshwater sources
Waitj	emu
Wama blossoms	makes a sweet drink
Wamulu	bush tomatoes
Wana	bush honey (Kalumburu area)
Wana	digging stick (Western Desert area)

Wanda	basket
Wardung/wardang	crow
Warlitji	eagle hawk
Warra, Worra	not good, bad
Windemarra	mulga
Winji/winjie	question, like 'what's going on?'
Wirnis	coolamons, wooden oval-shaped bowls
Wongki	Aboriginal person from the Goldfields area
Winjana, Wunjana	Kimberley region deity, mythical being
Wuurdatji	little hairy man
Yamatji	Aboriginal person from the north-west of Western Australia, that is the Pilbara, Gascoyne and Murchison areas
Yilwei	green ants
Yonga/Yongka	kangaroo
Yorga	south-west Bibbulmun woman
Yuwinji	woollybut seeds

Notes on Contributors

Josie Boyle was born in the Western Australian mining town of Morgans in 1941. At the age of two years she was placed in Mt Margaret Mission, where she remained until she was sixteen years old. She then travelled to Perth, where she still lives. Josie now works as a storyteller, sharing her experiences of desert life with pre-primary school children. She is currently working on her autobiography.

Septu Brahim was born in Port Hedland in 1932. His father came from Java, and was of Arab origin, and his mother came from the Fitzroy Valley, of the Bunuba Tribe. Septu has lived and worked in Broome, Port Hedland and Perth, where he now resides with his family.

Robert Bropho has written the important book *Fringedweller* (1980). He presently lives at The Swan Valley Nyoongar Community.

Irene Calgaret was born in Bunbury in 1945, and was stolen and taken to Roelands Mission at the age of six. Irene left Roelands at sixteen, married three years later, and worked, mainly in nursing, for many years. More recently, she continued her education at Edith Cowan University. Irene's writing is dedicated to her four grandsons.

Ambrose Chalarimeri (born Mungala Chalarimeri) was born into a traditional lifestyle in the bush at Oomarri (King George River) between 1930 and 1940. After five or six years Mungala was taken to the Spanish Benedictine mission at Kalumburu. He was given the name Ambrose and stayed on the mission until he was about twenty years old. Since then he has lived and worked all over the Kimberley and in other places, some as far south as Perth. He is now working on more stories for a book.

Mary Champion is a Nyoongah woman who has been living in Kalgoorlie for thirty years. She has studied at Kalgoorlie College, and is currently running a hostel for children in Kalgoorlie.

Jimmy Chi came out of university studies in the early '70s disillusioned and rather bitter so he wrote the song 'Acceptable Coon' in a very critical way about education and the monocultural streamlining of the dominant Anglo-Saxon system. 'Acceptable Coon' describes the attempt of students to find identity and cultural survival amongst their own historical and cultural roots and, with their qualifications gained, to give something back to their own community and advance Aboriginal Australia. He is a playwright and song-writer and author of the internationally acclaimed *Bran Nue Dae* (1991) and *Corrugation Road*.

Ethel May Clinch (nee Green) was born in the Mount Magnet region in 1908. She enjoyed reading poetry as a child, and has written many poems for family and friends over the years.

Chantelle Corbett was born in 1981. She is a young Nyoongar woman who lives in Pinjarra with her parents and she wrote the story in this collection when she was fifteen. She hopes to study at TAFE to be a Child Care worker.

Victor Deeble was born in East Perth. He describes himself as 'a half-caste Nyoongah', whose mother came from a tribe in the south-west. After his involvement in a devastating car crash as a young adult, he began to write, 'to lose myself in the written word'. Victor is presently working on a family history and a collection of short stories.

Pat Dudgeon grew up in Darwin but her people are in Broome. She came to Perth to study psychology and decided to stay. She is currently Head of the Centre for Aboriginal Studies at Curtin University. She lives in St James with four cats and a dog.

Walter Eatts was born in 1937, and worked as a horsebreaker, stockman, and cattle drover in Western Australia and Queensland before becoming a registered painter. He worked in that profession from 1958 to 1979, when he decided to further his education. The qualifications he gained have led to his current employment in the Juvenile Justice Division of the Ministry of Justice.

Robert Eggington has worked extensively in a number of Aboriginal organisations in Perth for the past eighteen years. Robert was the founder of the highly acclaimed Kyana gatherings held in 1991–1993. He has also represented the Nyoongah people on a number of national bodies and has instigated and co-ordinated international strategies for campaigns regarding intellectual property rights and cultural ownership issues.

Rodney Ellis is from the Yamatji people, and was born in Carnarvon in the late 1950s. He was brought up in missions and foster homes from the 1960s to the early 1970s. He has lived in Kalgoorlie and travelled a lot. Rodney currently lives in South Hedland.

Denise Groves is from the Pilbarra and was born in Marble Bar. She has a Masters degree from Murdoch University, where she now works in the area of Aboriginal and Islander Studies. She lives in Fremantle with her son.

Matthew Haltiner is in Year 9 at Kelmscott Senior High School. His interests include writing, football and cricket, music, working on the computer and cooking.

Chanelle Hansen is fifteen years old and lives in Armadale, Western Australia. Her interests include creative writing, basketball and netball. When she leaves school she would like to be a film director.

Fabien Nialle Hansen was born in Broome in 1971 and raised in the wheatbelt area of Hyden. He went to school at Hyden Primary School and Thornlie and Beverley High Schools, and continued at Bunbury Regional Prison.

Colin Indich was born in Northam in 1944 and grew up in the wheatbelt area, where he worked as a farm labourer and on the railways.

Betty Indich was born in 1947 in Merredin. At the age of eleven years she was placed in Norseman Mission, where she remained until she began working as a domestic. Betty and Colin now live in Kalgoorlie.

Clarrie Isaacs was born in 1948 and his country is around Margaret River. He is one of seven children, and was educated in Perth. In recent years he has played an active role in many protests, including the Cockatoo Dock Strike (1989) and the Tent Embassy (1972).

Kristy Jones' father's family come from South Australia and Victoria, while she, her mother and brother come from Carnarvon. Family, her small town upbringing, and the environment of her youth have all contributed to her view of life. She dedicates this contribution to her friends and family, and especially to her grandad.

Alan Knapp is a Nyoongah from the south-west of Western Australia. He has worked as a boxer and is currently writing his autobiography with help from David Whish-Wilson.

Lorna Little is a Nyoongah and a Custodial Elder of her clan, as well as being a mother, grandmother and great-grandmother. She has a BA degree in Social Science from Curtin University. She is also a practising Christian and a Parish Councillor with the local Anglican Church. She has been widely published in multicultural and Aboriginal anthologies.

Tom Little was born at Pinjarra in 1958 and his family belongs to the Bilyaduk Bindjareb people. He has been a professional sportsperson, playing cricket, football and basketball. He was also a member of the police force for nine years, before becoming a student at the University of Western Australia. Tom is a talented musician as well as a writer. He is married with two daughters.

Helen Lockyer is from the Roebourne area and is currently working at the Centre for Aboriginal Studies at Curtin University as a tutor in the Aboriginal bridging course. She is committed to working in the area of Aboriginal education.

Rose Murray is a Nyangumarda woman from the Pilbara region of Western Australia. She now lives and works in Port Hedland. She has completed tertiary studies in Primary Teaching and Art, and in her current position as a community worker, Rose is doing community education about family violence. She has collected oral histories from Pilbara women between the ages of eighteen and eighty years.

Stephen Narkle was born in 1983 and lives in Armadale. He is a Nyoongar. When he leaves school he hopes to be a Physical Education teacher or a Recreation Officer. He also hopes at some stage to write a book of short stories for children.

Charmaine Papertalk-Green is a Nyarlu (woman) with cultural ties to Wajarri and Bardimaya. She was born at Eradu, on the Greenough River, Western Australia, to Charlie Green and Margaret Green (nee Papertalk) and has four brothers and five sisters. She was raised in Mullewa and educated at Mullewa District High School. She lives with her partner, Tom, and two sons, Mark and Tamati, at Utakarra in Geraldton.

Fred Penny was born in Narogin in 1957. He spent twelve years in Wandering Mission, before being sent to the Pallotine Mission at Rossmoyne. He is married with four children, and describes himself as 'a Christian who writes and sings about the injustices committed against Aboriginal people in the hope that there will be a greater understanding of and tolerance towards Australia's indigenous people for the benefit of the whole community.'

Doris Pilkington (Nugi Garimara) has written two books, *Caprice* (1991) and *Follow the Rabbit-proof Fence* (1996), the latter of which is currently being made into a film. She is currently writing her mother's biography. She was the inaugural David Unaipon Award winner and has sat on the Australia Council.

Tracie Pushman. Unfortunately the editors have lost contact with Tracie Pushman since she submitted her story 'Junkie Man' for this anthology.

Tom Quartermaine was born at the Mogumber Mission, Western Australia, in 1944. He was looked after by his grandparents, and at the age of nine, was taken to a mission called Marybank, where he was supposed to stay until he was eighteen. He ran away at fifteen and worked wherever he could. Tom now works as the Peer Support Officer at Greenough Regional Prison.

Lloyd Riley is a Nyoongar man who is studying Education at Curtin University, Perth. He has a special interest in Nyoongar culture and wants to pass it on to others, especially young people. He strongly believes that older Nyoongars should share their culture with their young people and others. Lloyd has written a book, which was submitted for the David Unaipon Award and was highly recommended.

Jennifer Sabbioni was formally a senior lecturer in Aboriginal Studies and Director of Research at the Kurongkurl Katitjin School of Australian Indigenous Studies at Edith Cowan University. She is a Nyoongah woman actively involved in her community.

Vivienne Sahanna was born in 1937 at the Moore River Native Settlement in Western Australia. She has combined a long career in nursing with an active involvement in the Anglican Church, representing Australia internationally as a member of the National Aboriginal and Torres Strait Island Anglican Council. She is currently a practicing Remote Area Nurse in the Kimberley region of Western Australia.

Kim Scott was born in 1957 and grew up in Albany, Western Australia. He has published two acclaimed novels, *True Country* (1993) and *Benang: From the Heart* (1999).

Janice Slater was born in Perth in 1950. She belongs to the Badimya people of the Yamatji Nation, and has four children and five grandchildren. Janice has worked in Aboriginal education, employment and research, and has been writing poetry and short stories since 1984. She now lives in Coff's Harbour, New South Wales, where she is working on a collection of stories and poetry.

Barbara Stammner was born at Picton Junction near Bunbury in 1938, the youngest of thirteen children. Her people are the Winjan/Bibbulmun people, and she has lived around the Bunbury, Busselton, Roelands area all of her life. She has been married twice and has seventeen grandchildren and three great-grandchildren.

Alf Taylor has written two books of poetry, *Singer Song Writer* (1992) and *Winds* (1994), and is presently working on his autobiography, *God, the Devil and Me*, dealing with his childhood in New Norcia Mission. He has also written a play and is currently compliling a collection of poetry and a collection of short stories. He plans to write the biography of his mother.

Pat Mamajun Torres has a BA and a Diploma of Education. She aims through her writing and painting to educate the non-Aboriginal community about the rich and dynamic cultures of Aboriginal Australia. Her books include *Ngay Janijirr Ngank: This is my word* (1999).

Kathy Trimmer was brought up in the North Eastern Goldfields, and lived there until the age of 19 when she moved to Perth. She has worked at the Kalgoorlie Language Centre as a linguist for three years and also at the Nyoongah Language Centre compiling Wongtha dictionaries. Kathy is a well-known songwriter and storyteller, and her knowledge of traditional arts has enabled her to teach in schools. Since 1982 she has worked promoting cultural awareness in hospitals, schools, universities and the police department.

Rosemary van den Berg is a Nyoongar woman who comes from Pinjarra, in the south-west of Western Australia and now lives in Armadale. She is married with five adult children and twenty-two grandchildren and she is considered an Elder among her people. She is an author, historian and doctoral student at Curtin University, Perth. She has also co-edited this anthology of Western Australian Aboriginal writers. She has written *No Options! No Choice!* (1994), her father's biography. She recently completed her PhD at Curtin University.

Glenyse Ward lives in Broome. She is the well-known writer of *Wandering Girl* (1987) and *Unna You Fellas* (1991) and is currently working on another book. In her travels Glenyse has met Renee Owens from *Once Were Warriors* who has shown a keen interest in her books and hopes to make them into full-length feature films in the not-too-distant future. She also gives talks in schools.

Chantelle Webb was born in 1981 in Derby, Western Australia. She is the third child in a family of six children. Her mother is a Nyoongar woman who has family affiliations with Pinjarra, Perth, the Moore River Native Settlement, and Noonkanbah in the Kimberley. Her father comes from Fitzroy Crossing and has Nyoongar and English family affiliations as well.

Richard Wilkes was born in 1943 in Kununoppin, near Merredin, in the Western Australian wheatbelt. His father was a member of the Darbalyung Nyoongah community of the Swan River, and Richard was educated at Eden Hill and Mogumber primary schools. Richard met and married his wife, Olive, in the wheatbelt, and they later moved to Perth. Richard is the author of a novel, *Bulmurn: A Swan River Nyoongah.*

June Williams was born at Moore River settlement. Her mother was one of the Stolen Generation and came from a station near Derby, while her father grew up in New Norcia. She has four children, six grandchildren and two great-grandchildren. She works as an Aboriginal Student Support Officer at Curtin University's Kalgoorlie campus, and she is presently working on her autobiography.

Diana Rose Yoka was born in Subiaco in 1942. Until very recently, she was denied knowledge of her real identity, to protect her and her family from being put in missions. She belongs to the Garadjari people of Bidyadanga. She is a self-taught writer and artist.